Managing political change in Singapore

The Singapore Parliament's creation of an elected presidency in 1991 was the biggest constitutional and political change in Singapore's modern era.

This multi-disciplinary study gathers papers from leading local scholars in law, history, political science and economics to examine how political change is managed in Singapore. Through their analyses of the elected presidency, the contributors shed light on the other political institutions, processes and personalities in Singapore, providing a valuable source for those studying the recent politics of the region.

Managing Political Change in Singapore uses the presidency as a case study beyond the Singaporean context, adding to the debates surrounding the management of political change in developing countries throughout the world.

Kevin Tan is Senior Lecturer at the Faculty of Law, National University of Singapore, and specializes in Constitutional and Administrative Law, as well as in Legal History. **Lam Peng Er** is Lecturer at the Department of Political Science, National University of Singapore, and specializes in Japanese politics and one party dominant political systems.

Politics in Asia Series
Edited by Michael Leifer
London School of Economics and Political Science

ASEAN and the Security of South-East Asia
Michael Leifer

China's Policy Towards Territorial Disputes
The Case of the South China Sea Islands
Chi-kin Lo

India and Southeast Asia
Indian Perceptions and Policies
Mohammed Ayoob

Gorbachev and Southeast Asia
Leszek Buszynski

Indonesian Politics Under Suharto
Order, Development and Pressure for Change
Michael R. J. Vatikiotis

The State and Ethnic Politics in Southeast Asia
David Brown

The Politics of Nation Building and Citizenship in Singapore
Michael Hill and Lian Kwen Fee

Communitarian Ideology and Democracy in Singapore
Beng-Huat Chua

Politics in Indonesia
Democracy, Islam and the Ideology of Tolerance
Douglas E. Ramage

The Challenge of Democracy in Nepal
Louise Brown

Japan's Asia Policy
Wolf Mendl

The International Politics of Asia-Pacific 1975–1995
Michael Yahuda

Political Change in Southeast Asia
Trimming the Banyan Tree
Michael R J Votikiotis

Hong Kong
China's Challenge
Michael Yahuda

Korea versus Korea
A case of contested legitimacy
B. K. Gills

Managing political change in Singapore
The elected presidency

Edited by Kevin Tan and Lam Peng Er

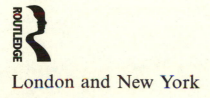

London and New York

First published 1997
by Routledge
11 New Fetter Lane, London EC4P 4EE

Simultaneously published in the USA and Canada
by Routledge
29 West 35th Street, New York, NY 10001

Typeset in Times by Routledge
Printed and bound in Great Britain by
T J Press (Padstow) Ltd, Padstow, Cornwall

British Library Cataloguing in Publication Data
A catalogue record for this book is available from the British Library

Library of Congress Cataloging in Publication Data
Managing political change in Singapore: the elected presidency /
edited by Kevin Tan and Lam Peng Er.
1. Singapore–Politics and government. 2. Presidents–Singapore–
Election. 3. Singapore–Economic conditions. 4. Singapore–
Social conditions. I. Tan, Kevin. II. Lam, Peng Er,
1959– .
JQ745.S5M36 1997   96–23824
320.95957–dc20   CIP

ISBN 0–415–15632–7

Contents

List of illustrations   vi
Notes on contributors   vii
Preface   xi

1 **Introduction**
   Kevin Tan and Lam Peng Er   1

2 **The head of state in Singapore: an historical perspective**
   Huang Jianli   9

3 **The presidency in Singapore: constitutional developments**
   Kevin Tan   52

4 **The election of a president in a parliamentary system: choosing a
   pedigree or a hybrid?**
   Valentine S. Winslow   88

5 **The elected president and the legal control of government:** *quis
   custodiet ipsos custodes?*
   Thio Li-ann   100

6 **Chaining the Leviathan: a public choice interpretation of
   Singapore's elected presidency**
   Tilak Doshi   144

7 **Singapore's first elected presidency: the political motivations**
   Hussin Mutalib   167

8 **Notes from the margin: reflections on the first presidential
   election, by a former Nominated Member of Parliament**
   Chia Shi Teck   188

9 **The elected presidency: towards the twenty-first century**
   Lam Peng Er   200

   Postscript   220
   Index   223

Illustrations

FIGURE

9.1 Typology of power relations between the EP and the PM   202

TABLES

9.1 Projected GDP growth,1993–8   208
9.2 Affluence and creature comforts of Singaporeans, 1973–92   210
9.3 Education of subsequent age cohort in Singapore   210
9.4 Affluent countries and GNP per capita   211
9.5 Affluent countries by purchasing power   212

Contributors

Chia Shi Teck became a school teacher after graduation before embarking on an entrepreneurial career in the clothing industry. He is now Chairman of Heshe Holdings Pte Ltd and was appointed Nominated Member of Parliament from 1991–3. When Mr Ong Teng Cheong's candidacy for President was announced, Chia offered to stand against him if no one else could be found.

Tilak Doshi was, until recently, a Fellow at the Institute of Southeast Asian Studies and the Coordinator of its Energy Project. Prior to that appointment, he served as Tutor in the Department of Economics at Victoria University, Wellington; Research Officer in the Department of Statistics, New Zealand; Robert S. McNamara Research Fellow, Economic Development Institute, World Bank; Visiting Scholar, East–West Centre, Honolulu; and Head of Research, Louis Dreyfuss Energy (Asia Pacific) Pte Ltd. His main specialty is in energy resource economics, but he maintains research interests in development economics. His recent publications include: *Houston of Asia: the Singapore Petroleum Industry* (ISEAS, 1989), *Country Report Singapore* for the Asia-Pacific Energy Series (United States Department of Energy, 1988), and *Vietnam: Asia's Newest Oil Exporter* (ISEAS-East-West Centre, 1993). He is currently Director, Economic and Industry Analysis, Corporate Planning, Atlantic Richfield Company, Los Angeles.

Lam Peng Er is Lecturer at the Department of Political Science, National University of Singapore, having joined the department in 1986 after a brief career in banking. He has spent the last few years doing fieldwork for his recently completed PhD dissertation entitled 'The network movement and old politics parties in urban Japan' for Columbia University. During 1991–3 he was a Visiting Scholar at the Law Faculty of Keio University, Japan. In addition to specializing in

Japanese politics, he has continued to pursue his longstanding interest in the one party dominant systems of Singapore and Japan.

Huang Jianli lectures on the history of China and Japan at the History Department of the National University of Singapore. He obtained his PhD from the Australian National University in 1987. Apart from specializing in Chiang Kai-shek's China from the 1920s to the 1940s, he is also doing research on the historical development of the Chinese entrepreneurial and intellectual elite in postwar Singapore. He is the author of *The Politics of Depoliticization in Republican China: Guomindang Policy Towards Student Political Activism, 1927–1949* (Peter Lang, 1996) and he has published in journals such as the *Journal of Oriental Studies and the East Asian History.*

Hussin Mutalib joined the Department of Political Science at the National University of Singapore in 1981. A Senior Lecturer, he specializes in comparative politics with particular reference to Singapore, Malaysia and the ASEAN States, and the Muslim World. He is a regular participant in discussions about Singapore society and politics, and his writings have appeared in international journals. Attached to Harvard University in 1993 as Fulbright Visiting Scholar, he is also the author of *Islam and Ethnicity in Malay Politics* (OUP, 1990), *Islam in Malaysia: from Revivalism to Islamic State?* (Singapore University Press, 1993), and *Islam, Muslims and the Modern State: Case Studies of Muslims in Thirteen Countries* (Macmillan Press, 1994).

Kevin Tan is Senior Lecturer at the Faculty of Law, National University of Singapore, where he has taught since 1986. He obtained his Masters of Law and Doctor of Juridical Science degrees from the Yale Law School and has since specialized in constitutional and administrative law. He is the co-editor of *Constitutional Law in Malaysia and Singapore* (MLJ, 1991), which is the standard casebook for Malaysian and Singaporean law students, and has also published widely, mainly on constitutional law and legal history.

Thio Li-ann is a Lecturer at the Faculty of Law, National University of Singapore. She read jurisprudence at Oxford University and, in the interest of enhancing a comparative perspective on Anglo-American public law, obtained her Masters of Law from Harvard Law School. The subject of her Masters thesis was constitutional law theory, and she has published a comprehensive article on the institutional development of the Singapore legislature. Her fields of interest are primarily constitutional and administrative law, and public international law. She intends to pursue further research and to write on the need for the articulation of constitutional law theory in Singapore – the basis for religious freedom and other civil liberties and human rights in general. In 1995 she assisted counsel for the President in the first ever *Constitutional Reference.*

Valentine S. Winslow is Associate Professor at the Faculty of Law, National University of Singapore. He specializes in constitutional and administrative law and the law of evidence and has published widely on these topics. In 1995, he assisted counsel for the President in the first ever *Constitutional Reference.*

Preface

Heads of state in parliamentary systems in which executive powers are vested in cabinet government led by a prime minister do not normally assume office through a direct electoral process. In the case of Singapore from its independence in August 1965, the Republic has enjoyed the services of several presidents as ceremonial heads of state who assumed office after nomination by government and approval by parliament. In August 1993, however, direct elections were held for a president with veto powers over budget decisions, the scale of spending from financial reserves and the appointment of senior officials. The direct election of a president with such powers within a replica of the Westminster Model would seem to mark a constitutional change of potentially great significance. That change was introduced, in particular, because of the brooding concern of Singapore's former Prime Minister and incumbent Senior Minister, Lee Kuan Yew who continues to exercise a unique political influence. His anxiety about the wisdom of succeeding generations of leaders in managing the affairs of the vulnerable island-state has been translated into a constitutional change intended to provide a safeguard against abuse or misuse of power and other failings of good government, including indulging undue popular demands for public welfare. Singapore lacks credible political opposition as well as the facilities of civil society which serve the cause of accountability. In their absence, the object of the elected presidency is to ensure that the material and honest bureaucratic legacy of the founding generation of Singapore's leaders is not dissipated to national disadvantage.

This collection of essays is the first systematic attempt to examine and assess the historical context, legal content and political and economic significance of Singapore's novel constitutional change. It takes the form of a scholarly collaboration between students of history, law, politics and economics who have overcome divisive disciplinary bounds to the readers benefit. The value of this volume is manifold. It brings an important inter-disciplinary perspective to an important subject. Through special attention to Singapore, it also makes a signal contribution to the study of comparative constitutions and to that of comparative politics. Conventional wisdom upholds the superiority of a government of laws over one of men. The radical constitutional change which has been effected in Singapore, expresses itself, however, in a distribution of powers between holders of high offices likely to be strong personalities. As such, it may have sown the seed of a structural tension between prime minister and president within a political system distinguished by interventionist government. This collection of essays makes a stimulating contribution to the current debate over the future of Singapore in the inevitable absence of the awesome moral authority of its supreme 'old guard' political leader.

Michael Leifer

1 Introduction

Kevin Tan and Lam Peng Er

[K]ingdoms which depend on the virtue of one man do not last, because they lose their virtue when his life is spent, and it seldom happens that it is revived by his successor. . . . The security of a republic or a kingdom, therefore, does not depend upon its ruler governing it prudently during his lifetime, but upon his so ordering it that, after his death, it may maintain itself in being.[1]

Niccolò Machiavelli, *The Discourses*

But if it is true that great princes seldom appear, how much more rare must a great lawgiver be? A prince has only to follow a model which the lawgiver provides. The lawgiver is the engineer who invents the machine: the prince is merely the mechanic who sets it up and operates it. Montesquieu says that at the birth of political societies, it is the leaders of the republic who shape the institutions but that afterwards it is the institutions which shape the leaders of the republic.[2]

Jean-Jacques Rousseau, *The Social Contract*

This book examines the office of the elected presidency, the political context and rationale for its introduction, the political process which led to its adoption, its unique constitutional features *vis-à-vis* the executive, legislature and the judiciary, and its potential impact on the politics of Singapore. It also analyses the state's first presidential election in 1993. The study of a key political institution which is now tightly woven into the country's political fabric from a multi-disciplinary approach (law, political science, history and economics) has much to inform us about the dynamics and dilemma of the city-state's quest for political survival and institutionalization beyond the era of its Founding Fathers. Contemporary Singapore politics cannot be understood without examining the central institution of the elected presidency. In terms of per capita purchasing parity, the nation has become one of the globe's top ten richest countries; it also possesses one of the most impressive financial reserves in the world. The elected presidency is, in part, specifically designed to safeguard its reserves which the country will draw upon for its survival in a domestic or international crisis.

CHARISMATIC FOUNDING FATHER AND THE ELECTED PRESIDENCY

Since 1959 when Singapore attained self-government, it has been governed by the People's Action Party (PAP) led by Lee Kuan Yew. Few elected political leaders in the world can match Lee's political longevity. Because he dominated the country's politics uninterruptedly since 1959, he was in a unique position to shape its political landscape. Lee did not single-handedly build the nation but was aided by a team of able lieutenants. He was a necessary though not a sufficient factor for the impressive development of the city Republic.[3] Despite abdicating his formal leadership positions[4] and taking a back-seat role as senior minister, Lee remains extremely influential. Often considered to be modern Singapore's Founding Father, Lee has left an indelible personal mark on its politics and society. He has anticipated potentially disruptive political changes and challenges, and has sought to bequeath Singapore a constitutional legacy which will ensure the long-term survival of the country. One such constitutional device is the elected presidency. Lee as the Founding Father is in a unique role to shape the Constitution. He proposed the scheme and helped to carry it through.

When Lee first formed the government in 1959 he was, as the prime minister, merely first among equals; over the years, he emerged as the undisputed leader who towered over his colleagues in the PAP. Although the first generation, old-guard PAP leaders were undoubtedly a capable lot, few had Lee's charismatic touch. Even the pugnacious Devan Nair acknowledged Lee's headship when he was the president, although protocol dictated otherwise:

> [Nair] knew his place. For his abiding faith was that Singapore's and his own leader was Mr Lee Kuan Yew. Even after he became Head of State, he would forget protocol when with close friends and refer to his Prime Minister as The Boss.[5]

In the decades after independence in 1965, the PAP succeeded in consolidating its position in Singapore. Since the opposition Barisan Sosialis' abandonment of Parliament in 1968, the PAP has secured a near-monopoly of seats, and with that, the power to change the Constitution at will.[6] Its hegemony of Parliament, and its strict adherence to the party line and insistence on party discipline through the party Whip enabled the PAP easily to secure the special majority of two-thirds required for Constitutional amendments. Amendments made to Singapore's Constitution number, on average,[7] one per year and several of the more recent amendments – including the elected presidency – evince a clear preoccupation with the issue of political change and succession.

New institutions and safeguards which promoted the PAP's and probably Lee's vision of a good state were entrenched in the Constitution. Clearly, these institutions were intended to outlast Lee's tenure as Singapore's paramount leader. These new and often innovative devices were not intended to apply to Lee or his current group of PAP stalwarts for they are 'good rulers'. Instead, they were to be invoked at times when good rulers could not be found to run government, and when the weaknesses of human nature threatened the existence of Singapore. At such critical moments, these constitutional devices would be activated and good institutions would, hopefully, save the day.

When Singapore's elected presidency was first introduced, the experiment was considered unique because the president has the mandate to veto certain governmental decisions, but lacks the power to initiate policies. While the mechanics of Singapore's presidential system may appear unique, the underlying concern to build institutions to manage political and socio-economic change is universal. Samuel Huntington believes that the process of rapid modernization, social mobilization, urbanization, rising mass education and expectations, and democratization is potentially destabilizing. Instead of an emerging stable democratic polity with sustained economic growth, the upsurge of mass participation in politics may overload fledgling political institutions, resulting in political breakdown.[8] Huntington advocates the strengthening of political institutions to contain and accommodate mass political participation as a prerequisite to political stability and economic development. Implicit in this authoritarian approach is the idea that mass democracy is potentially irrational but political executives may be counted upon to exercise their power wisely and rationally to promote political and economic development. In reality, the concentration of power in the hands of the executive is inherently problematic and dangerous; the axiom that absolute power corrupts absolutely should be a counterfoil to Huntington's prescription for a powerful executive to manage change.

Singapore, like other political systems, faces the perennial question: how can we ensure that the political executive remains clean, accountable and effective? The office of the elected presidency would be unnecessary if the former British colony retained a functioning parliamentary Westminster system where a sizeable loyal opposition exists and checks the ruling party. In the absence of a credible political opposition in the nation, the executive is not seriously subjected to parliamentary checks and balances. Lee's solution is to create another political institution, the elected presidency, to check the prime minister and his Cabinet. Conceivably, another plausible approach to prevent the abuse of executive power is the presence of a strong civil society which can check the state. However civil society is depoliticized and weak in Singapore. Professional bodies, the mass media, interest groups and intellectuals exercise little influence over an autonomous and powerful administrative and developmental state. Thus civil society cannot presently check the state in Singapore. The lack of a viable loyal opposition and a strong civil society, a peculiar situation created in part by the ruling PAP, necessitates the search for an institutional check on the executive.

STRUCTURE OF THE BOOK

In Chapter 2 historian Huang Jianli traces the antecedents of the elected presidency. He compares the terms of the first four presidents, who were elected by parliament rather than directly by the electorate, and argues that even though the office was essentially symbolic and ceremonial, the regime used the institution to promote nationhood and enhance ethnic harmony in a newly independent state with only a nascent sense of national identity. A unique unwritten convention was adopted: the highest office in the land was symbolically rotated among its ethnic groups; the first president was a Malay, followed by a Eurasian, an Indian and a Peranakan[9] Chinese. Ethnic peace is an important prerequisite for the political stability and economic growth of multi-racial Singapore. With the aim of managing delicate ethnic relations, the norm of rotating the presidential office among different racial groups was one strategy to legitimize the ideology of a multi-ethnic nation rather than a Chinese state even though Singaporean Chinese form an overwhelming 75 per cent of the population. Given the county's geopolitical location in a Malay sea (Malaysia and Indonesia), this approach seemed the most practical and sensible one.

Huang chooses a thematic rather than a chronological approach towards the office. He examines the process by which presidential candidates were selected, the influential politicians who nominated them, contrasting presidential styles, the doggedness of the Presidents in performing their roles even though most were plagued by ill health, their political contributions and problems, especially during the term of the third presidency which was marred by controversy and tragedy. Huang notes that contrary to the conventional wisdom that the earlier presidential system was apolitical since it lacked executive and other veto powers, it was indeed a politicized office which was used to serve the interest of nation building. It was an institution which helped to manage political change – the highest representation of the national ideology of multi-ethnicity and the creation of a new nation underpinned by such values.

The next three chapters by constitutional lawyers explore various legal aspects of the elected presidency. Kevin Tan begins with a conspectus of the key legal changes that have taken place from the first public articulation of the concept by Lee in 1984, through the two White Papers and the version of the Constitution (Amendment) Act 1991 that was finally adopted and passed. He goes on to argue that the transformation of the presidential office can be seen in the context of a recurring pattern of constitutional changes in Singapore to meet the political agenda of the ruling party. The PAP does not consider any aspect of the Constitution to be sacrosanct. Instead, it periodically changes the Constitution to fulfil its vision of a 'good' political system. Tan contextualizes the elected presidency amendments within other key significant constitutional changes which depart from the inherited Westminster system: Non-Constituency MPs, Nominated MPs, and Group Representation Constituencies where single member electoral districts are combined into bigger electoral districts and a single slate of candidates with different ethnic representation from a single party competes against another from a different party. Tan goes on to examine in detail the constitutional amendments made to the elected presidency and their legal and political implications. In his conclusion, Tan points out that while the institution must be tested before we can make a fair assessment of its effectiveness, 'we have made the stakes much too high, and on those grounds alone, the scheme must be considered much too volatile for comfort'.

In the following chapter Thio Li-ann considers the perennial problem: who guards the guardians? This is an especially critical problem in Singapore where state and society are shaped by a one party dominant system. Unlike the British Westminster parliamentary model of politics which assumes a constant checking and balancing of power between two major parties, Singapore's single party dominant system precludes the existence of viable opposition parties.[10] As such, the problem of who should be made to check the executive in the exercise of its power and authority is especially acute in Singapore.

Thio argues that the introduction of the elected presidency can be understood against this backdrop of a 'parliamentary gap'. Although Singapore inherited the formal structures of the British Westminster system upon independence, a two party system did not emerge. Because of the need to check the guardians, the elected presidency – like the other major institutional amendments made since 1984 – was introduced to fill the missing 'gap' in the Westminster transplant. Of these amendments, Thio opines that the elected presidency is the most 'revolutionary' and that Singapore's system of government stands at a threshold between presidentialism and parliamentarianism. She concludes by questioning the efficacy of this scheme as a device to deal with the 'problem of over-centralized power'.

Valentine Winslow's chapter focuses on the qualifications of the presidential candidate, and the process of electing a president. Analysing the relevant provisions, Winslow argues that the Constitution, as it stands, neither guarantees that the president shall be elected directly, nor that he shall be elected freely on the basis of universal franchise and equality in voting, and that a preferable enactment should follow the South Korean example. Winslow further argues that by pitching the qualifications of the presidential candidate in such elitist terms, Singapore has tried too hard to ensure a safe result, attempting to 'write the Constitution like an insurance policy – so much so that the right of electors to choose the president who appeals best to them is diminished'.

In the next section, economist Tilak Doshi makes a thorough survey of the literature on political economy and constitutionalism. Basing his analysis on the work of leading scholars like James Buchanan and F. A. Hayek, Doshi points out that electoral democracies tend to be subjected to voters' insatiable demands for increased consumption of public welfare. These electoral demands inevitably lead to the depletion of the national reserves and the accumulation of a deleterious public debt. Doshi argues that current intellectual understanding of public finance and government supports the Singapore government's underlying arguments for introducing the elected presidency scheme. And if the scheme can truly check such populist pressure, it should be evaluated in a positive light.

Two chapters in the next section cover the first presidential election conducted in 1993. Entrepreneur and ex-Nominated Member of Parliament Chia Shih Teck presents a semi-autobiographical account of his public decision to offer himself to be a presidential candidate if no one else were willing to take up the challenge. For a brief moment Chia basked in the national limelight as a potential presidential candidate until an opponent – the reluctant Chua Kim Yeow – was persuaded to offer himself to run against the PAP-endorsed candidate. This chapter is not meant to be a heavy academic piece but to convey the atmosphere and the angst of the times from a perceptive participant-observer. Chia's account offers a 'ring-side seat' at the contest.

Political scientist Hussin Mutalib perceives the elected presidency scheme as part of a continual process by the ruling party to tinker with various constitutional devices to perpetuate its power, especially in the wake of falling electoral support for the PAP. Hussin argues that the elected presidency and other institutional changes were made to manage and contain a younger and better educated electorate with rising expectations and a predilection to vote for political pluralism.

In the final chapter political scientist Lam Peng Er examines the public debate on the possible impact of the elected president on the future of Singapore politics. He conceives four different scenarios concerning the power relationship between the president and the prime minister in the post-Lee era. Lam argues that even in the best scenario where a 'responsible president' is faced with 'good' prime minister, there is still room for conflict and gridlock. So while the elected presidency may have been designed to safeguard the well-being of Singapore, a clash between two strong personalities with differing conceptions of a 'good' government is still possible and potentially catastrophic. Lam suggests that a confrontation between the dual centres of power may well be precipitated by a threatening regional and international milieu, Singapore's acute sense of vulnerability, and a lack of political consensus between the president and the prime minister to deal with external dangers. Ironically, Singapore, a country characterized by an able and interventionist government that thrives on anticipating and managing change, may have created an institution which has the potential to paralyse the political system if the president and prime minister collide.

NOTES

1 Niccolò Machiavelli, *The Discourses*, Introduction by Bernard Crick (Harmondsworth: Penguin Books, 1970): 141–2.
2 Jean-Jacques Rousseau, *The Social Contract*, translated by Maurice Cranston (Harmondsworth: Penguin Books, 1968): 87.
3 Lee acknowledged that even he could not have built Singapore without the support of the PAP old guards, especially Goh Keng Swee, S. Rajaratnam, Toh Chin Chye and Ong Pang Boon. See *Straits Times*, 17 September 1993. Besides strong PAP leadership, there are many factors that have contributed

to Singapore's remarkable economic growth. They include: the strategic location of Singapore as an international port, access to relatively open global markets and thus the ability to adopt an export-led growth, a regional balance of power maintained by the US, the deterrence offered by the Five Power Defence Pact (Singapore, Malaysia, Britain, Australia and New Zealand), peaceful relations with its neighbours, a reliable state bureaucracy inherited from the British colonial masters, and a hardworking population.

4   Lee left the premiership and the general secretaryship of the PAP to Goh Chok Tong in 1990 and 1992 respectively. However he remains a member of the Central Executive Committee, the PAP's highest decision-making body. Lee nonetheless continues to sit in on Cabinet meetings.

5   *Straits Times*, 29 March 1985.

6   Although Singapore has free and regularly held elections based upon the British Westminister model, and the presence of opposition parties, the electorate has returned the PAP to power in every general election. Thus Singapore has a one party dominant system. This is different from the one party state of various totalitarian and authoritarian regimes which do not recognize the existence of opposition parties and their right to compete for power. Theoretically, the PAP can be voted out of power. The British first-past-the-post system has benefited the PAP. In the 1991 general elections, the PAP captured 77 out of 81 seats with only 59.3 per cent of the popular vote.

7   See Kevin Tan Yew Lee, 'The Evolution of Singapore's Modern Constitution: 1945 to the Present Day', *Singapore Academy of Law Journal* (1989) 1: 1.

8   Samuel Huntington, *Political Order In Changing Societies* (New Haven, CT: Yale University Press, 1968).

9   Peranakan Chinese are also known as Straits Chinese whose ancestors often intermarried with the local Malay population, adopted some aspects of the indigenous culture such as language and food. This resulted in a unique blend of Chinese and Malay culture.

10   The one party dominant system of Japan, Italy, India and Sweden did not preclude the existence of viable opposition.

2 The head of state in Singapore

An historical perspective

Huang Jianli

INTRODUCTION

This chapter is a historical analysis of a comparatively new institution: the presidency of the Republic of Singapore. Created only when full independence was suddenly forced upon Singapore in 1965, the presidency was bereft of a long historical tradition. As such, it was impossible to write down all the rules of office from the start. Its evolution was shaped by the imperative of forging a nation-state out of a multitude of ethnic groups and by the political leadership of Lee Kuan Yew and his People's Action Party (PAP). To a lesser extent, the personality of incumbents also played a role in its development. Taking a broad look at the presidency from 1965 to 1993, the evolution of the office has been characterized by a deft balancing act between stability and experimentation to develop a constitutional headship that suits the moods and needs of a fledgling city-state. In this sense, the new presidential era in 1993 featuring the first popularly-elected president was merely the continuation of this search for the right formula.

For most of its modern history before 1965, Singapore was governed as an integral part of the British Empire. It was only in 1959, when a partial transfer of power to the local people was effected through internal self-government, that the office of the British governor was replaced by the 'Yang di-Pertuan Negara' or 'Head of State of Singapore', although he still represented the British monarch. To facilitate a smooth transfer of power, Sir William Goode, the then British Governor, was made the interim head of state on 3 June 1959. Six months later, he relinquished the post to Yusof bin Ishak. When Singapore gained independence from the British through a merger with the Federation of Malaya, Sabah and Sarawak on 16 September 1963, Yusof remained the 'Yang di-Pertuan Negara' but he was now the representative of the Malaysian king, the 'Yang di-Pertuan Agong'. On 9 August 1965, full independence was forced upon Singapore through its expulsion from Malaysia. The Constitution was amended and the title of head of state was changed to that of 'president'. Yusof bin Ishak became the first president and head of state of an independent Singapore.

From 1965 to August 1993, we have had a total of four presidents. Yusof was the first and, after he died on 23 November 1970, Benjamin Henry Sheares was appointed by Parliament on 30 December 1970 as his successor.[1] This second presidency lasted until 12 May 1981 when Sheares passed away from a cancer-related illness. C. V. Devan Nair was the third president of Singapore from 23 October 1981 to 27 March 1985, but his tenure ended in controversy and he resigned from office. It was left to Wee Kim Wee, who held the post from his appointment on 30 August 1985 to his retirement on 31 August 1993, to restore the prestige of the office. His term of office was unique in that he actually held the expanded powers of an elected presidency for nearly two years, between the empowering on 30 November 1991 through the passage of a parliamentary bill for elected presidency and the first presidential election in August 1993. Winning 58.7 per cent of valid votes, Ong Teng Cheong was sworn in as the fifth president of Singapore and the first popularly elected head of state.

Taking a closer look at the first four presidencies from Yusof to Wee, we will try to understand some of the key processes and issues involved in the selection of appointees and their fulfilment of presidential responsibilities before the onset of popular presidential elections. This chapter will touch on the shortlisting of candidates as well as the important influence of Lee Kuan Yew and the ethnic factor. The degree of political engagement before and after each of the candidates assumed the presidency will also be explored. Illness was a noticeable feature in all the four presidencies and it appears (at least in the eyes of the political leadership) that ill-health does not and should not disqualify one for the presidential office. Part of the health problem was related to the difficult adjustment each of them had to make when entering the presidential world with all its trappings. Devan Nair's failure to adjust, for example, contributed to his controversial exit. Two of the presidents (Yusof and Sheares) died while still in office and their deaths provided occasions to take stock of the nation-building process. Attention will also be drawn to the various ways in which the epithet of 'People's President' has been used and how the term can be seen in the larger context of an attempt to politicize the presidency of Singapore. The epilogue focuses on the beginning of Ong's elected presidency and draws some historical parallels with the previous four.

SHORTLISTS AND PERSUADERS

The transition in presidencies is usually met with much speculation and claims to privileged information on the likely choices, but the selection process remains beyond the realm of public information. In 1965, Yusof was a logical choice for the presidency as he was already the 'Yang di-Pertuan Negara' before Singapore's independence. Moreover, given the sudden change of events and the need for stability in the heady days following Singapore's expulsion from Malaysia, it seemed prudent not to call for a new selection or make drastic alterations save for a mere change of nomenclature of the office.[2] But what about Sheares, Nair and Wee?

When Yusof passed away in November 1970, the government was able to elect Sheares as the new head of state within a month. Owing to the early warning given by Yusof's long illness, Lee Kuan Yew and his Cabinet were able to hold deliberations spread over two and a half years.[3] Although the detailed shortlist of candidates was never officially released, it was reported in the media that 'political and professional circles' were pointing their fingers at Wee Chong Jin, Yeoh Ghim Seng, Punch Coomaraswamy, A. P. Rajah, Othman Wok, and Ismail bin Abdul Aziz.[4] Wee Chong Jin was a Chief Justice and the next three had previously been speakers of parliament. Wee, Yeoh and Punch Coomaraswamy had also occasionally acted as president when Yusof was indisposed. Othman Wok was the Minister of Social Affairs and Ismail was then Head of the Muslim Religious Council. The eventual selection of Sheares, a leading obstetrician-gynaecologist in private practice, was 'not an obvious choice and his name was never heard in public or private speculation'.[5]

Lee's personal relationship with Sheares apparently played a major role in this selection. Explaining his part, Lee noted that Sheares was 'so obviously a suitable choice' and with the Cabinet's agreement, he approached Sheares personally who in turn was 'surprised', 'delighted' and 'apprehensive'.[6] Lee was also on record as being the one who was instrumental in persuading Sheares to extend his term of office during the last of his three four-year terms.[7] Upon Sheares' death in 1981, Lee disclosed that he first knew Sheares 41 years earlier when the latter moved into a house diagonally opposite Lee's home in Norfolk Road.[8] Through the years, Lee also may have come to know Sheares much better when his (Lee's) wife came under Sheares' medical treatment.[9]

The lapse between Sheares' death and the appointment of the next president was longer: five months. This was due mainly to the preparations needed to extricate Devan Nair from his labour and political commitments.[10] Nair was approached as early as June 1981, some three weeks after Sheares' death. This time, Lee specifically stated that the Speaker of Parliament and a few others outside the Cabinet were asked to help in the search and that the final shortlist comprised another three unnamed persons, 'only one was not connected with the PAP' and 'he was colourless compared to Devan Nair'.[11] Lee's relationship with Nair dated back to 1952 when Lee, then a lawyer, first met Nair as a political detainee at the St. John's Island detention centre. Over the three decades after 1959, following Nair's ideological reversal and Lee's electoral triumph, they worked closely together to fight the communists within the PAP, to represent the party's interests in the Malaysian Parliament and to control the Singapore labour movement. It would not be surprising if Lee turned out to be Nair's original proposer, especially since he had said that he had approached Nair personally and urged him to accept the post.[12]

There was also a five-month lapse between Nair's departure and the appointment of Wee Kim Wee. This time, the delay arose from the abruptness and circumstances of Nair's resignation in March 1985. Apart from thinking it 'better to take our time', Lee also felt it prudent to disclose even less about the shortlist except to say that 'several names were proposed' and 'the Cabinet took quiet soundings'.[13] He did not repeat his previous argument that anyone worth his salt would in all likelihood be related to the PAP. Ong Teng Cheong, however, was one of those Lee approached, although he immediately ruled himself out as being 'too young' to take on the job.[14] A foreign news report also named Lim Kim San, a former PAP minister, as a possible successor to Nair.[15] The eventual candidate was Wee, and Lee made it clear in his nomination speech that his senior colleague in the Cabinet, S. Rajaratnam, was responsible for putting forward Wee's name for consideration. Rajaratnam and Wee were both newspapermen and had known each other for over 30 years. It was Rajaratnam who first encouraged Wee to leave the post of editorial manager of the *Straits Times* to serve as Singapore's High Commissioner to Kuala Lumpur – one of the most significant and sensitive diplomatic posts in the Singapore foreign service in the early 1970s.[16] As for the presidency, Rajaratnam spent one whole month persuading Wee who subsequently reminisced that 'Raja twisted my arm so hard'.[17] Although Rajaratnam was the prime mover, Lee added his own endorsement. He had encountered Wee in the 1950s in the latter's capacity as a reporter and editor and was retrospectively pleased to note that, during the tumultuous 1950s and 1960s, Wee 'watched, with barely concealed alarm, the agitation, the protests, the strikes, the demonstrations, and the violence that sporadically broke out'. Lee also learned 'how shrewd' Wee was when he read Wee's 'perceptive despatches from Kuala Lumpur'.[18] There were also ties between the two families. In 1974, Wee wrote the foreword for a cookbook by Lee's mother in which he acknowledged that she was his cousin and that he had benefited from her culinary skills through the years.[19]

The entire process of selecting the president was therefore a low-key closed-door affair in which only senior Cabinet ministers, the Speaker of Parliament and a privileged few outside the Cabinet were consulted confidentially. Such informal quiet soundings meant more room for personal preferences. While the Cabinet endorsement should probably have been in order before any name was forwarded to Parliament for appointment, it remains uncertain whether the entire Cabinet ever debated and voted on a shortlist of several candidates. Lee seems to have played a very important role in the selection process. It was after all his responsibility as the Prime Minister to put forward the names of candidates and approach them. The fact that Lee knew all four presidents well before their appointments clearly facilitated his decision-making.

ETHNICITY AS A SELECTION CRITERION

As the holder of the highest office in the land and the embodiment of the values and aspirations cherished by the society, a president was expected to have qualities such as profound learning, good character, high reputation, distinguished public service and strong moral fibre. The selection process naturally paid attention to these qualities and all four presidents were said to have possessed them in varying degrees. However, one striking feature running through all the selections which deserves closer discussion is the ethnic factor.

Given the multi-racial composition of Singapore, its geographical location in the Malay Archipelago, its recent history of a failed merger with Malaysia and Indonesia's confrontation with Malaysia, the ethnic background of its head of state became a primary consideration. A pattern of rotating the post among the various ethnic groups can clearly be observed. The presidency became part of what might be termed 'the institutionalization of ethnicity' in Singapore.[20] Yusof was a Malay, Sheares an Eurasian, Nair an Indian and Wee a Chinese. Before Ong Teng Cheong formally announced his candidacy for the elected presidency, there was speculation that Ridzwan Dzafir, a Malay community leader and a senior civil servant, would be the 'establishment's candidate', thus prompting the remark that 'it was time for the "ethnic" wheel to come full circle'.[21]

In fact, the ethnic factor was played out in varying ways, including a straightforward denial of its significance in the early days. When Yusof was proposed for a further term in 1967, a Malay PAP MP spoke in Malay to support the motion:

> [I]n making our choice, we are not influenced by his religion or race. He is elected [by the Parliament] solely on the basis of his merit, his character, his devotion to duty and the esteem in which he is held by the people.... [It would be] unfair to Inche Yusof and even to my community to say that he has been nominated to this office simply because he is a Malay.... It is his qualities as a man and a citizen of Singapore and nothing else which recommend him for this high office.[22]

A new twist to this ethnic concern was added when the next MP, who spoke in Mandarin in support of Yusof, qualified Yusof's Malay background as follows:

> First, like most of us in Singapore – whether Chinese, Indian or Malay – Inche Yusof is of immigrant stock. He is a Malay of Sumatran descent. On the paternal side, he can trace his ancestral stock to Minangkabau and on the maternal side to Langkat. Inche Yusof himself was born in Perak.... In this, Inche Yusof's story is not unlike that of the vast majority of us whose fathers and forefathers emigrated from other countries to settle in Singapore and make it their permanent home.[23]

The next PAP MP to rise in support of Yusof was an Indian who spoke in Tamil. As on all other occasions when the prime minister tabled a motion to appoint a president (from Yusof to Wee), parliamentarians from the respective ethnic communities took turns to speak in their ethnic tongues in order to emphasize the multi-racial support given.[24] This orchestrated pattern of presentation itself reflects the importance of ethnicity in the presidency.

As for the uniqueness of Yusof's Malay background and how it differed from the *bumiputra* approach of Malaysia, Lee himself stressed:

> [Yusof] was keen that in this multi-racial milieu, our Singapore Malays should break out from the bounds of customs which were preventing them from making the same progress as the other

communities. He believed in policies to modernize our society, including our Malays. He believed that all men should be equal, or at least be given equal opportunities to advance themselves through their own effort.[25]

Upon Yusof's death, Othman Wok, the then Minister of Social Affairs and well-known Malay leader, was apparently on the shortlist to succeed him. However, 'many felt that to avoid a precedent being set, the new president should not be drawn from the same community'.[26] Depending on the timing and circumstances, a candidate's ethnic background can prove critical, either working to his advantage or disadvantage. Eventually it was the Eurasian Sheares who succeeded Yusof, and Devan Nair, an Indian, held the next presidency.

When Devan Nair resigned, it seemed the time had come for a Chinese to assume the presidential position. Yet, it had been said that Lee Kuan Yew and the Cabinet initially felt that Singapore was still not quite ready for it. They 'had originally been searching for someone from a minority community' but it was Rajaratnam who urged them not to do so and he proposed Wee Kim Wee. He contended it was time that the minorities realized that 'whether Indian, Eurasian, Malay or Chinese, we are all here as Singaporeans'.[27] A PAP Malay MP, speaking in Malay, in support of making Wee the president, admitted openly that a key consideration behind Wee's selection was race, and this in a way marked the maturity of the society:

> Mr Wee's election as president marks an important change in the history of Singapore. It reflects the maturity of thought on the part of the multi-racial people of Singapore. This is the first time that a citizen from a non-minority community has been proposed for election as president, the highest office in the land.[28]

Just as compensatory factors such as the non-indigenous, immigrant background and independent modernizing spirit of Yusof were invoked to bolster his acceptance by the wider society, Lee Kuan Yew stressed that Wee was an English-educated Straits-born Chinese, when moving the parliamentary motion for Wee's election.[29] When Wee himself retired, he emphasized the syncretic Peranakan dimension of his Chinese ethnicity:

> A lot of Straits-born Chinese can't speak a work of Peranakan.... I speak Peranakan well and my native language, Hokkien, fluently. I can save my neck with Mandarin, which I learnt through part-time study... I can write with a Chinese brush. I would be able to mix

with the Chinese crowd. . . . When I mix with Malays, they would accept me not as a Malay, but as a true Singaporean.[30]

Women shared the limelight of the presidential office as well as its ethnic sensitivities. The activities of the First Lady usually received a fair portion of attention in the mass media. Apart from ceremonial and protocol matters, the government was conscious of her importance since very few presidential candidates are available at each round of selection. Any disagreement from their spouses could easily disrupt the process.[31] Hence, praises were often heaped upon Noor Aishah, Mrs Sheares, Mrs Devan Nair and Mrs Wee for sharing the burden of presidential duties. But in the context of the present discussion, it was significant that the image of the First Lady was at times deliberately or unconsciously intertwined with the ethnic sensitivities surrounding the presidential office. For instance, Lee Kuan Yew commented on Yusof's wife as follows:

Eight years ago, Puan Noor Aishah did not speak any English. Now she speaks it easily. The willingness to learn, the keenness of Singapore and her people – a striving, thrusting society – are personified in the president and his wife.[32]

Another example is Sheares' wife. Since he was born of a Eurasian father and a Japanese mother and spoke no Mandarin or any Chinese dialects, his China-born wife came to be regarded by some as a 'major asset' and her 'Fukien background' was expected to provide 'a link with the majority [Hokkien Chinese] community' in Singapore.[33] When proposing that the Parliament accept Sheares as president, Lee made a point of saying that 'his wife, Mrs Sheares, speaks Chinese, English and some Malay. She can lend support to the president in his social duties'.[34] As for Devan Nair, in facilitating the acceptance of his impending presidency, Nair described his wife as 'a traditional, homely, Hindu housewife who has very multi-racial tastes'.[35]

DEGREE OF POLITICAL ENGAGEMENT

Some see the elected presidency, particularly with Ong Teng Cheong being formerly a senior Cabinet member and prospective prime minister, as the beginning of the politicization of the presidency. Such a view is too narrow. While Sheares and Wee were not actively involved in party politics, Yusof and Nair were very much in the political fray before becoming constitutional heads of state.

Sheares, as a gynaecologist with an international reputation and a distinguished record of service, confined his involvement in community affairs mainly to those related to his medical profession. Apparently, he was not active within his church circles either. The total absence of political involvement prompted an editorial to remark that 'any political associations he may have are known only to himself'.[36] Wee was less distant than Sheares from politics. As a senior editorial member of the *Straits Times* after 1959, Wee must at least have been politically attuned, although he seemed to have avoided direct political participation and affiliation. After he left his newspaper job in 1973, his various positions as ambassador in Malaysia, Japan and Korea and chairman of the Singapore Broadcasting Corporation made him somewhat of a 'faceless' senior civil servant. Lee Kuan Yew admitted later that when Wee was first made president in 1985, he was 'not well-known to Singaporeans'.[37]

Unlike Sheares and Wee, Yusof had a solid political background leading up to his appointment as the head of state in 1959.[38] He began his political march in secondary school when he joined the youth wing of the Singapore Malay Union (*Kesatuan Melayu Singapura*), arguably the first politically motivated Malay organization in Singapore and Peninsular Malaya. By 1938, he had assumed the position of secretary-general of this organization. About the same time, he also founded and managed the *Utusan Melayu*, a Malay newspaper which helped lay the foundations of modern Malay journalism and which gave a voice to the Malay nationalists and radicals who championed an end to colonial rule. In 1956, he was the only Malay leader invited by David Marshall's government to sit on a committee to expedite the 'Malayanization' of the civil service. When Lee Kuan Yew won power in 1959, he asked Yusof to head the Public Service Commission and, shortly after, his government appointed the latter as the 'Yang di-Pertuan Negara'.

Among the presidents, Nair was the most political prior to assuming the presidency.[39] Indeed, politics was his vocation. His political activities began during the Japanese Occupation when he assisted the Malayan People's Anti-Japanese Army, providing underground fighters with information and food supplies. After the war, he became active in the teachers' union and joined the Anti-British League which had links with the Malayan Communist Party. In January 1951, together with a number of other English-educated leftists such as Samad Ismail of *Utusan Melayu*, he was arrested and detained on St. John's Island for one-and-a-half years. After his release, he continued with left-wing union activism and, in 1954, worked with Lee Kuan Yew and a number of others to launch the PAP. When the PAP first participated in general elections in 1955, Nair was one of its four candidates but he lost the contest for Farrer Park Constituency by 200 votes. In another major crackdown on communists, the British detained him again in 1956. It was about this time, when Malaya gained independence, that Nair began to abandon his support for leftist insurrectionary struggles, but he did not turn his back on politics. When the PAP took power in 1959, Lee secured his release from detention and made him the political secretary to the Minister of Education. He left shortly after, preferring to re-immerse himself again in union work and subsequently rose to become the secretary-general of the National Trade Union Congress in 1962. Then there was an interlude of four years when he was the PAP's only representative in the Malaysian Parliament. In 1969, he returned to Singapore to spearhead Lee's grand design to convert the labour movement 'from a confrontational to a cooperational one'. Ten years later, having successfully engineered what Lee regarded as a 'difficult U-turn at great speed',[40] he re-entered Singaporean parliamentary politics when he won the Anson seat first in a by-election and later in the December 1980 general election with 81 per cent of the votes.

Nair's record was therefore not just one of heavy political commitment but one which was intensely partisan to the ruling party. He also had 'a reputation and style for saying and doing things in a forceful and colourful manner' and there was 'vehemence in some of his oratory'. His accusation that Singapore Airline pilots taking part in industrial action were guilty of treason and his lambast at 'snooty, arty-crafty Singaporeans' already earned him the epithet of 'Divine Nair' from some quarters.[41] Most Singaporeans were said to have regarded him as 'the doyen of trade unionists with a penchant to let his mouth run over'.[42] His own comrades from the labour movement called him a 'fire-breather'.[43] It was therefore hardly surprising that the proposal to make Nair the third president immediately aroused public controversy. As a *Business Times* editorial put it:

> [S]ince it leaked out that Devan Nair was the hot favourite to be the next president, the most frequently stated objection in coffee-shops and at cocktail parties has been that he had spent too long in the hurly-burly of politics and the cut, thrust and parry of industrial affairs to make successfully the transition to the non-partisan still waters of the presidency.[44]

Lee Kuan Yew justified his proposal on grounds that it was exactly these 30 years of political involvement which provided the irrefutable proof that Nair had the 'total dedication to a cause bigger than ourselves' and the 'moral fibre [to withstand] the pressures and the heat of crises'. Moreover, Lee said that in considering distinguished men in their fifties and sixties, 'anybody with any strength of character' in this generation would have entered the political fray and taken sides.[45] Without providing the names, he mentioned that three of the four 1981 candidates shortlisted were connected with the PAP. There is, however, dubious validity in Lee's second argument. Even during the most critical national crises, not everybody would be enticed into active party politics; many would probably still have chosen to contribute in other ways. As for how the overwhelming majority in the 1981 shortlist were related to the PAP, it all depends on how Lee and the Cabinet went about their selection.

To gain greater public acceptance, Lee also reiterated the position that, after assuming the presidency, Nair 'should be non-partisan' and 'he had to rise above the fray between the PAP and the other political parties who aspired to be the government'. He urged that Nair could 'still be colourful, still be approachable, still be pungent', but he 'must be above the political fray' and 'would have to represent all Singaporeans'.[46]

Prior to his appointment to the presidential office, Nair resigned from all union, party and political posts, including his parliamentary seat in the Anson constituency, to comply with the constitutional provisions of the presidency. A by-election for Anson was subsequently held on 31 October 1981, in which the PAP candidate managed to obtain only about half of the 81 per cent votes Nair captured during the December 1980 general election, and was defeated. The PAP's defeat had been attributed mainly to other problems, especially those relating to housing and the cost of living.[47] However, the public apprehension surrounding Nair's previous political engagement and his impending presidency might have contributed to a view that in 1981 the PAP had 'become progressively arrogant and self-righteous about its intelligence and its definitions of "what is good for the people" '.[48] The irony of the by-election result was that 'the very people of Anson, who had earlier elected an MP who is now president, the embodiment of the nation's unity, now elected the first opposition MP in almost 20 years'.[49]

Having been elected into office despite their various degrees of prior political experience, to what extent were the first four presidents of Singapore able to stay 'above politics'? When Lee defended Nair's candidacy in Parliament, he chose his words with care. Apparently, he was only concerned with avoiding political confrontations resulting from partisan party politics. Nonetheless, it was clear that even before the onset of the elected presidency, he knew that the presidential office could not be completely insulated from politics. In fact, throughout the first four presidencies, Lee repeatedly stressed the need for presidents to be 'politically well-informed' and, in line with Westminster practice, he, as prime minister, briefed the presidents regularly.

When he was proposing Yusof for a further term in 1967, Lee observed that the previous long years of briefings Yusof received as the head of state on 'all the matters and the crucial issues which have affected our lives and fortunes' gave him 'the added aplomb, the *savoir faire*'.[50] As for Sheares, Lee praised him for his keen and lively interest to keep 'abreast of what is going on in government' and 'all important matters of state' on at least three different occasions. Sheares received copies of all important papers and knew of Cabinet decisions and Lee called on him regularly once a month to keep in touch. Lee noted that 'Whenever I referred to sensitive developments concerning our security and our economy, there was always immediate cognizance of the dangers that could unfold, and he would twinkle his eyes or give one of his quizzical looks'.[51]

No praises were sung about Nair in this regard because he left office in ignominy. But Nair certainly had his share of the usual confidential papers to read during his term of office, if not more. After he resigned from office and kicked up a public row with Lee and the government, it was disclosed that an Internal Security Department investigation was launched to see if Nair had inadvertently leaked any official secrets, especially to a physiotherapist from South India who became very close to him.[52]

Wee was more than just a 'politically informed' president. He was perhaps the only one of the four to test the boundary of political engagement without stirring up government objections or public controversy. In paying a tribute to Wee at the end of his presidency, Goh Chok Tong who had taken over as prime minister in 1990 said that although Wee 'reads all the Cabinet papers', he 'felt it useful to let him know my thinking face to face' and thus called upon the president regularly for about an hour (frequency of visits undisclosed) to 'brief him on the Government's agenda and priorities'. But Goh noted that Wee was not just listening. At times, Wee even urged Goh directly towards a certain policy direction, such as correcting the adverse side-effects of meritocracy which measured a man's worth by his car and house. Occasionally, Wee would even send ministers 'politely couched notes offering his views and concerns on certain matters based on his own personal experience and observations, or feedback which he had received'.[53] Speaking after Goh, both the PAP MP Tan Cheng Bock and Nominated MP Chia Shi Teck acknowledged receiving personal advice from Wee on the need to be 'honest and brave enough to speak up' and 'never fear the truth'. Chia once asked Wee whether he had the chance to speak up as a president and the reply was an unequivocal yes. Chia was therefore very much touched, inspired and encouraged that Wee was 'not just taking his role as a ceremonial one'.[54]

Constitutional amendments conferring upon Wee the powers of an elected presidency came into effect on 30 November 1991, but even before that, Wee had already been adopting a relatively more active presidential style. During this time, the Elected Presidency Bill was in the process of being drafted and the long process of legal preparation must have encouraged the government to give him some leeway to experiment with a more participatory form of presidency. Moreover, the prime ministership changed hands midway through Wee's presidency and the younger and less assertive Goh may have created a more conducive environment for feedback on political or other matters. Goh's open acknowledgement of Wee's more active involvement certainly helped in projecting the image of his proposed consultative and consensus-building style of government and in further preparing the public for elected presidency. The fact that these limits were tested at all must also be attributed to the personality and temperament of Wee himself. He seemed eager to strike a balance between principles and activism and yet he was astute enough to know the parameters of his prescribed environment and the extent to which he could push them. As he revealed upon retirement, 'I came in with full knowledge of what I am expected to do. The only thing I can embark on is to change the style or the role of presidency without going into sensitive or policy issues'.[55]

ILLNESSES

Another striking feature of the first four presidents was that they coincidentally had significant health problems. Three of them suffered from various natural illnesses and one apparently from alcoholism (Devan Nair's alcoholism will be discussed in the next section of this chapter).

Yusof's health apparently deteriorated during the Japanese Occupation due to the harsh living conditions.[56] When the 'Yang di-Pertuan Negara' post was offered to him in 1959, he was hesitant to accept it partly because of health reasons. By 1966, he was afflicted with tuberculosis and high blood pressure. During a holiday planned as a '53-day health cruise' to Australia, Yusof collapsed from a heart attack, on 13 March 1968, and had to be taken off the ship at Port

Moresby and flown to Melbourne for treatment. The diagnosis of the Australian specialists was not encouraging and it was believed that he had only a few more months to live. The doctors and nurses who took care of him were credited for stretching that to two and a half years. As Lee Kuan Yew observed, these were unpleasant years for Yusof as well as his family and friends:

> The long illness over nearly three years reduced him slowly to an invalid. It was painful and sad to watch him go down little by little after each relapse of his cardiac and respiratory problems. ... As his condition deteriorated, his usually composed demeanour was affected. He was beset by anxieties.[57]

Sheares also had serious health problems before and during his presidency.[58] He was a chain smoker, puffing 'tins of fifties continuously from morning till night'. He had a lung operation in 1953 and was suffering from acute gastric ulcers. In 1961, he resigned from government service on grounds of ill health. Five years before his nomination as president, Sheares underwent another major operation, this time for stomach ulcers. Moreover, despite official pronouncements that he enjoyed 'good health' on the day of election as the second president, Sheares became 'gravely ill' shortly after and required surgery for vascular disorder in early 1971 and for abdominal aneurysm in December 1971. However, Sheares recovered well enough to be nominated for a second term in November 1974 and later a third in December 1978. By 1978, Sheares had passed his seventieth year and was 'conscious that he had slowed down' and was 'concerned he might not have the strength to see through another term'. Yet, Lee remained very keen on Sheares continuing in office and persevered in persuading him to keep the job. Sheares 'agreed only after the third discussion', and Lee conveyed to the Parliament that 'I believe some thoughtfulness on the part of the Government can lighten the physical demands of the office'. In early 1981, Sheares had pneumonia and, in the course of treatment, cancer was detected. In his 'thorough, methodical way', Sheares sorted out his affairs before his death on 12 May 1981 from a cerebral haemorrhage.

Wee's health problem was the least serious of the three cases.[59] He assumed office in August 1985 apparently without any record of significant illnesses. But four years later, he underwent two consecutive operations in January and February 1989, one for cancer of the rectum and the other for a prostate problem. He lost some weight but recovered well enough for Lee to nominate him for a second term in August. Wee completed this term and retired from office in August 1993.

The presidential office was therefore often plagued by health problems. The government disclosed most of these cases openly in the Parliament to keep the public informed, albeit without much detail. Through these limited disclosures, it was obvious that there were occasions when it seemed more appropriate to let the incumbent leave and to appoint another person to take on the job. However, the Cabinet opted not to disrupt the prevailing term of office, and allowed it to continue and even extended it when the incumbent showed signs of recovery. The government chose to rely on reducing the physical demands of the office and, when the president was incapacitated, to rely on his wife or the acting president (usually the Speaker of Parliament or the Chief Justice) to fulfil the role. The prolonging of the Yusof presidency was particularly excruciating and it is uncertain if legal and parliamentary complications in arranging a pension or gratuity for Yusof and his family had any bearing on this.[60]

Perhaps, the Government's underlying assumption was that any presidential candidates in their fifties and sixties were likely to have medical problems, be they major or minor ones. It was also believed that the best doctors and nurses available to the presidential office would facilitate a good chance of recovery. Moreover, illnesses were not necessarily bad for the image of the presidency. By carrying out the duties of the office even when ailing, the president might reaffirm the sterling qualities of tenacity and courage, set a tradition of service and sacrifice for the country, and help generate a flood of public concern, sympathy and respect for the Citizen Number One and his office.[61] Even death in office and the subsequent nationwide mourning provided the people with an occasion to reflect on the more abstract meaning of statehood symbolized by the office of the president.[62] Ultimately, it might have been the mainly symbolic and constitutional role of the head of state in Singapore which prompted the PAP Government to consider it desirable to have stable and longer-term presidencies rather than have frequent changes.

ENTRY AND EXIT

Entering the Istana was a major and difficult decision for all the four presidents. Apart from being a little overawed by the significant constitutional role they were to play, they were deeply concerned about whether they could adjust to the trappings of presidential life. In the end, most of them had some difficulties and had to resort to various means to surmount them.

'Loneliness' of the office was a major problem for Yusof. He had a yearning to keep up with his old friends even when he was in high office. Hence he often tried to meet up with them either in or outside of the Istana. However, it was obviously a complicating and frustrating exercise. 'I would like to meet all my old friends again', he complained, 'but getting through the red tape and security boys exhausts me.'[63] To provide him with company, Lee Kuan Yew was said to have made the unprecedented arrangement of allowing Othman Wok, then the Minister of Culture and Social Affairs and close friend of Yusof from the days of *Utusan Melayu*, to stay in one of the bungalows within Istana grounds.[64] When Yusof collapsed during the cruise to Australia, it was Othman Wok who flew over immediately in order to be with the ailing president to 'cheer him up'.[65]

Being able to keep in close touch with old friends was also Wee's deep concern. Before accepting the post, he explicitly asked for and received Lee's assurance that he need not change his social life and could keep up with his circle of friends and his usual social activities.[66] As if to obtain a surer guarantee of greater freedom of movement, Wee decided not to stay in the Istana and opted to continue living in his home in Siglap and commute to the Istana for work and functions.[67] He also broke with tradition by shopping personally in departmental stores. 'When I first came to the Istana', the President proudly proclaimed, 'I was not even supposed to go to a bookshop to buy a book, my PS or ADC had to go. But I preferred to go there myself and take a look at the range, sizes, colour, prices…so I broke tradition. I went to Tangs'.[68]

Given Nair's intense union and political engagement before his assumption of the presidency, it was not surprising that he had the hardest time adjusting to a new life in the Istana. As discussed, there were early public concerns about how well he would be able to make the transition. Nair himself shared some of these. After the initial stage of being 'taken aback' by Lee's nomination, he deliberated for two weeks and then asked Lee 'if he could continue to move freely and informally as he had always done, without the trappings of the President' as he 'feared that these would cut him off from his old friends and fellow workers'. Lee assured him that he need not always be attending official parades and functions, and 'there is no reason why, however, at ease and in mufti, he should not continue to be his old self'.[69] This reassurance paved the way for Nair to enter the Istana but its inadequacy was amply demonstrated by his quick exit.

In a letter to Lee about two weeks after his resignation, Nair described his 'Greek tragedy' as follows:

The drastic change in life-style, the highly uncongenial protocol constraints, the loneliness and isolation of my office, bereft of the normal and easy companionship of the majority of my personal friends and colleagues, the absence of my sons in the States, all provided fertile ground for increasing recourse to alcohol. . . . I found it extremely difficult to adjust to life as president. Instead of rude prison warders who were my keepers when I was a political prisoner, I now found myself surrounded by polite and sometimes resplendently dressed gentlemen, who were nonetheless my keepers and prompters. I had managed to restrain my recourse to alcohol after three months of battle. Nevertheless, the loneliness of my job, the absence of the exhilaration of relating to crowds, committees and friends, relentlessly drew me back to the bottle. I tried to fight back, sometimes won, but more often lost.[70]

Lee, however, swiftly denied that the isolation and loneliness of the presidency was responsible for Nair's alcoholism:

To make a fresh start you have to cut out the make-believe. T[t]hat you were the President, and isolated in the Istana, had nothing to do with your alcoholism. Your two brothers and three sisters, your father, your mother, and two uncles, they all had alcoholism. They were not isolated in any Istana. [*sic*] Unless you stop rationalizing and making excuses for yourself, you cannot concentrate on the realities of the present.[71]

Nair's exit was therefore fraught with several related controversies. One was the precise juncture when Nair's alcoholism was supposed to have begun and whether this was closely associated with the burdens of the presidential office.[72] The government's position was that Nair used to drink heavily and continuously during three periods: a) when Phey Yew Kok, a former NTUC chairman and PAP MP was arrested and charged with misappropriating a large sum of union funds, b) in the period before his nomination and after his installation as president, and c) after the 1984 general election when the PAP suffered significant electoral set-backs. At first Nair admitted having the problem of alcoholism although he himself had known it for sure only about a year earlier. However, months later, Nair began denying that he had ever been an alcoholic and mounted a strong public defence through local and foreign publications, thus prompting the government to issue a parliamentary paper which collated medical and security investigations and private confidential correspondence on the subject.

Another controversy surrounding Nair's exit was his eligibility for a pension.[73] Nair had asked for a pension 'to live on, at least in ex-presidential dignity'. Lee was not in favour of granting him one, but the majority of his Cabinet prevailed on him and offered Nair a package which was conditional upon Nair abiding by the advice of a medical panel. Nair claimed to have rejected the idea of such an offer right from the beginning and was angry that the government proceeded to table it in Parliament and gave 'the unfortunate impression that [he] would accept a pension, with conditions, and that [he] required continuing medical attention'.

The third controversy was over the manner of his resignation.[74] Nair claimed that two days before his fateful trip to Kuching, Sarawak, he had told Lee about being 'seized by an unappeasable restlessness' and had reached an agreement with Lee to 'consider the possibility of [him] stepping down from the presidency straightaway, without waiting for [his] term to expire in October, and to arrange for Parliament to appoint Raja[ratnam] as president'. Moreover, he stated in the official letter of resignation tabled and read out in Parliament that 'I should feel obliged to step down from my high office. I make it abundantly clear that the decision to do so is entirely my own'. The government, however, remained curiously silent on Nair's purported resignation offer before the Kuching trip but its parliamentary paper left little doubt that Nair was forced from office. At first Nair had refused to resign but Lee and Rajaratnam met him at the hospital bed and threatened to remove him from the post through the constitutional provision of a two-third majority vote in the Parliament.

Nair's exit was not just controversial, it inflicted grave damage to the dignity of the presidential office. Supposedly under the influence of alcohol, Nair acted in the most unpresidential manner during his unofficial visit to Sarawak, 'behaving uninhibitedly with women, outraging their modesty, propositioning, fondling and molesting them'. The victims allegedly included nurses, young and old Malay women, Iban maidens, European ladies and wives of Sarawak ministers.[75] Subsequent investigations suggested that, prior to the Sarawak trip, Nair was already having an affair with a German woman whom he knew from his old union days and that he had also secretly left the Istana driving around and walking in Orchard Road unescorted and in disguise.[76]

While Nair resigned under such dramatic circumstances, the first two presidents died in office. Their deaths and the state funerals which followed provided the opportunity for an extended display of the presidential office's power in rallying the citizens and for a chance to take stock of the success in nation-building.

Yusof died of heart failure at the then Outram Hospital at 7.30 a.m. on 23 November 1970 after a long illness. The state burial was held promptly in the evening of the following day. Alluding to the Islamic practice of a quick burial, a statement from the prime minister's office explained that this was done 'in deference to the wishes of the family'.[77] Notwithstanding this, pomp and pageantry were not absent from the occasion. His body was rushed from the hospital to the Istana and almost all the Cabinet ministers turned up to pay their last respects by the late afternoon of 23 November. Members of Parliament, government officials and the diplomatic corps had their turn in the following morning. At 11.30 a.m. on 24 November, a gun carriage carrying the coffin drawn by 100 cadets from the Singapore Armed Forces Training Institute and escorted by Cabinet ministers, mourners, Muslim religious officials and members of the diplomatic corps made their way on foot from the Istana to the City Hall, a procession which lasted for nearly one-and-a-half hours. At the City Hall, the commonfolk were initially given only three hours to pay their final tribute. The public response was beyond the Government's expectation – apart from the countless number who thronged the streets to view the foot procession despite being drenched by rain midway, about 7,000 people turned up at the steps of the City Hall. At one point in time, crowd hysteria erupted and the doors had to be closed for 20 minutes until police reinforcements arrived. The public viewing time was subsequently extended by 40 minutes before the body was moved again from City Hall to reach Kranji Cemetery by 6.00 p.m. for the performance of the last rites which ended with a 21-gun salute and buglers sounding the *Last Post*.

Officials of the Muslim Religious Council played a key role in the funeral arrangements, but the secular influence of the state was visible. While the Muslim Religious Council marked out the precise spot for burial, it was the Government who decreed that Yusof was to be the first person to be buried at a new National Cemetery created for 'those who made major contributions to Singapore during their lifetime'. Situated next to the existing Kranji War Memorial for soldiers who died during the Second World War, the two-acre plot of land was now designated a cemetery which would reportedly be 'styled after America's Arlington National Cemetery where the late President John F. Kennedy lies'.[78] Moreover, while women, in accordance with Muslim custom, ought to be absent from the scene of burial, Puan Noor Aishah followed the secular requirement of a state funeral and was at Kranji to lay the first wreath over the grave.[79]

To underscore the fac that Yusof was the president of a

broad-based multi-racial society, tributes from leaders of the National Trade Union Congress, Singapore Employers' Federation, Chinese Chamber of Commerce, Indian Chamber of Commerce, International Chamber of Commerce, Nanyang University and Singapore Medical Association were solicited and publicized.[80] Apart from those held in mosques and by other Muslim organizations, memorial services were also held on the day of burial by the Singapore Buddhist Federation, the Inter-Religious Organization and the St. Andrew's Cathedral. The Jewish Welfare Board conducted its memorial service on the following day.[81]

While Yusof's death provided an opportunity to rally the nation, the government decided in its usual pragmatic manner that the normal affairs of the state should not be overly disrupted. No public holiday was declared for the day of the state funeral although government offices and many private businesses closed at 1.00 p.m. as 'a mark of respect'. Buses ran as usual and students were reminded to attend their on-going final examinations for secondary four and pre-university two certificates.[82]

When Sheares died of cancer on 12 May 1981, there was again no declaration of a public holiday, and this time government offices did not grant their employees a half day off to pay their respects to the departed president. This led someone to comment: 'I don't understand why the Government has not declared a public holiday as a mark of respect for the president's death. How many working people can come today to pay their respects?' Another very unhappy man said, 'Without a public holiday, I simply cannot make it here in time to pay respects. There was no time to come during lunch hour. I am very disappointed'.[83] Despite the limitations, the public response was again beyond the expectation of the organizers. Within a span of eight hours, 85,000 Singaporeans forming a one-kilometre queue starting from Orchard Road eventually bade farewell to the late president as his body lay in state at the Istana. More than half the number were teenaged school-children, some of them arriving with their teachers but many groups said they came without being asked by the schools. Initially, the crowd was allowed to bow, salute or say a silent prayer. When the crowds started swelling rapidly, they were hurried past the coffin without being allowed to linger for a while.[84]

Sheares was the second person to be buried at the designated National Cemetery. With the coming of age of television, the last rites beginning at 3.55 p.m. were televised live but this too generated controversy:

> Because there was no public holiday, many missed the direct telecast of the Sheares funeral procession, graveside service and

burial.... The fact that there would be no repeat telecast put a damper on things. Many might have been looking forward to seeing a piece of Singapore history in the making. Now it is considered inappropriate to telecast the state funeral again. Is it in bad taste to re-broadcast 'a sad and solemn occasion'? American presidents and British monarchs would probably say it's a fact of public office. But, in Singapore, public office is cloaked and shrouded as much as possible. Perhaps Singapore is too small an island and even national leaders need some assurances of privacy.[85]

The unexpectedly large turnout and strong public reaction to missing out on 'a piece of Singapore history' prompted many to feel that Singapore had reached a new level in its nation-building process. A *Straits Times* commentary noted that the large crowd at the Istana was 'a clear demonstration of a common identity among the people, and it was the strongest, most visible statement yet that said yes, Singapore is indeed a country and its people, when it comes to the crunch, are one'.[86] Wong Lin Ken, then the Raffles Professor of History at the University of Singapore, concluded firmly that 'we have definitely made significant progress in developing a sense of national identity'. Several sociologists and political scientists interviewed were reported to have echoed this view.[87]

The exit of the fourth president, Wee Kim Wee, was under much more propitious circumstances. In fact, it was a delayed exit of what was originally intended as a stop-gap presidency. When Lee Kuan Yew as Prime Minister first recommended Wee to the Parliament, it was made clear that Wee might not complete his full term and the government was finalizing the terms of an elected presidency. He even discussed with Wee at the beginning of the appointment the possible trauma in adjusting to ordinary life after leaving high office.[88] The legal and political process of pushing through the scheme of elected presidency took much longer than expected. Wee completed his first full term and was renominated and went on to finish his second term, making it a total of eight years. In the last two years of his tenure, he was the 'unelected elected president', one who was appointed only by the Parliament but vested with the power of an elected president.

Wee was the only president so far to retire from office graciously and gracefully. In his own words on the eve of his departure,

all good things must come to an end sometime. We must adjust to meet a given situation in our lifetime, either upward or downward.... You strip me of my presidency, what am I? I am just an ordinary man, a Singapore citizen.[89]

When asked to come up with five adjectives which sum up best his two terms, he suggested 'satisfying, interesting, fascinating, illuminating and understanding'.[90] His retirement evoked a stream of responses from many segments of the society. The accolade of being the 'People's President' was effusively showered upon him by both benches in the Parliament, by journalists and letters to the press.

Wee's retirement plan included some travelling 'to the other end of the earth', but he intended to spend the bulk of his time writing a memoir about his immediate and extended families and his various careers, a recollection which would unfortunately just be his family heirloom and not for publication.[91] While the idea of returning to the life of an ordinary citizen was natural to him, some others reacted strongly against it. Chia Shi Teck, a Nominated MP, observed:

> But do we, Singaporeans, now that we are talking about a more compassionate society, like to see the [ex-president and his wife] fade into the wilderness or into the unknown? I suppose the Government will give him some form of pension. But, sometimes, it is not a question of dollars and cents. It is a question of privileged treatment. So can the Government, or the state, not provide him with some properly accorded protocol, an office or a driver, or maybe, an official title or role to tap on his vast experience? I do not know whether we could make him an honorary president. In the French system, an ex-president or ex-prime minister is still entitled to use the title. It is just like in the army, where above a certain rank, he could keep his title. . . . I am not saying all this out of fun. I am thinking more on how we can set a precedent to recognize and reward great leaders who have contributed to the nation. I hope the Government can look into this area.[92]

Several readers also wrote to the press to request for 'a more concrete or tangible way of expressing our warm and sincere respect for a most beloved president'. A commemorative stamp and a bust at one of the national parks were some of the suggestions made.[93] In the end, Wee's exit was kept fairly low-keyed. A brief government gazette issued soon after his departure, announced that the former president was henceforth appointed a Deputy Registrar of Marriages, one of the several hundreds who were given the power to solemnize and register marriages outside of the Registry, such as at the couple's home, at a religious place, or in a restaurant.[94]

According to Goh Chok Tong, Wee's exit from the Istana could well have been delayed once more. Goh disclosed in Parliament that Wee was 'the Government's first choice to be Singapore's first elected president' and he had personally invited him as early as January 1993 to stand for election when his current term expired.[95] A month later, Wee declined the invitation, explaining that having been president for eight years, he would find it awkward to now ask the people to vote him in as president. Moreover, he could not reconcile himself with the need to campaign for votes and, at his age, another term of six years was too long. Goh's late disclosure only after the end of the presidential election was partly forced by public opinion. As Walter Woon, another Nominated MP, had noted:

> President Wee has attracted broad support from all sectors of the population. In fact, during the course of the presidential elections, one refrain I often heard was 'Why doesn't President Wee stand? We will have no problems electing him'. This came from all sides, people who supported Mr Ong [Teng Cheong], people who supported Mr Chua [Kim Yeow], all were equally comfortable with President Wee standing.[96]

Ling How Doong, Member of Bukit Gombak and a leader of the opposition Singapore Democratic Party, shared similar views: 'I dare say that had he run for the elected presidency, he would have received an overwhelming mandate from the people.'[97]

Such support for Wee to stand as a candidate for the 1993 presidential election, however, should not be overstated as there was at least one clear dissenting voice. S. Rajaratnam, who first recommended Wee for the presidential job in 1985, argued on the eve of Wee's departure from the Istana that Wee was ill-suited for elected presidency:

> I cannot imagine him standing up at elections to plead a cause and you have Chiam See Tong and others challenging him. I would have dissuaded him. I would say, 'lay off', because it would ruin him. An elected presidency would be unfair to him. Kim Wee is not a political personality. He is a personality. And he was a success. He was the People's President.[98]

THE TITLE OF 'PEOPLE'S PRESIDENT'

Wee's exit as the 'People's President' raised a number of interesting issues. First and foremost was the question of whether the other three presidents before Wee were therefore *not* 'People's Presidents'. Wee claimed that it was a journalist who first gave him this title and he is glad that the label stuck. In his view:

Every Singaporean has the right to have a People's President. You want someone who is approachable. Yusok Ishak, Benjamin Sheares and Devan Nair mixed with everybody too. So there's nothing really amazing that the President of Singapore should be close to the people.[99]

Indeed, both Yusof and Sheares, were sometimes also regarded as having been able to forge close ties with the people. In 1966, for example, Yusof made at least three widely publicized tours of constituencies during which he met up with many community leaders, school children, farmers, fishermen and kampong folk.[100] When he died, the *Straits Times* presented from its photo library a pictorial tribute to 'a man who believed his people came first'.[101] As for Sheares, he continued to attend to poor patients and to teach graduates and undergraduates at Kandang Kerbau Hospital two mornings a week even after becoming president.[102] Upon Sheares' death, Chiam See Tong, then secretary-general of the opposition Singapore Democratic Party, praised him as a president who 'endeared himself to all the people of Singapore'.[103] As the head of the Singapore Federation of Chambers of Commerce and Industry, Wee Cho Yaw offered the view that 'the late president was well known for his empathy for the common man and his concern for the welfare of the underprivileged. . . . Truly, he was one of those rare individuals who could walk with kings and yet not lose the common touch'.[104]

Despite recognizing their ties with the people, the accolade of 'People's President' was never given to Yusof and Sheares. Instead, it was apparent that some considerable distance remained between them and the people and it appeared that most Singaporeans did not get to know their first two presidents well. In a tribute on Yusof as a 'pioneer with a proud record', the *Straits Times* commented:

His constant message was that peoples of all races should be progressive, forward-looking, keen and prepared to take on challenges of the time. With him it was the message, not the man that mattered. And so it was that as publisher and editor and later President of Singapore he was never really known. He was also cloaked from the public by his modesty and a nature tending to the austere. . . . That Singapore is what it is today is due in some degree to a man it never fully knew, its first president.[105]

For Yusof, at least the public had some knowledge of the man through his early involvement in promoting Malay nationalism. Comparatively, Sheares was a much more distant figure for most Singaporeans, except perhaps for the medical fraternity. His son, Dr Joseph Sheares, said in an interview in 1987 that his father's main weakness was his extreme shyness, being in his element only among intimate friends and appearing distant and aloof to others.[106] Even the common friends of both presidents, as well as those who had worked under them, found Sheares much less accessible to the masses.[107] It was only at the point of his death and the subsequent media coverage of his life and times that many Singaporeans suddenly seemed to have 'rediscovered' Sheares and his presidency. A *Straits Times* journalist who was then 'a 31-year old son of Singapore' who 'felt he spoke for his generation of Singaporeans', wrote:

> I did not know many things about my president. He was always out there, I knew, the way the Singapore River was out there, a presence I somehow took for granted. I saw his picture occasionally in the papers, a long gaunt face with two deep lines running down his cheeks. I remembered that his speeches were rarely strident or exhortative, unlike many of my other leaders', and I had a vaguely outlined mental picture of my president as a humane person. On Wednesday, after reading the anonymous tribute in my paper, I was greatly moved; and later when I went through a file on him in the library, I knew in my heart that here was a person who deserved my greatest respects...[108]

A 17-year-old Ngee Ann Technical College student who was standing in the queue to pay his last respect to Sheares was interviewed and he earnestly said, 'I did not know much about the president when he was alive, I read the *Straits Times* and found out that he was such a good president. That's why I am here, to pay my respect'.[109] Similarly, a 24-year-old handicapped man who rolled his wheelchair all the way from his Jalan Besar home to the Istana disclosed, 'I am so moved by what I read in the papers that I feel I must come and show my respects as a citizen of Singapore'.[110] It was seemingly the posthumous heavy media coverage and the 'rediscovery process' it invoked which, more than anything else, brought Sheares' presidency a step closer to his people.

Given his controversial exit, it now appears ironic that the title of 'People's President' was in fact first given to Nair. The term crept into the political vocabulary of Singapore soon after it became clear that Nair was likely to assume the presidency after Sheares' death. The first recorded usage was probably the headline given to a news article which gave a profile about the prospective presidential candidate: 'Man who will be the People's President'.[111] The article itself did not use these words and had merely outlined Nair's political background, trade union connections, oratorical bluntness and family ties. The intentions behind the coining of such a headline became a little clearer when *The Sunday Times* came out with an editorial on 18 October 1981 entitled 'Of Presidents and Precedents', calling for a new 'concept of People's President'.[112] Without discrediting the Yusof and Sheares presidencies, it argued that some changes in the Singapore presidency would be welcome and that the nomination of Nair might

> help correct the fixed image in the minds of some of a presidential candidate who has a stately bearing, has ascended the pinnacle of his chosen profession, and has some of the trappings of material success.... Instead of clinging to some faded notions of what the presidency is all about, we should look forward to changes which may bring new dimensions and verve to the office.

The proposed concept of a People's President was regarded to be a 'bold and exciting image that is more in keeping with the changed times' and the editorial alluded to three essential qualities. Such a president should first of all have 'amply demonstrated that his heart is in the right place where Singapore is concerned'. It suggested 'someone who has dedicated the better part of his life to the country and has contributed much to the present state of its development'. Political leaders from the ruling party would fit this criterion well. Second, hinting at the much wider spectrum of grassroot contacts which Nair commanded when compared to Yusof and Sheares, the new president should be one who was able to reach out to *all* Singaporeans, 'workers, professionals and intellectuals alike'. Third, and this was the part which differed the most from precedents, the president should be 'more than just a figurehead and a benevolent patron to boy scouts and charities'. Putting in the careful qualification of 'without politicizing the office' and 'a leadership that rises above the polls', the editorial championed for a president who would have 'an important role to play in maintaining continuity of vision, purpose and direction', amidst 'the challenges of the Eighties and the inevitable change of political leadership'.

To realize this new concept of People's President, the editorial raised a number of questions, and with them the prospect of constitutional changes to the presidential office: 'Should we find a man who is likely to fit the job or should the job be shaped to fit the man?' 'Is our third Head of State to concern himself purely with perfunctory and ceremonial functions or will his role be enlarged?'[113] A day after Nair was duly elected, it was reported that there was no indication in the parliamentary proceedings that 'the duties of the office would be altered, as speculated by some, to accommodate the personality and abilities of the new president-elect'.[114] The title of People's President, however, stayed in vogue and it solidified further when the National Trade Union Congress rushed out a new pictorial publication entitled *Devan: Nation Builder, People's President, the Singaporean.*[115]

Although the choice of language was far from precise and the proposed concept of 'People's President' remained largely ambiguous, this campaign to rationalize Nair's presidency seemed to aim at preparing Singaporeans for a new era, an era where a degree of politicization of the presidential office was not only inevitable but was perceived as necessary for the long-term interest of the nation. At the very least, the incumbent would henceforth be drawn from within the existing pool of frontline political leaders. The presidential seat as the rallying apex of the nation-building process would now be claimed by the nation-builders themselves. A partial marriage of the symbolic office and the pioneering political executives was to be the new political setting for Singapore.

While the idea of 'People's President' was originally tailored specifically for Nair and was probably intended to usher in a new trend in the presidency for Singapore, these efforts suffered a severe setback when Nair was suddenly forced out of the Istana under a dark cloud of controversy. With his exit, the notion of 'People's President' slipped temporarily into disuse. It was revived in a full-blown manner only at the end of the first as well as the second term of Wee's presidency. However, the original politicized dimension had been pushed aside and Wee's claim on the title of 'People's President' rested essentially on his image as a caring, approachable and fatherly figure.

When Wee was initially recommended to take over from Nair in 1985, he had been called 'Mr Average'[116] and 'was not well-known to Singaporeans'.[117] By the end of his first term and when he was up for renomination, Lee Kuan Yew noted:

> Sir, today Wee Kim Wee needs no introduction. Most Singaporeans have seen and many have met their President and like him. They speak of him with affection. He has time and a kind word for everybody. He is an outgoing person who has reached out to a wide range of people.... And he does not distinguish between VIPs and ordinary Singaporeans.[118]

Speaking in support of Wee's renomination, the then Senior Parliamentary Secretary to the Minister for Education, Sidek bin Saniff, praised Wee for 'his concern for the people, for people of all strata and of all walks of life, from the healthy to the feeble, from the common man to men of position'. To him, Wee therefore embodied 'the meaning captured by the concept of "a People's President"', and fully deserved to be called one.[119] Member for Tampines, Aline Wong, also agreed that 'by his quiet dignity, his friendly and courteous disposition, a common touch and a genuine concern for the unfortunate in society', Wee had 'earned the very enviable reputation of being the People's President'.[120] The then Parliamentary Secretary to the Minister for Education and the Minister for Home Affairs, Tang Guan Seng, regarded Wee as 'truly the People's President' because Wee had won the hearts of all the races, including the minorities, and noted that this success of course had to do with his 'sociable personality'.[121]

This unanimous chorus of praises was repeated in Parliament at the end of Wee's second term of office.[122] However, during this occasion, enough time had elapsed for parliamentarians to reflect and comment on the Nair episode amidst their cheering for Wee. Government backbencher Tan Cheng Bock claimed that all Singaporeans applauded Wee as 'the *ideal* People's President',[123] raising the possibility of regarding Nair also as a People's President, albeit an imperfect one. More direct references comparing Wee with his disgraced predecessor were made by parliamentarians outside of the ruling party. Opposition member Ling How Doong noted that it was almost a cliché now to say that Wee was a 'People's President' but that he supported this notion partly because

> [Wee] accepted the heavy responsibility of the presidency in 1985 after an unfortunate episode. At the time when the nation needed someone to restore the dignity of the institution of the presidency, he did not fail us. By his humility and his approachable manner, he returns the presidency to the people.[124]

In similar vein, Nominated MP Chia Shi Teck observed:

> The first two presidents that we had, President Yusof bin Ishak and President Benjamin Sheares, died in office. Our third president, Mr C. V. Devan Nair, left unfortunately. Now, President Wee Kim Wee is stepping down most graciously and gracefully after eight good years of his life. [Wee and his wife] have toiled hard to earn back the prestige and respect of the office of the president. He became a truly People's President, loved by one and all, including the Opposition in this House.[125]

The revival of the 'People's President' notion describing Wee's two terms of presidency was prompted very much by the exceptionally good rapport which Wee managed to establish with a wide range of people. On the other hand, we cannot rule out the possibility that this unabashed loud acclamation of Wee's presidency constituted an unconscious, or even a deliberate, government-endorsed attempt to repair the damage caused to the office by Nair's sudden expulsion. The revival also meant a re-definition of the term. Under the original conception tailored for Nair's presidency, the 'People's President' had a strong political dimension. This was now shoved aside and Wee's claim to the title lay essentially upon the apolitical basis of unadulterated public admiration of him as an avuncular figure. Moreover, while the prestige of the head of state was rescued through the undisputed crowning of Wee as the 'People's President', it also left the new President Ong Teng Cheong with a hard act to follow.

EPILOGUE

The presidential office played an important role in Singapore's nation-building process. As the rallying point and embodiment of values and aspirations of the people, the head of state naturally had a role to play in nation-building. This role is critical in a multi-racial country with a Chinese majority and situated in the heart of the Malay Archipelago. Inevitably, a high degree of ethnic sensitivity surrounded the first four presidencies. The choice of president was determined largely in terms of race. He was carefully chosen from the various racial segments of the society: Malays, Eurasians, Indians, and Chinese. The order of succession was from the minority to the majority race, beginning with the dominant stock within the region. To make the candidate more acceptable to the other racial groups, his ethnic background was often diluted or qualified, such as reminding Singaporeans that Yusof was an immigrant of Sumatran descent and that Wee was an English-educated Straits-born Chinese. The ethnic and linguistic backgrounds of the first ladies were also occasionally discussed. Parliamentary presentations either supporting the appointment of a president or paying tribute to one upon his death or retirement were carefully choreographed with parliamentarians of different races speaking in sequence using their mother tongues even if all of them had a good command of English. A multi-racial, multi-religious dimension was equally visible during the funeral services for Yusof and Sheares. The public responses to their last rites were also used as barometers to take stock of how successfully Singapore had gelled as a nation.

For the first 28 years of its nationhood, Singapore had the service of only four presidents. Government believed that stable, long-term presidencies would make the arduous task of nation-building easier. At times, they even prolonged the tenure of the office-holders despite problems with their health, as in the cases of Yusof and Sheares. This preference for continuity and stability, however, did not mean that the government was averse to the idea of reshaping the presidential office to suit the local socio-political environment. As a young nation having seen only two generations of political leaders, several of Singapore's political institutions and practices underwent major modifications. The presidency was not spared although the degree of change was less than the others.

The most significant revision was of course the conversion of the figurehead presidency into a popularly elected one with some forms of executive power. Although the first elected president was sworn into office only on 1 September 1993, a proposed overhaul of the presidential office can be traced back more than a decade. Lee and his Cabinet colleagues reportedly began confidential deliberations on the matter as early as 1982, and he broached the subject publicly in April and August 1984. A government White Paper was issued subsequently in July 1988.[126] Wee Kim Wee then assumed the powers of an elected presidency from 30 November 1991 and became unofficially the 'unelected elected president' during the last two years of his tenure. Therefore, Singapore's presidency actually functioned in an atmosphere of imminent major change for more than a third of the first 28 years. A spirit of experimentation had therefore very much co-existed with the preference for stable long-term presidencies.

Significantly, Nair's nomination as the third president of Singapore foreshadowed the institutionalization of an elected presidency. It was probably no coincidence that Nair was nominated in October 1981 and that the Cabinet began confidential deliberations on elected presidency in 1982. At the point of Nair's nomination, Lee as Prime Minister argued that it was inevitable that more and more potential presidential candidates would have been caught up in the political struggles of decolonization and anti-communism and have played an active role in the management of Singapore. Simultaneously, the media clamoured for a departure from the precedents set by Yusof and Sheares and pushed for a new 'concept of the People's President'. As we have seen, the title of 'People's President' was first conferred on Nair at the start of his presidency and the purpose was apparently to secure public acceptance of a new kind of president who would play a direct and key part in shaping the development of Singapore and in 'maintaining continuity of vision, purpose and direction' amidst the 'inevitable change of political leadership'. In other words, the presidential office as the highest focus for the process of nation-building would be brought one step closer to the executive branch of the political system. The president himself was to have been an active nation-builder, in particular from within the ranks of the ruling politicians, and he would help steer the nation through future changes in political leadership. This scheme therefore was a departure from Yusof's and Sheares' presidencies and called for a degree of politicization of the office.

The sudden exit of Nair from the Istana upset such a plan but did not put a stop to it. The government in fact contemplated appointing Ong Teng Cheong, another PAP party leader, to be the next immediate president.[127] But with Ong's own disinclination at that time and with the restoration of the dignity of the office as a prime consideration, Wee who was essentially a non-political figure was chosen to replace Nair. The government, however, continued its planning and deliberations and eventually put the elected presidency into effect, according much more power to the president, especially in terms of controlling the financial reserves and key appointments to the civil service and some statutory boards. Having been a Cabinet minister for at least three years became one of the optional prequalifying conditions to run for the presidency.[128] The captains of the first and second generations of PAP leaders who steered Singapore through troubled waters would now enjoy the chance of becoming more than just an elder statesmen in retirement; a prospective presidentship with special powers had become a distinct possibility. In August 1993, Ong Teng Cheong resigned from his deputy prime ministership and chairmanship of the PAP and was the first to take on the job of an elected president. His elevation marked the success of the ruling party's attempt to claim the presidency for the foremost leaders of the early generations of nation-builders, possibly in the hope that this would solidify the process of nation-building but interpreted by some as yet another attempt to perpetuate the political hegemony of the PAP.[129]

While the election of Ong as the fifth President of the Republic ushered in a new era, there are historical continuities as certain issues observed in the previous four presidencies remained relevant even at the beginning of Ong's elected presidency. For instance, there was still a great deal of ethnic sensitivity surrounding the office. At the National Trade Union Congress (NTUC) press conference announcing Ong's candidature, the panel of 15 NTUC central committee members led by their president Oscar Oliverio was asked point-blank if Ong's role as an advocate of Chinese language and culture would affect his standing among the ethnic minorities. In response, the Malay, Indian and Eurasian unionists who were present quickly jumped in to endorse Ong as one who believed in multi-racialism and cared equally for all races.[130] About two weeks later, Ong himself had to address the same issue candidly:

> I am a Chinese Singaporean. I know Chinese. It is not a sin, right? I understand their culture, their thinking, better than other Singaporeans who do not know Chinese. But basically, I am Singaporean. I know a bit of Malay, but that doesn't mean I would not like to know more. In fact, that is the way to be truly Singaporean – to know as much about the various ethnic communities, as much as possible.... So to those who want to say that because I am Chinese-educated I will not be able to relate to the other communities, I think it is not true.[131]

Illness, which touched the previous four presidencies in varying ways, was another issue that troubled Ong's presidency right from the start as he had been diagnosed to be suffering from cancer barely a year before he was put up for the presidential election. On 16 November 1992, partly forced by public 'whispers' which had led to a 32-point drop in the *Straits Times* stock-market index, the government issued a statement and called for a briefing to disclose that Ong was found to have cancer in late April while Leé Hsien Loong, the other Deputy Prime Minister, found out about his cancer on 16 October.[132] Due to the slow growing nature of his cancer, Ong and his specialist doctors decided not to undergo any treatment but merely to continue close follow-up. The diagnosis and watch-and-wait approach cast a shadow over Ong's nomination and eventually also his presidency. At the nomination press conference, Oscar Oliviero, who was the NTUC chairman and later the chairman of Ong's election campaign steering committee, brushed aside questions on Ong's health by asserting that the illness 'doesn't affect him at all at this moment' and 'in fact, he is much healthier than many of us here'.[133] Two weeks later, Ong put up his own defence:

> I am fine. I don't worry or think about it. The problem is around the neck. I was operated on, they took a lump out and diagnosed it as malignant. But because of the operation, some nerves were pulled. That's why my mouth is a bit crooked. There you can see. It is improving slowly. You can see I have a dimple here which I was not born with! So I am slowly recovering. But being old, you know, it

takes longer to recover. Other than this, in recent months, there has been no other activity. In that sense, I am healthy.[134]

Having won the election campaign, Ong was sworn in as the fifth president on 1 September 1993. Less than a year after this, Ong's health problem surged to the forefront of public attention again when he had a medical examination and lost his voice, forcing him to cancel a major Istana tea party for 300 students and to be warded for rest and observation. The prime minister's office quickly issued a statement denying that the loss of voice was related to the low-grade lymphoma and attributed it to an inflammation of the throat caused by an endoscopic examination.[135] Five days later a front page photograph and news item reported that Ong was 'looking well' after his discharge from hospital and was able to attend a philharmonic orchestra performance.[136] Two days after this, during the intermission of another cultural performance, Ong spoke to reporters saying that he had recovered fully from the loss of his voice and had resumed normal duties. He reassured the public that since he was diagnosed as suffering from cancer, he had been going for blood tests every two to three months and other tests, such as computed tomography scans and X-rays, once or twice a year. 'I lead a normal life,' he said, 'I don't suffer from pain, so everything is normal.'[137]

Another public concern at the onset of Ong's presidency was his strongly partisan political background, demonstrating a close parallel with the public unease over Devan Nair's nomination as the third president. This was no surprise. After all, Ong shared with Nair very similar backgrounds in past partisan political activities and labour union connections. In fact, as argued earlier, the elected presidency scheme and Ong's nomination for the post could be seen as continuation of a long process to politicize the presidential office since Nair's time.

Ong's election campaign was forced to put in special efforts to allay the public concern. The NTUC press conference launching Ong's candidacy presented Ong's long political experience as a 'tremendous advantage', especially since he would better understand the workings of government and possess the necessary political judgement. Responding to a query on whether Singaporeans would prefer a President with no past party links, the panelists argued that Ong had shown himself to be independent-minded on at least two occasions.[138] First, it was claimed that Ong had been 'very critical of the party' in his analysis of the PAP's performance in the 1991 general election. Second, during the economic recession of the mid-1980s, Ong was said to have 'resisted government pressure' to impose too severe a wage restraint on the labourers.

The most significant step taken to reassure the public of Ong's political independence was to choose the NTUC to spearhead Ong's nomination and election campaign.[139] As indicated by the following news analysis, pains were taken to try to convince the public that Ong was asked independently by the labour movement to run for the presidency and the PAP's hand was not behind the NTUC's move:

> It is no secret that the trade union body is closely linked with the PAP. So it is hardly surprising that many Singaporeans wonder if the PAP was behind all of this. Was the NTUC operating on its own steam? And what are the implications of it taking on such a high-profile political role? Insight posed these questions to NTUC president Oscar Oliveiro at a press conference on Monday, and in a subsequent interview. He maintained that it was he who had initiated the move to draft Mr Ong into the post.... He said that the grassroots leaders had come up with the idea on their own, without any prompting from any quarter. Even the four PAP MPs on the NTUC's CEC were excluded from the group's initial discussions, although they later backed the committee's decision. This was because it was important for the NTUC to make clear that Mr Ong's nomination was not initiated by the PAP MPs in the labour movement, he said. We wanted the nomination to come from the grassroots. We wanted a *People's President*, who is above party politics.[140]

This brief reference to 'People's President' might well be the only instance of its use in Ong's campaign. By this time, the term 'People's President' was so overused and well-claimed by Wee that it was not suitable to be invoked to promote Ong's candidacy. This was just as well because votes were cast and tallied in choosing an elected president and there was always the likelihood of not securing an overwhelming support. Indeed, the outcome of the election was that Ong in a contest against Chua Kim Yeow, a former accountant-general and one who hardly put in any serious effort in the presidential campaign, garnered only 58.7 per cent of the valid votes. While Ong had certainly won the mandate to preside over Singapore, a substantial number of people in Singapore had voted against him. To what extent would he then still be regarded as the 'People's President'?

Alluding to Wee's claim on the title of 'People's President', Lee Kuan Yew was asked at the reception following Ong's swearing-in ceremony as to whether Ong should try and emulate Wee's personalized approach. Lee replied firmly that 'it would be "madness" as Mr Ong was not Mr Wee'.[141] He in fact reminded Singaporeans quickly that the office of the president had changed and there must now be a different kind of president. To him, the elected president would hitherto have to take a stand from time to time, a stand which might be unpopular. In a thrust against Wee's style of 'People's President' and the quest for popularity, he asserted that an elected President's job was not to be popular but to be strong. He added: 'To do his job, he has to keep abreast of developments in the fields where he had responsibilities and that is going to take some time. In other words, he can't just go around shaking hands.'[142]

In evaluating Ong's presidency in the future, either a new epithet would have to be coined to depict his presidency or the title of 'People's President' would have to be redefined once more. The redefinition may well mean a return to the political dimension already prescribed when the title was first coined in 1981.

NOTES

1 Even before the onset of the elected presidency, the official words used were 'election of president'. Strictly speaking, however, the first four presidents of Singapore were 'appointed' rather than elected because candidates could not nominate themselves, nor had there ever been more than one name on the slate for Parliament to 'elect' from.

2 See the Constitutional Amendment Act and Independence Act in *Singapore Government Gazette Acts Supplement*, No. 1 dated 23 December 1965 and No. 2 dated 28 December 1965. I wish to thank Sai Siew Min for her help in the writing of this research article, especially in locating and photocopying source materials. This chapter focuses on the period between 1965 and August 1993 and thus will leave out a discussion on why Yusof was chosen in the first place in 1959 to be the Yang di-Pertuan Negara.

3 'Election of President of Republic of Singapore', *Parliamentary Debates Singapore*, 30.7 (30 December 1970): 378.

4 'Who will be the next Head of State?' *Straits Times*, 25 November 1970. Yeoh Ghim Seng, A. P. Rajah, and Othman Wok were also named as prospective candidates in 'Times Change', *Far Eastern Economic Review*, 9 January 1971.

5 'Times Change', *Far Eastern Economic Review*, 9 January 1971. It was reported here that 'some PAP members believe that the post was offered to and refused by A. P. Rajah, Singapore's High Commissioner in London'.

6 Lee speaking on 'Tribute to the late President Dr Benjamin Henry Sheares', *Parliamentary Debates Singapore*, 41.1 (12 June 1981): 9; Ranjit Kaur, 'The Life of Benjamin Henry Sheares, 1907–1981', Academic Exercise, Department of History, National University of Singapore, 1987/88: 34, suggested that Goh Keng Swee, then the Minister of Finance, was

the 'prime mover in nominating Sheares'. There is, however, inadequate evidence and Goh was probably merely helping to gather information about Sheares from some of the latter's close friends.

7 Lee speaking on 'Election of President of the Republic of Singapore', *Parliamentary Debates Singapore*, 38.2 (29 December 1978): 58.

8 Lee speaking on 'Tribute to the late President Dr Benjamin Henry Sheares', *Ibid.*, 41.1 (12 June 1981): 8.

9 James Minchin, *No Man is an Island* (Sydney: Allen and Unwin, 1990): 213. The source of his information on Lee's wife having been one of Sheares' eminent patients is not indicated here; 'Times Change', *Far Eastern Economic Review*, 9 January 1971, referred to Sheares as having treated the 'wives of three senior Cabinet ministers'.

10 Changes in appointments were made in the International Confederation of Free Trade Unions – Asian Regional Organizations, the Singapore Airline and the National Trade Union Congress from July and they were all related to Nair's imminent presidency. See 'Nair to become President', *Business Times*, 13 October 1981.

11 Lee speaking on 'Election of President of the Republic of Singapore', *Parliamentary Debates Singapore*, 41.5 (23 October 1981): 232.

12 *Ibid.*

13 Lee speaking on 'Election of President', *Ibid.*, 46.4 (30 August 1985): 313.

14 Ong's disclosure in Singapore Lianhe Bao (ed.) *Wang Dingchang: Zouxiang Zongtongfu zhilu* [Ong Teng Cheong: Road to the Istana] (Singapore: Singapore Press Holding, 1994): 125.

15 'A Stab in the Heart', in *Far Eastern Economic Review*, 11 April 1985, also pointed to Choor Singh, a retired High Court judge, as another possibility.

16 Lee speaking on 'Election of President', *Parliamentary Debates Singapore*, 46.4 (30 August 1985): 313.

17 'The President who Put People Before Pomp and Protocol', *Straits Times*, 31 August 1993.

18 Lee speaking on 'Election of President', *Parliamentary Debates Singapore*, 46.4 (30 August 1985): 313–14.

19 Mrs Lee Chin Koon, *Mrs Lee's Cookbook: Nonya Recipes and Other Favourite Recipes* (Singapore, 1974). Foreword was written on 21 October 1974 when Wee was then Singapore's High Commissioner to Malaysia.

20 Sharon Siddique, 'The Phenomenology of Ethnicity: A Singapore Case-Study', in *Sojourn: Social Issues in Southeast Asia*, 5.1 (February 1990): 35–62. Here, the author was pointing to other aspects such as the Housing Development Board's allocation of public flats along racial proportions, Group Representative Constituencies for parliamentary elections and immigration policies. She argued that the government's intention was to create a Singaporean multi-racial model which would be interactionist, rather than integrationist or assimiliationist.

21 'Power Watch', *Straits Times*, 31 July 1993. Ridzwan Dzafir was then a director-general at the Trade Development Board, one of Singapore's roving ambassadors, and a member of the Presidential Council for Minority Rights.

22 Rahmat bin Kenap, Member of Geylang Serai, speaking on 'Election of President of Republic of Singapore', *Parliamentary Debates Singapore*, 26.7 (30 November 1967): 412–13.

23 Lim Guan Hoo, Member of Bukit Merah, speaking, *Ibid.*: 414.
24 For Sheares' first term appointment, parliamentarians who spoke in their mother tongues were Rahmat Kenap, Chng Jit Koon and P. Govindasamy. They repeated their act when Sheares was up for his second term. For his third term, it was Sidek Saniff and Yeo Choo Kok (no Tamil speaker on this occasion). The parliamentary motion for Devan Nair's appointment was supported by Ahmad Matter, Yeo Choo Kok and M. K. A. Jabbar, while that for Wee Kim Wee was supported by Yatiman Yusof and Chng Jit Koon (also no Tamil speaker this round). See *Ibid.*, 30.7 (30 December 1970): 380–2, 33.14 (6 November 1974): 1082–4, 38.2 (29 December 1978): 57–60, 41.5 (23 October 1981): 234–40 and 46.4 (30 August 1985): 317–21.
25 Lee speaking on 'Obituary on the Late President Yusof Bin Ishak', *Ibid.*, 30.7 (30 December 1970): 375.
26 'Times Change', *Far Eastern Economic Review*, 9 January 1971.
27 'The President Who Put People Before Pomp and Protocol', *Straits Times*, 31 August 1993.
28 Yatiman Yusof, Member of Kampong Kembangan, speaking on 'Election of President', *Ibid.*, 46.4 (30 August 1985): 320.
29 Lee speaking on 'Election of President', *Ibid.*: 313.
30 'The President Who Put People Before Pomp and Protocol', *Straits Times*, 31 August 1993.
31 This awareness is best captured by comments made by Goh Chok Tong on Ong Teng Cheong's elected presidency, but which could be applied easily to the earlier presidencies: 'So we are really talking of two people, not just one, when we look for suitable presidential candidates. A President and a First Lady'. See 'Teng Cheong Gets PM's Vote', *Straits Times*, 16 August 1993.
32 Lee speaking on 'Election of President of Republic of Singapore', *Parliamentary Debates Singapore*, 26.7 (30 November 1967): 408.
33 'Times Change', *Far Eastern Economic Review*, 9 January 1971.
34 'Election of President of Republic of Singapore', *Parliamentary Debates Singapore*, 30.7 (30 December 1970): 379.
35 'Man who will be the People's President', *Straits Times*, 13 October 1981.
36 'President To Be', *Straits Times*, 28 December 1970.
37 Lee speaking on 'Election of President', *Parliamentary Debates Singapore*, 54.6 (31 August 1989): 489.
38 The following brief account on Yusof's political background is based upon 'He was a Pioneer with a Proud Record', *Straits Times*, 24 November 1970; and Bruno Lopez, 'Yusof bin Ishak: Journalist and Head of State', Academic Exercise, Department of History, National University of Singapore, 1987/88, chs 1–4.
39 The following general account is compiled from: 'Comrade President', in *The Monitor: Journal of the United Workers of the Petroleum Industry*, Special issue of October 1981, Singapore; *Devan: The Nation Builder, People's President, the Singaporean*, National Trade Union Congress (ed.) (Singapore: NTUC, 1981); Lee speaking on 'Election of President of the Republic of Singapore', *Parliamentary Debates Singapore*, 41.5 (23 October 1981): 228–31; 'Man who will be the People's President', *Straits Times*, 13 October 1981.

40   Lee speaking on 'Election of President of the Republic of Singapore', *Parliamentary Debates Singapore*, 41.5 (23 October 1981): 230–2.
41   'Man who will be the People's President', *Straits Times*, 13 October 1981.
42   *Ibid.*
43   'Devan is Right Choice, Say Labour Leaders', *Ibid.*, 20 October 1981.
44   'Devan Suitable for Presidency', *Business Times*, 24 October 1981.
45   Lee speaking on 'Election of President of the Republic of Singapore', *Parliamentary Debates Singapore*, 41.5 (23 October 1981): 232–3.
46   *Ibid.*
47   Chan Heng Chee, 'Singapore in 1981: Planned Changes, Unplanned Consequences', in *Asian Survey*, 22.2 (February 1982): 219–25; Chua Beng Huat, 'Singapore in 1981: Problems in New Beginnings', *Southeast Asian Affairs, 1982* (Singapore: Institute of Southeast Asian Studies, 1982): 315–20; and Ong Sing Keh, 'The Anson By-Elections of 1961 and 1981: A Comparative Study', Academic Exercise, Department of History, National University of Singapore, 1983/84.
48   Chua Beng Huat, 'Singapore in 1981: Problems in New Beginnings': 320.
49   *Ibid.*
50   Lee speaking on 'Election of President of Republic of Singapore', *Parliamentary Debates Singapore*, 26.7 (30 November 1967): 409.
51   Lee speaking on 'Election of President of Republic of Singapore', *Ibid.*, 33.14 (6 November 1974): 1081; 38.2 (29 December 1978): 56 and 'Tribute to the Late President Dr Benjamin Henry Sheares', *Ibid.*, 41.1 (12 June 1981): 10.
52   The Indian national was Kalu Sarkar, see *C. V. Devan Nair: Circumstances Relating to Resignation as President of the Republic of Singapore*, Paper presented to Parliament on 29 June 1988, Comd 8 of 1988: 3, B4 and C1.
53   Goh speaking on 'Tribute to President Wee Kim Wee', *Parliamentary Debates Singapore*, 61.6 (31 August 1993): 525–7.
54   Tan (Member of Ayer Rajah) and Chia speaking, *Ibid.*: 530 and 543–4.
55   'The President who put people before Pomp and Protocol', *Straits Times*, 31 August 1993.
56   The following account on Yusof's health is compiled from: Bruno Lopez, 'Yusof bin Ishak: Journalist and Head of State': 29–30, 62, 83–5; 'Yusof may be out in a Week, Says Hospital', 'Yusof: Further Improvement' and 'President Yusof', *Straits Times*, 15 and 16 March and 20 April 1968; 'He was a Pioneer with a Proud Record', *Straits Times*, 24 November 1970; and Lee speaking on 'Obituary on the Late President Yusof bin Ishak', *Parliamentary Debates Singapore*, 30.7 (30 December 1970): 374–5.
57   Lee speaking on 'Obituary on the Late President Yusof bin Ishak', *Parliamentary Debates Singapore*, 30.7 (30 December 1970): 374–6.
58   The following discussion is based upon: Ranjit Kaur, 'The Life of Benjamin Henry Sheares, 1907–1981': 8–9, 25, 41 and 53. The information on chain-smoking is from Ranjit's interview with Sheares's son, Dr Joseph Sheares, on 27 October 1987; Lee speaking on 'Election of President of Republic of Singapore', *Parliamentary Debates Singapore*, 30.7 (30 December 1970): 378–80, 33.14 (6 November 1974): 1081–2 and 38.2 (29 December 1978): 55–7, and 'Tribute to the Late President Dr Benjamin Henry Sheares', *Ibid.*, 41.1 (12 June 1981): 7–14.

59 Lee Kuan Yew, Dr Lee Siew Choh (Non-Constituency Member) and Chiam See Tong (Member of Potong Pasir) speaking on 'Election of the President', *Parliamentary Debates Singapore*, 54.6 (31 August 1989): 491 and 495–6; Goh Chok Tong speaking on 'Tribute to President Wee Kim Wee', *Ibid.*, 61.6 (31 August 1993): 527.

60 A Civil List and Pension Bill providing money for the president and his family upon departure from office was first passed by the Parliament in May 1970 and yet very quickly amended to provide for additional financial support in December 1970. See *Ibid.*, 30.2 (21 May 1970): 43–5 and 30.7 (30 December 1970): 376–8. The new financial arrangement was confirmed only when Hon Sui Sen moved the motion on 'Pension for Widow and Children of the Late President', *Ibid.*, 30.8 (11 January 1971): 531–2. Replying to a written query from me, Noor Aishah (Yusof's First Lady) has not shed light on this issue. She attributes the prolonging of the presidency solely to Yusof's own determination 'to finish his work and complete his term'. Letter from Noor Aishah, dated 21 December 1994.

61 See for example, Lee's praise of Sheares in 'Election of President of Republic of Singapore', *Ibid.*, 33.14 (6 November 1974): 1081; 'The Substance and the Trappings', *Straits Times*, 17 May 1981.

62 This subject will be raised again in the following section on 'Entry and Exit'.

63 'He was a Pioneer with a Proud Record', *Straits Times*, 24 November 1970. Noor Aishah, in a letter to me dated 21 December 1994, claims that Yusof 'was never lonely whilst in office' and 'he had many friends from his earlier days', including 'Mr Wee Kim Wee, the late Justice Chua and Dr Ee Peng Liang'.

64 Bruno Lopez, 'Yusof bin Ishak: Journalist and Head of State': 84. This information is based upon his interview with Othman Wok.

65 *Straits Times*, 14 March 1968.

66 Lee speaking on 'Election of President', *Parliamentary Debates Singapore*, 46.4 (30 August 1985): 317.

67 'Wee Sworn in as President', *Business Times*, 3 September 1985; 'Thirty Seconds Later, Our New President', *Straits Times*, 3 September 1985. Sheares was the first President who opted not to reside at the Istana, seeking solace in his own home at Holt Road. See Ranjit Kaur, 'The Life of Benjamin Henry Sheares, 1907–1981': 40.

68 'The President who put People before Pomp and Protocol', *Straits Times*, 31 August 1993.

69 Lee speaking on 'Election of President of the Republic of Singapore', *Parliamentary Debates Singapore*, 41.5 (23 October 1981): 232–3.

70 Letter from Devan Nair to Lee Kuan Yew dated 11 April 1985: 4, in *C. V. Devan Nair: Circumstances Relating to Resignation as President of the Republic of Singapore*, presented to the Parliament on 29 June 1988: C11–17. In a public speech made about four months earlier, Nair was already drawing a parallel between the Istana and Changi Prison: 'They are both cages, the one harsh, grim and grey, the other gilded and red-carpeted. I was escorted by police officers in and out of the Changi residence. I am still escorted by police officers in and out of the Istana, but without handcuffs, of course', *Straits Times*, 8 December 1984.

71 Lee's reply to Nair, dated 22 April 1985, in *C. V. Devan Nair: Circumstances Relating to Resignation as President of the Republic of Singapore*: C18.

72 The following discussion is based upon *Ibid.*:1–2, 7–8, Medical Reports in Section A, C6–7, C11–18.

73 See documents in *Ibid.*: C4 and C20–4.

74 The following discussion and quotes are taken from *Ibid.*: 1–2, C4–5 and C16.

75 The discussion in this paragraph is based upon documents in *Ibid.*: 1–6 and A1–7.

76 *Ibid.*: 1–5, B1–7 and C16.

77 'President Yusof Dies', *Straits Times*, 24 November 1970.

78 'A Hero's Rest . . . ' *Ibid.*, 24 November 1970. Today, the cemetery remains in a neglected state. Apart from the two tombstones of Yusof and Sheares, there are no other markings or structures befitting a National Cemetery.

79 'Nation pays its final tribute', *Straits Times*, 25 November 1970.

80 'Tributes to the President', *Ibid.*, 24 November 1970.

81 'Mosques, Churches, Temples Hold Memorial Services', in *Ibid.*, 24 November 1970 and 'Bells Toll 20-Min as the Cortege Passes', in *Ibid.*, 25 November 1970.

82 'President Yusof Dies', *Ibid.*, 24 November 1970.

83 'The People's Tribute', *Ibid.*, 15 May 1981. The first comment was made by G. Prakash (age 17) and the second Tay Hee Teck (age 34).

84 *Ibid.*

85 'The Appropriate Attitude', *Ibid.*, 17 May 1981.

86 'The President and I. . . . By a 31-Year-Old Son of Singapore', by Richard Lim, *Ibid.*, 16 May 1981.

87 'The Substance and the Trappings', *Ibid.*, 17 May 1981.

88 Lee speaking on 'Election of President', *Parliamentary Debates Singapore*, 46.4 (30 August 1985): 316–17.

89 'Looking Back, 1985–1993', *Straits Times*, 31 August 1993.

90 'Never Shun the Common People', *Ibid.*, 22 August 1993.

91 'Never Shun the Common People', *Straits Times*, 22 August 1993, this was billed as his 'farewell interview'; Goh Chok Tong also made reference to Wee's private memoir when speaking on 'Tribute to President Wee Kim Wee', *Parliamentary Debates Singapore*, 61.6 (31 August 1993): 528–9.

92 Chia speaking on 'Tribute to President Wee Kim Wee', *Parliamentary Debates Singapore*, 61.6 (31 August 1993): 545.

93 Letters from Anthony Hooi Liang Kwan and Pang Boon Chye, respectively in *Straits Times*, Forum page, 6 and 10 September 1993.

94 As reported in 'Wee Kim Wee Made a Deputy Registrar of Marriages', *Ibid.*, 1 January 1994.

95 Prime Minister Goh speaking on 'Tribute to President Wee Kim Wee', *Parliamentary Debates Singapore*, 61.6 (31 August 1993): 528.

96 Woon speaking on 'Tribute to President Wee Kim Wee', *Ibid.*, 61.6 (31 August 1993): 546.

97 Ling speaking, *Ibid.*: 539.

98 'The President who put People before Pomp and Protocol', *Straits Times*, 31 August 1993.

99 'Never Shun the Common People', *Straits Times*, 22 August 1993.

100 'President Meets the People', *The Mirror*, 2.28 (11 July 1966) and 2.40 (3 October 1966).
101 'Smiles that Span the Years', *Straits Times*, 24 November 1970.
102 Lee Kuan Yew speaking on 'Tribute to the Late President Dr Benjamin Henry Sheares', *Parliamentary Debates Singapore*, 41.1 (12 June 1981): 9.
103 'Tributes from Those Who Lost an "Old Friend",' *Straits Times*, 13 May 1981.
104 *Ibid.*
105 'He was a Pioneer with a Proud Record', *Straits Times*, 24 November 1970. On Yusof's lack of inter-personal skill, A. Samad Ismail, *Ketokohan dan Kewartawanan* [Personalities and Journalism] (Kuala Lumpur: Dewan Bahasa dan Pustaka, 1991): 136 and 139, noted that Yusof was rather harsh towards his subordinates at the *Utusan Melayu*.
106 Ranjit Kaur, 'The Life of Benjamin Henry Sheares, 1907–1981': 8.
107 Bruno Lopez, 'Yusof bin Ishak: Journalist and Head of State': 82.
108 'The President and I. . . . By a 31-Year-Old Son of Singapore', by Richard Lim, *Straits Times*, 16 May 1981.
109 *Ibid.*
110 'The People's Tribute', *Ibid.*, 15 May 1981.
111 'Man who will be the People's President', by Ivan Fernandez, *Ibid.*, 13 October 1981.
112 The following discussion and quotes are taken from 'Of Presidents and Precedents', *Sunday Times*, 18 October 1981.
113 *Ibid.*
114 'From the Gallery', by Ivan Fernandez, *Straits Times*, 24 October 1981.
115 *Devan: Nation Builder, People's President, the Singaporean* (Singapore: National Trade Union Congress, November 1981). The text of this book, however, makes no direct reference to the term 'People's President'. It merely emphasizes Nair's grassroots links with the labour movement. The NTUC also published in the following year, a 413-page volume on *Not by Wages Alone: Selected Speeches and Writings of C. V. Devan Nair, 1959–1981* (Singapore: National Trade Union Congress, 1982).
116 Yatiman Yusof, Member of Kampong Kembangan, speaking on 'Election of President', *Parliamentary Debates Singapore*, 46.4 (30 August 1985): 320.
117 Lee Kuan Yew speaking on 'Election of President', *Ibid.*, 54.6 (31 August 1989): 489–90.
118 *Ibid.*: 489–50.
119 Sidek speaking, *Ibid.*, 54.6 (31 August 1989): 492.
120 Wong speaking, *Ibid.*: 497.
121 Tang speaking, *Ibid.*: 493.
122 See for example the speeches of Sidek bin Saniff (Minister of State for Education), Ow Chin Hock (Member of Leng Kee) and Ho Kah Leong (Senior Parliamentary Secretary to the Minister for Information and the Arts) speaking on 'Tribute to President Wee Kim Wee', *Ibid.*, 61.6 (3 August 1993): 534, 537 and 541.
123 Tan, Member of Ayer Rajah, speaking on 'Tribute to President Wee Kim Wee', *Ibid.*: 530.
124 Ling speaking, *Ibid.*: 538.
125 Chia speaking, *Ibid.*: 544–5.

126 Exchanges between J. B. Jeyaretnam and Lee Kuan Yew on 'President of the Republic of Singapore (Choice of electorate)', *Parliamentary Debates Singapore*, 43.20 (19 October 1984): 2083–4; Goh Chok Tong speaking on 'Constitutional Amendments to Safeguard Financial Assets and the Integrity of the Public Service (White Paper)', *Ibid.*, 51.9 (29 July 1988): 479.

127 Ong's disclosure in Singapore Lianhe Bao (ed.) *Wang Dingchang: Zouxiang Zongtongfu zhilu* [Ong Teng Cheong: Road to the Istana]: 125. See also the previous discussion under the section on 'Shortlists and Persuaders'.

128 Article 19 (2) (g) (i) of the *Constitution of the Republic of Singapore* (1992 Reprint).

129 For interpretations on linking the elected presidency to the perpetuation of PAP's power, see Lily Z. Rahim, 'Singapore: Consent, Coercion and Constitutional Engineering', in *Current Affairs Bulletin*, 70.7 (December 1993/January 1994): 20–26 and Hussin Mutalib, 'Singapore's Elected Presidency and the Quest for Regime Dominance', Working Paper No. 9 (1994), Department of Political Science, National University of Singapore, 51 pp. The latter has been revised for publication in this present volume.

130 'Teng Cheong to Run for President', *Straits Times*, 3 August 1993.

131 'Teng Cheong on his links with the Chinese Community', *Ibid.*, 16 August 1993.

132 'Bourse Suffers Biggest Fall Since Mid-August', and 'Both DPMs Have Cancer', *Ibid.*, 17 November 1992. Investigation of Ong's cancer was said to be conclusive only with a surgical excision and biopsy performed on 25 August 1992, see 'Painless Swelling in the Neck Noticed in April', *Ibid.*, 17 November 1992.

133 'Ong Teng Cheong to Stand for Executive President Post', *Business Times*, 3 August 1993.

134 'Teng Cheong on: His Cancer', *Straits Times*, 16 August 1993.

135 'President Ong Warded for Rest and Observation', *Straits Times*, 10 June 1994.

136 'President Looks Well at Concert', *Straits Times*, 15 June 1994.

137 'President Ong: My Voice is Fine and I'm Back at Work', *Straits Times*, 18 June 1994.

138 'Ong Teng Cheong to Stand for Executive President Post', *Business Times*, 3 August 1993; 'Teng Cheong to Run for President', *Straits Times*, 3 August 1993. The first instance probably refers to Ong's Mandarin speech on 'My Views on the 1991 General Election', given to the Singapore Chinese Press Club on 16 September 1991. This speech (attributing a plunge in PAP electoral support to (a) the middle class and English-educated's desire for political pluralism, (b) the feeling of neglect by the Chinese-educated, (c) the rising cost of living for low-income citizens, and (d) the perennial anti-government votes) is available in Singapore Lianhe Bao (ed.) *Wang Dingchang: Zouxiang Zongtongfu zhilu* [Ong Teng Cheong: Road to the Istana]: 310–15.

139 There were other considerations to take such a step. Warren Fernandez in an analysis quoted partially below pointed out that a NTUC campaign as opposed to a political party campaign would also prevent a 'demeaning

political scramble to the Istana' and set the precedent that the nominee need not always be put up by the government or a political party.

140 'What are the Implications of the NTUC's Move to Nominate Mr Ong Teng Cheong for President?', by Warren Fernandez, *Straits Times*, 7 August 1993. Paragraphs for this quotation have been rearranged and italics added.

141 'Elected President's Job is to be Strong, not Popular – SM Lee', *Ibid.*, 2 September 1993.

142 *Ibid.*

3 The presidency in Singapore
Constitutional developments

Kevin Tan

INTRODUCTION

In many of the former British colonies, the idea of a non-executive head of state was an alien one. To many politicians in these nascent states, it seemed illogical that the person occupying the country's highest office should hold little actual power.[1] As far as they were concerned, a leader of a country should lead, and it mattered little that the Westminster system of parliamentary government, after which their new constitutions were patterned, owed its structure to a quirk of history. As a result, many of these societies soon abandoned their colonial constitutions and the Westminster parliamentary model in favour of a limited presidential executive where the head of government and head of state reposed in a single office, and where the president, as head of government, wielded more effective power.

Like many other former colonies of Great Britain, Singapore inherited the Westminster parliamentary system of government when she attained independence. But neither Singapore nor any of these former colonies benefited from the same political experience and history as Great Britain. As such, the Westminster system was made to operate in an environment which was fundamentally different – in both its socio-political structures and cultures – from that of its country of origin.

Among post-colonial states, Singapore was unique in refusing to follow this trend. From independence in 1965 to 1991, she had a non-executive president with very limited powers – discretionary and otherwise. During that period, the president's functions were largely ceremonial and real power resided in the prime minister and his Cabinet. However, in 1991, a major amendment was made to Singapore's Constitution to transform the office of the president into an elected one.

This chapter discusses the new elected presidency as well as some of its attendant problems and prospects. I have divided the chapter into five sections. The first is a short historical account of the office of the president, whereas the second discusses the new constitutional arrangements for the elected president. In the third section, I highlight some unique aspects of the scheme, and in the last two sections I elaborate upon the problems and prospects of the scheme.

SINGAPORE'S PRESIDENTIAL EXECUTIVE: A SHORT HISTORY

During the colonial era, Singapore's chief executive was the governor.[2] He was appointed by the Crown and acted on its behalf. In 1959, when Singapore was granted self-governing status, the office of the governor was transformed into that of the Yang di-Pertuan Negara.[3] Like the governor, the Yang di-Pertuan Negara was appointed by the Queen, but after consultation with the government.[4] During the transition from colony to self-governing state, the then-governor of Singapore, Sir William Goode, became the first Yang di-Pertuan Negara.[5] At the same time, he was also appointed by the Queen as the first United Kingdom Commissioner.

To complete the transition, Goode resigned his office as Yang di-Pertuan Negara and Encik Yusof bin Ishak, a former journalist succeeded him to the post. He thus became the first and only Malayan-born Yang di-Pertuan Negara of Singapore. When Singapore entered the Federation of Malaysia in 1963, Encik Yusof continued in office as Yang di-Pertuan Negara. However, in 1965, when Singapore became independent, the post of Yang di-Pertuan Negara was abolished and replaced by the office of non-executive president. Encik Yusof became the first president of the Republic of Singapore. Since then, Singapore has had four other presidents.[6] President Wee Kim Wee became head of state in 1985, following the resignation of his predecessor Mr C. V. Devan Nair. When the amendments providing for an elected presidency were made in 1991, President Wee also became the first elected head of state in Singapore's history.[7] In 1993, Mr Ong Teng Cheong became Singapore's first popularly elected President.

THE ELECTED PRESIDENT

In 1984, then-Prime Minister Lee Kuan Yew mooted the idea of having an elected president.[8] However, four years were to elapse before the first White Paper on the Elected President[9] was issued. The paper aroused considerable controversy and the public debate that ensued was really a mixture of rumour, conjecture and pure speculation since the specific provisions and powers of the president were never explicitly spelt out. In August 1990, a second White Paper[10] outlining the specific proposals was issued with an accompanying Constitution Amendment Bill.[11] Following lengthy debates in Parliament, a Select Committee was appointed.[12] Several amendments were made to the original bill and it was finally passed into law in January 1991.[13]

The rationale and the initial proposals

In the first White Paper, the government stated its rationale for the creation of an elected presidency as follows.

1 In many countries, irresponsible governments have mismanaged their nations' finances and economically ruined their countries. This is done to win votes by providing handouts and heavy subsidies which naturally make those governments very popular.[14]
2 Singapore has so far been fortunate to have a responsible government, but with over US $30 billion in the national reserves, the temptation for a future irresponsible government will be very great. Indeed, in times of economic strife and flagging support, an irresponsible government will find this temptation irresistible. Hard earned money will be spent on short-term vote buying and on popular measures.[15]
3 One of the cornerstones of Singapore's success has been its public-service sector. The key appointment holders in Singapore's public service and statutory boards are men and women of integrity and ability. This, too, may be destroyed if an irresponsible government makes key appointments based on considerations other than merit. Nepotism and corruption may result and the public service will collapse.[16]
4 There is nothing in the Constitution to prevent any such present or future government from squandering all the nation's reserves, leaving it economically ruined. Nor is there any safeguard against the irresponsible appointment of important civil servants. The prime minister and his cabinet have untrammelled power.[17]
5 It is therefore necessary to have some constitutional safeguard to secure the future for Singaporeans and to prevent an irresponsible Government from ruining Singapore.

In designing a constitutional safeguard, the White Paper also found the following considerations vital.[18]

1 The Parliamentary system of government should be preserved in the sense that the prime minister and his cabinet should keep the initiative to govern the nation.
2 The safeguard mechanism must enable quick action. In this respect, the procedures must be such that the authority charged with the responsibilities of protecting the reserves and key appointments can act swiftly to control a potentially disastrous situation.
3 The person must have moral authority, and such moral authority is derived from the will of the people as expressed in an election.
4 The person must have ministerial, high executive or administrative experience since he has to 'balance the demands of political expediency and the public interest'.
5 The Constitution should require presidential candidates to have such experience and qualities.

These considerations appear to have precluded the possibility of creating any other constitutional mechanism to safeguard the national reserves and the integrity of the public service. Indeed, while the White Paper stated that 'the government . . . considered many alternatives; creating an upper legislative body, reposing the power of the veto in the Presidential Council for Minority Rights or some other body analogous to the Federal Reserve Board, or requiring decisions on financial assets to be subject to the approval of the electorate in a referendum',[19] these options were deemed by the government to be unsuitable.

Thus, under the original proposal, the office of the president would be transformed into an elected one so that the president would hold the 'second key' to the nation's financial reserves. Also, the presidential candidate and the vice-presidential candidate were to be voted in as a team, and the president was to have limited executive powers. His powers were to be confined to two specific areas – government spending and the appointment of key posts in the public service.

The second White Paper

The original scheme outlined in the first White Paper was given a more concrete framework in the second White Paper. While most of the proposals and recommendations were the same as in the first White Paper, several additional considerations were brought into play.

First, the elected president was further tasked with checking the possible abuse of power by the executive in preventive detention cases under the Internal Security Act.[20] Second, the elected president's discretion was extended to the making of prohibition orders under the Maintenance of Religious Harmony Act.[21] And third, in the interests of upholding the integrity of the Cabinet, the Director of the Corrupt Practices Investigation Bureau was to report directly to the president.[22]

A fourth change related to the president's advisory panel. The original 'Presidential Committee for the Protection of Reserves' was renamed Council for Presidential Advisors (CPA)[23] and would comprise six members instead of the original five.[24] The president, the Chairman of the Public Service Commission and the Prime Minister would nominate two members each.[25] In addition, the role of Council of Presidential Advisors was defined as giving the president advice on all matters in which he has discretionary powers, although the president is legally obliged to consult the Council only on questions involving the budgets of the Government, statutory boards and key government companies.[26]

Finally, a new provision was introduced to allow Parliament to override the presidential veto.[27] In addition to these changes, other provisions relating to the qualification and disqualification of candidates, terms of office, specific government statutory boards and companies to be included under the president's purview were specifically spelt out.

The Select Committee's Report

Parliament debated the bill vociferously during the Second Reading before committing it to Select Committee. The Select Committee's Report[28] was presented to Parliament on 18 December 1990. A month later, the Bill and its amendments were passed into law.

The Select Committee comprised 12 members including several key cabinet ministers and one opposition member[29] and was headed by the speaker, Mr Tan Soo Khoon. It received a total of 40 written representations, of which 34 were considered by the Committee. A total of four meetings were held, two of which were to hear oral representations.[30] In its 33-page report, the Committee considered numerous issues and made their recommendations thereon. Of particular interest and relevance to us are the following:

Qualifications for presidential candidates   The Committee favoured retaining the pre-qualifying requirements for presidential candidates. It did not accept the view of some representors that anyone who was not obviously disqualified should be permitted to stand for elections. Its position was that it 'is not the right of every citizen to stand for election as President' but to 'ensure that voters are given qualified and suitable candidates to choose from'.[31] This is because the elected president has far greater and more crucial responsibilities than a member of parliament.

Another issue which the Committee considered was whether the Constitution should require candidates to be persons of 'integrity, good character and reputation'[32] and concluded that Article 18 should be amended to ensure that candidates satisfy the PEC accordingly. The Committee also recommended that a minimum age of 45 years be set for presidential candidates though no upper limit was specified.

Candidate's political affinity   A hotly contested issue was whether a candidate who is a member of a political party should be required to resign from the party. The main arguments for resignation were based on the idea that the president should be non-partisan. Accordingly, candidates for presidential office should be seen as being non-political. The Committee was in two minds on this point, but decided in the end to recommend that candidates not be members of any political party and that if they were, that they should resign from the party before the presidential elections. In the words of the Committee:

> If a candidate belonged to a political party, formally cutting this link cannot really obliterate his sympathy for the party's goals. . . . However, when the president is elected he must represent, and be seen to represent, the collective interests of all its citizens. He must rise above personal interests and the interests of his family, his friends and his political party. He must act according to his own judgment of what is in the best national interest. On occasion he may have to take strong stands on matters coming within the president's purview against the political parties which supported him.
>
> It does not follow that a president who is a member of a political party is incapable of discharging his functions impartially. . . . However, the Committee noted the views of representors that the president must not only be above party politics *but be manifestly seen to be so*. If he continues to be a member of a political party there may be lingering doubts that the president is still subject to party discipline and is thus constrained to act in accordance with decisions of his party caucus. It may be more reassuring to the public if the president stood for election in his own right and not on a party platform.[33] At the same time, the Committee also recommended that the President takes an Oath of Office which

explicitly declares that in carrying out his duties, 'he will not allow any past affiliation with a political party to affect his judgment'.[34]

Establishment and composition of the Presidential Elections Committee (PEC)   Several representors pointed out that the original bill failed to spell out the actual composition of the PEC. The Committee accepted that this needed to be done since the PEC fulfilled an extremely important role in the pre-qualification of candidates. They recommended that the PEC comprise:

1   Chairman of the Public Service Commission to sit as Chairman of the PEC;
2   Member of the Presidential Council for Minority Rights nominated by the Chairman of that Council; and
3   Chairman of the Public Accountants Board.[35]

President's powers and functions   The proposed Article 5(2A) provides that unless the president directs otherwise, amendments to certain critical provisions will require the support of two-thirds of the voters at a referendum. The question was whether these critical provisions, most of which pertained to the office of elected president and his powers, should be extended to other provisions as well. The Committee recommended that it should be extended to the whole of Part IV of the Constitution which contains all the fundamental liberties provisions. It felt that '[n]o Government should be allowed to amend these provisions without being subject to the scrutiny of the President, who will have to consider if the amendments are justified'.[36]

Another important question was whether the president should have the final say in issuing a Proclamation of an Emergency. The proposed new Article 20(2)(f) gave the president discretion in 'the withholding of consent to a request for the issue of a Proclamation of Emergency under Article 150'. After some deliberation, the Committee recommended against such an amendment on the grounds that 'the decision to proclaim an emergency should be entrusted to the Prime Minister and Cabinet, not the President' and that the 'process of satisfying the President of the need for a Proclamation and obtaining his concurrence may unnecessarily delay the Government's response to an emergency'.[37]

The Committee also recommended that the president's concurrence for key public service appointments also·be extended to the Chairman and members of the Presidential Council for Religious Harmony and the Chairman and members of the Advisory Board constituted under the Internal Security Act.[38] At the same time, it also recommended that the President's role in safeguarding CPIB investigations concerning ministers be extended to 'any person' since it is possible that 'a complaint may implicate the Prime Minister himself' and it is possible for the Prime Minister to 'obstruct investigations of individuals which may eventually implicate a Minister'.[39]

Council for Presidential Advisors (CPA)   The amending bill provided for six members in the CPA. However, the Committee felt that this was problematic if there were a tie, and recommended that the CPA should comprise only five members, with two nominees coming from the president, two nominees from the Prime Minister and one nominee from the Chairman of the Public Service Commission (PSC). The Committee recommended that for the first appointments to the CPA, half the appointees of the President and the Prime Minister serve three-year terms, while the other half serve six years together with the Chairman of the PSC's nominee. This staggering of terms will ensure that 'an incoming President or Prime Minister cannot immediately replace the incumbent Presidential Advisors with his own personal nominees'.[40]

The Committee also recommended that the CPA be given powers to examine 'any public officer, or officer of a key statutory board or Government company'.[41] In respect of key appointments, the Committee felt that the president should be required to consult the CPA but left the final decision with the president. It felt that there was no need for the President to consult the CPA on questions of detentions under the Internal Security Act (ISA), or Restraining Orders under the Maintenance of Religious Harmony Act, or in approving CPIB investigations.[42]

Acting president   The Committee accepted several representors' views that the Chief Justice should not act as President in the President's absence since the chief justice could be placed in a position of conflict. In any case, they felt that the presidency was a political position and 'judges should not make political decisions'.[43] Accordingly, the Committee recommended that the persons exercising the functions of the president should be (in order): the Chairman of the Council of Presidential Advisors, the Speaker, or a person appointed by Parliament.

Removal of president and immunity from suits The amending bill was vague on what grounds the president could be removed. The Committee proposed that the following grounds be included:

1 being permanently incapable of discharging the functions of his office by reason of mental or physical infirmity;
2 intentional violation of the Constitution;
3 treason;
4 misconduct or corruption involving abuse of the powers of his office; and
5 any offence involving fraud, dishonesty or moral turpitude.

The Committee also recommended that the president's immunity from suits be extended to cover his official actions during and after his term of office, and that the immunity for his private actions cover only his term of office.[44]

Financial provisions The financial provisions are extremely complicated and many of the matters dealt with in the Select Committee Report concern methods of accounting and budgeting. The main points are as follows:
    The Committee recommended that

1 the chairmen and chief executive officers (CEOs) of the key statutory boards and government companies be required to declare whether their budgets are likely to draw on the reserves;[45]
2 appointments to the boards of directors of the key statutory boards and government companies be for a period of three years only. This will allow the president to 'revoke their appointments where they subsequently are suborned or they collude with the plans of a profligate Government'. These directors can be re-appointed but such appointment will require the concurrence of the president;[46]
3 the president should not control investment decisions of the key statutory boards and government companies since this would 'involve him in the actual operations' of these boards and companies;[47]
4 as a matter of practicality, Telecoms, the Port of Singapore Authority and the Public Utilities Board be omitted from the list of companies under the president's purview. This was because they would soon be privatized. At the same time, any amendment to this list would be difficult if companies were privatized. As such, the Committee felt that the list of statutory boards listed in Article 22 be set out in a Schedule which can be amended by the president on the Advice of the Cabinet by way of subsidiary legislation;[48]

5 the President's approval need not be obtained for the incurring of any debt since this was highly impractical. Instead, the Committee suggested that a duty be imposed on the Auditor-General and the Accountant General to inform the President of any proposed transaction 'which in their knowledge is likely to draw on reserves'.[49] At the same time the Minister of Finance would submit to the president a statement of outstanding guarantees and other financial liabilities at the close of each financial year.[50] If the President is of the opinion that 'certain outstanding liabilities are likely to draw on the reserves, he shall formally inform the Prime Minister and shall cause his opinion to be published in the *Gazette*'. This will enable the president to draw the attention of the public even if the transactions may not require his approval.[51]

6 if the President fails to convey a decision on any Supply Bill or Supplementary Supply Bill within 30 days, he shall be deemed to have assented to the Bill;[52] and

7 different aspects of the Bill should have different commencement dates. This is necessary for all the administrative and practical problems to ironed out before they become almost impossible to amend.[53]

Two other issues were raised and considered but not accepted by the Committee. The first was whether the number of terms for the president should be limited. In particular, it was suggested that a cap of two terms be placed on the President. The Committee rejected this since it might deprive 'the country of the services of someone who has in fact a proven track record of being a good President'.[54] The second issue was whether the list of people deemed automatically qualified could be expanded to include ambassadors, professors and the Solicitor-General, etc. The Committee also rejected this suggestion since the PEC has sufficient discretion to qualify such people.[55]

Parliament's response

The Report of the Select Committee was debated in Parliament on 3 January 1991. In moving the Third Reading, Prime Minister Goh Chok Tong chose to concentrate on three 'politically significant' areas:

- the pre-qualifying of candidates;
- the requirement that candidates who are members of political parties resign from their parties before nomination day; and
- the requirement that the President consults the Council of Presidential Advisors.[56]

He commended the Select Committee on its thoroughness and work and supported the pre-qualifying requirement on the grounds that in the event of a freak election result, 'whoever is chosen can do the job'.[57] He also felt that the requirement that the President consults with the CPA gives the CPA a larger role and strengthens it as a political institution.[58] However, he went to great lengths to discuss the question of political affinity and membership of a political party.

The Prime Minister felt that of the two recommendations, resignation from political party and the Oath of Office, the latter was the more important. His personal view was clearly reflected in his speech:

> In the elections, what would be at issue? Surely, it is the candidate's competence and experience for the job as well as his character and reputation, rather than his political affiliation. He either has, or does not have, these qualities. If he has them, being a member of a political party will not prevent him from dutifully discharging his duties. Also, once elected, the president has to take a solemn oath to discharge his duties to the nation as a whole. Note the words 'bear true faith and allegiance to the Republic'. He is bound by this oath which overrides his own personal interests and that of his party, family or friends.
>
> . . . it is fallacious to argue that one cannot live up to this oath just because he continues to be a member of his party.
>
> I do not therefore think that actual party affiliation is so critical that it should disqualify a person becoming the president. The election of the president is about electing a man of integrity, experience and ability who will put national interests above all other interests, including his own, and those of his family and friends and those of his party during his term of office.[59]

None the less, he was prepared to go along with the view of the representors on this point 'to make the proposal more acceptable to the public'.[60] Of the PAP MPs, Lim Boon Heng, Koh Lam Son, Goh Choon Keng, John Chen and S. Vasoo spoke in support of the Bill while Non-Constituency MP Lee Siew Choh made the longest speech during this reading with an impassioned tirade against the short-comings of the Bill. He concluded that 'a genuine parliamentary democracy will serve as a better check than an Elected President with veto powers' and that if these changes had to be made, it were better made through a referendum.[61] The Bill was finally passed with 75 votes for and one against. Chiam See Tong of the Singapore Democratic Party was the sole dissentient. Lee Siew Choh, being a Non-

Constituency MP, was not entitled to vote on a constitutional amendment.

The final scheme in 1991

Under the final scheme, the elected president is to be a citizen of Singapore,[62] aged 45 and above,[63] not be a member of any political party on the date of nomination for election,[64] have his name appear on the current register of electors,[65] be a resident of Singapore at the time of nomination, and have been a resident for period amounting in aggregate to not less than 10 years,[66] and not subject to any disqualification under Article 45.[67] In addition, he had to satisfy the Presidential Elections Committee (PEC)[68] that 'he is a person of integrity, good character and reputation',[69] and has for a period of not less than three years, held office in one of numerous capacities laid down under Article 19(2)(g). Specifically, these offices are: Minister; Chief Justice; Speaker; Attorney-General; Chairman of the Public Service Commission; Auditor-General; Permanent Secretary; chairman or chief executive officer of one of the statutory boards referred to in Article 22A read with Schedule 5 (*viz* Board of Commissioners of Currency, Singapore, Central Provident Fund Board, Housing and Development Board, Jurong Town Corporation, Monetary Authority of Singapore, and the Post Office Savings Bank of Singapore); chairman of the board of directors or chief executive officer of a company incorporated or registered under the Companies Act with a paid-up capital of at least $100 million or its equivalent in foreign currency; or 'in any other similar or comparable position of seniority and responsibility in any other organization or department of equivalent size or complexity in the public or private sector which, in the opinion of the Presidential Elections Committee, has given him such experience and ability in administering and managing financial affairs as to enable him to carry out effectively the functions and duties of the office of the President'.

Article 17(2) of the Constitution provides that the President 'shall be elected by the citizens of Singapore in accordance with any law made by the Legislature. To this end, the Presidential Elections Act 1991[70] was passed. Under the Act, elections will be held within six months after the office of the president becomes vacant, but not more than three months before the expiration of the incumbent.[71] The writ of election is issued by the Prime Minister addressed to the returning officer[72] who must give notice of the writ at least four clear days before nomination day.[73]

Section 8 also provides that any time after the notice of election and at least two clear days before nomination day, each candidate must apply to the PEC for a certificate stating that the PEC was satisfied that he is a qualified candidate under Article 19 of the Constitution.

The president's term of office is for six years.[74] Generally, he must exercise his functions under the Constitution, acting on the advice of the Cabinet or of a minister acting under the authority of the Cabinet.[75] However, he may act in his discretion when performing the following functions:

- appointment of the prime minister;
- withholding consent to a request for the dissolution of Parliament;
- withholding assent to any bill under Articles 22E,[76] 22H,[77] 144(2),[78] or 148A;[79]
- withholding concurrence under Article 144 to any guarantee or loan to be given or raised by the Government;
- withholding concurrence and approval of appointments and budgets of statutory boards and Government companies applicable under Articles 22A[80] and 22C;[81]
- disapproving of transactions referred to in Articles 22B(7), 22D(6) or 148G;[82]
- withholding concurrence under Article 151(4)[83] in relation to the detention or further detention of any person under any law or ordinance made or promulgated in pursuance of Part XII (Special Powers Against Subversion and Emergency Powers);
- the exercise of his functions under S12 of the Maintenance of Religious Harmony Act 1990;[84] and
- any other function the performance of which the president is authorized by this Constitution to act in his discretion.

In addition, the President is given the discretion to consent to investigations undertaken by the Corrupt Practices Investigations Bureau even if the prime minister has refused his consent.[85] When exercising his discretion, the president is, in some cases, bound to consult the CPA, and in others, may refer these matters to them for advice.

The president is immune from any court proceedings for anything done or omitted by him in his official capacity.[86] He may, however, be removed from office if he 'is permanently incapable of discharging his functions of his office by reason or physical infirmity'[87] or has been found guilty of the following:

- intentional violation of the Constitution;[88]
- treason;[89]
- misconduct or corruption involving the abuse of the powers of his office;[90] or
- any offence involving fraud, dishonesty or moral turpitude.[91]

To determine whether the president was guilty of the grounds stipulated under Article 22L, a tribunal appointed by the Chief Justice and consisting of not fewer than five Judges of the Supreme Court would be constituted.

More recent changes

In September 1994, the Constitution of the Republic of Singapore (Amendment No. 2) Act came into operation.[92] This is the first major amendment to the scheme discussed above. In moving the Bill, Deputy Prime Minister Lee Hsien Loong pointed out that the amendments were meant to plug some loopholes in the original scheme. This was the first major amendment to the scheme since its enactment. In his second reading speech, he said: 'We have discovered that the elected President mechanism is even more complex than we originally anticipated ... As we operate the mechanism day to day, we are still discovering implications of the provisions which we had not realized'.[93]

The Amendment Act is long and complicated, taking up close to 20 pages and some 32 sections in all. The main amendments made by the Act may briefly be discussed under the following headings.

President to state reasons for spending reserves   Under Article 22B(7), the president was empowered to disapprove any transaction which draws upon the reserves. The new amendment to Articles 22B(7), 148A and 148G requires the President to publish his reasons in the *Gazette* even if he agrees to allow the Government to draw on the reserves. In other words, the President must now publish the rationale for his actions, whether he chooses to use his presidential veto powers or not.

This amendment is welcomed since the elected President must justify his decision. The President can check an errant government, just as the president can easily collude with the same government. It cannot be that the president be made to explain his rationale only if he decides to exercise his veto powers.

Transfer of surpluses   Previously, under Article 22B, transfers of surpluses from statutory boards or government companies were considered a draw on their reserves. This accounting practice has been revised under the amendments to Articles 22B and 22D.

Council of Presidential Advisors   New articles were added to provide for remuneration of members of the Council of Presidential Advisors who shall be paid 'such fees as may be determined by the President'.[94] Such fees are paid out of the Consolidated Fund and 'shall not be diminished during the continuance in office of the Chairman and members of the Council'.[95] At the same time a new Article 37M allows the Council to 'appoint a Secretary to the Council and such other officers as may be required to enable the Council to carry out its functions'.

Advisory capacity of the Supreme Court   A new Article 100 establishes a special tribunal consisting of not fewer than three judges of the Supreme Court. The President may refer to this tribunal 'for its opinion any question as to the effect of any provision' of the Constitution. The Tribunal is under a duty to 'consider and answer the question so referred as soon as may be and in any case not more than 60 days after the date of such reference'.[96] Any dissenting opinions of any judge must accordingly be reflected in the opinion rendered to the president although the majority decision shall be considered the opinion of the Tribunal and shall be pronounced in open court. The opinion is not subject to question in any court.[97]

   This amendment was not only significant, but also proved to be a portent of things to come. BG Lee, in moving the amendment pointed out that unlike in Malaysia, the 'Singapore Constitution does not have any provisions for referring questions of interpretation of the Constitution to the Courts for an advisory ruling'.[98] Brigadier General Lee explained that having such a tribunal will be useful in resolving interpretations of the complex provisions of the elected presidency scheme, and that an issue with respect to the interpretation of Article 22H had already arisen. This issue will be discussed in Part IV of this chapter under the sub-heading 'When Executives Collide'.

Personnel boards   A number of the amendments were required by Parliament's creation of the establishment of various personnel boards designed to take over the functions of the Public Service Commission, the Education Service Commission and the Police and Civil Defence Services Commission.

No veto powers for defence and security measures A new Article 151A has been inserted which effectively makes the presidential veto ineffective in respect of 'any defence and security measure'.[99] For the purposes of this section, 'defence and security measure' has been defined as 'any liability or proposed transaction which the Prime Minister and the Minister responsible for defence, on the recommendations of the Permanent Secretary to the Ministry of Defence and the Chief of Defence Force, certify to be necessary for the defence and security of Singapore'.[100] This certificate is not justiciable and is 'conclusive evidence of the matters specified therein'.[101]

This amendment created the greatest uproar in Parliament. The Government's view is that since the Prime Minister and the Cabinet are responsible for deciding whether the country goes to war, they must have the power to execute the decision, and we cannot risk a tussle between the Prime Minister and the President over whether spending is necessary for defence and security. On the other hand, some members pointed out that the new Article 151A could be abused by unscrupulous politicians. Nominated MP Walter Woon put it succinctly thus:

> Imagine what an irresponsible prime minister could do. He could circumvent all the safeguards by certifying any transaction as necessary for national security – national security being such a wide thing that it would be possible to fit any sort of handouts within the rubric if your are intelligent enough. All you need is a smart and crooked lawyer to help you do this. And it should be possible, especially when nobody can challenge it.
>
> There is no point having two keys to the door, if the door is unlocked.[102]

Several other MPs, notably Tan Cheng Bock (PAP, Ayer Rajah), Low Thia Kiang (WP, Hougang) and Kanwaljit Soin (NMP) were equally concerned over the possible abuse of power. The Amending Act also dealt with other problems inherent in the method of accounting used in the Constitution. They are, however, of far lesser political and constitutional significance.

SOME UNIQUE ASPECTS OF THE SCHEME

Singapore's elected president scheme is unique in a number of ways. First, unlike the presidential executive model of the United States or France, Singapore's elected president's powers are greatly limited in their scope. Indeed, these powers are of a reactive rather than a proactive nature. As such, even though the president's power to say 'No' is an extremely potent one, he is in no position to formulate or promote particular policies or platforms.

Second, the elected president is political but non-partisan. Unlike the American president, who can hail either from the Democratic or Republican parties, the Singaporean president cannot be a member of any political party. If he is, he must resign from the party before Nomination Day. A great deal of debate was generated on this point during the Select Committee hearings. The main fear expressed by representors was that if any member of a political party should become the president, he would tend to be biased and would therefore not be effective as a check against a deviant or unscrupulous government.

Third, the new scheme transformed the office of the president into a competitive one. The electorate is thus called upon to vote twice: once for the government of the day, and another time for the head of state. While this is not, in itself remarkable – the French employ a similar system – it represents a marked departure from the established model of government. The office of the head of state has often been seen in the past as a unifying component in the Westminster constitutional set-up. The role of the ceremonial head of state, no matter how trivial and formal, is an important one. Loyalty is owed to the state as epitomized by the president, and it is he who provides the rallying point for all nationalist sentiment. This function is particularly so in multi-racial, multi-religious Singapore.

In the past, the presidency was a semiotic representation of Singapore's multi-racial and multi-religious make up. While Singapore has a predominantly Chinese population, Malays, Indians, Eurasians and other minorities are given due recognition by having members of their communities elected to the post of president. The first president, Encik Yusof bin Ishak, was a Malay. He was succeeded by Dr Benjamin Henry Sheares, a notable Eurasian gynaecologist and obstetrician and when Dr Sheares died, Mr C. V. Devan Nair, an Indian unionist and former PAP MP, succeeded to the post of president. The first Chinese president is Mr Wee Kim Wee. A former journalist and diplomat, Mr Wee is a Peranakan, a Straits-born Chinese whose ancestors came to this part of the world centuries ago, adopting many Malay customs and habits.[103]

Under the new scheme, this key function of the president is obliterated. No longer will the currency of race be exploited to unite the nation. The symbol of multi-racial Singapore is now lost.[104] Neither will the president be seen as the benevolent, elder statesman or father figure who soothes the nation over difficult times and patches up family quarrels, bringing diverse factions together for the common good. Indeed, with the office transformed into a competitive one, the candidate's personality, promises and outlook which will matter more than all else.

Fourth, the office of the elected president in Singapore is unique in that it is more tightly entrenched than most other provisions under the Constitution; and this includes the Parliamentary system of government, the judiciary and the fundamental liberties. This was achieved by amending the old Article 5 by adding a new sub-section 2A which now provides that:

> a Bill seeking to amend this clause, Articles 17 to 22, 22A to 22O, 35, 65, 66, 69, 70, 93A, 94, 95, 105, 107, 110B, 151 or any provision in Part IV or XI shall not be passed by Parliament unless it has been supported at a national referendum by not less than two-thirds of the total number of votes cast by the electors registered under the Parliamentary Elections Act.

The operative articles covered by Article 5(2A) are Articles 17 to 22, and 22A to 22O. Thus, as far as the presidency is concerned, the article operates to prevent any of its provisions from being amended unless a referendum is carried out. While Article 5(2A) is not yet in force,[105] it nevertheless poses two rather disturbing questions.

The first question pertains to the manner in which these provisions were introduced. Theoretically, I would argue that in order to introduce any constitutional provision which can be altered only by referendum, Parliament must do so by way of referendum. Indeed, this argument is even more compelling when one considers how radically the amendments alter the existing constitutional structure. Such a drastic change should only be made by referendum.

The second question concerns the need for entrenching these provisions so tightly in the Constitution. Indeed, the present scheme goes counter to the government's avowed predilection of preserving the parliamentary system of government. At best, the provisions relating to the elected president can be said to sit incongruously with the rest of the Constitution. The fact that the provisions relating to the office of the president are more entrenched than many other key provisions suggests that the Government considers it far more important an institution to protect and preserve than anything established in the Constitution itself. Indeed, provisions establishing the parliamentary system of government, guaranteeing the people's fundamental liberties provisions and constituting and protecting the judiciary are amendable by Parliament without referendum. On a more practical front, at least three major sets of amendments have been made to the Constitution since the elected presidency came into being, two of which affect the same provisions covered under Article 5(2A) directly. If we had allowed the scheme to take effect immediately, we would have had to call two referendums already. While adjustments can be made in the next few years, there is no telling when unforeseen problems brought about by unintended consequences will crop up. Already, the issue of whether the president could veto a bill to amend Articles 5(2A) and 22H of the Constitution had to be referred to the Special Tribunal for an advisory opinion.[106]

Finally, the elected president scheme adds a unique twist to the classic idea of the separation of powers doctrine. We are accustomed to constitutional set-ups where either the legislature or the judiciary provide checks and controls on the executive. However, under the elected president scheme one executive provides checks on the other.

SOME PROBLEMS

There are three main foreseeable problems I wish to highlight at this point. The first concerns the nomination process and the criteria for candidacy. The second problem arises when the prime minister and the president disagree, and the final issue deals with the president's removal.

Choosing a nominee

Under Article 19, very stringent requirements have to be satisfied before any person stands for presidential elections. There are two key objectives to be achieved by insisting on stringent pre-qualifications. The first relates to competence. Thus, only the best candidates – preferably those with experience in matters of state or in managing large financial resources – should be permitted to contest the presidential elections. The second consideration is independence of mind. The candidate must be politically neutral so that he may properly exercise restraints on an errant government.

However, the present requirements for candidates not only make the office of president fundamentally elitist, but are also likely to fail its acknowledged objectives. I shall deal with each in turn.

Competence   The Government's position on pre-qualifying candidates has its roots in its meritocratic philosophy. In respect of the elected president, it assumes that no one should be allowed to hold the reins of power unless he or she has a proven track record of effective management. Indeed, during the debates on the elected president amendments, Prime Minister Goh Chok Tong said:

> So what is democracy all about? It is not the right to stand for election. It is giving the electorate the right to choose good candidates to Parliament. If you do not give the people a choice, then they are choosing between two bad candidates. But if you pre-qualify them, and you allow good candidates to emerge and be chosen, you can be sure that only good ones will be returned to Parliament.[107]

Two basic problems arise here. First, Section 8 of the Presidential Elections Act 1991 requires any candidate to obtain a certificate from the PEC stating two things:

- that the PEC is satisfied that the candidate is a person of integrity, good character and reputation; *and*
- that the candidate satisfies the other requirements under Article 19(2).

I wish to emphasize the word 'and' here. The Presidential Elections Act makes it plain that the PEC must be satisfied on *both* counts – character as well as the requirement under Article 19(2) – and unless it is so satisfied, no certificate will be issued. There are two causes for concern. First the PEC is given great subjective discretion to determine the suitability of candidates. The Constitution provides no guidelines as to what is meant by 'integrity, good character and reputation', neither does it indicate the criteria which the PEC may use in deciding whether the candidate has held office

> in any other similar or comparable position of seniority and responsibility in any other organization or department of equivalent size or complexity in the public or private sector which . . . has given him such experience and ability in administering and managing financial affairs as to enable him to carry out effectively the functions and duties of the office of President.[108]

Second, the independence and objectivity of the PEC is called into question here. There are no constitutional guarantees to ensure independence of the PEC and with such wide discretionary powers and few objective guidelines, they wield an incredible amount of power in determining what the slate of candidates will be, especially in respect of the first criteria of 'integrity, good, character and reputation'. As Professor Winslow points out:

As the constitution nowhere provides for the independence of the PEC, this provision places an unseemingly great power in that body, by giving it discretionary power to determine who is fit enough to offer himself as a candidate, and providing for less than objective criteria.[109]

Independence and control   The second objective of pre-qualification is to ensure that the candidate, if elected, will have sufficient independence of mind and fortitude to act as an effective check against an errant or spendthrift government. He must thus be politically neutral and fiercely independent. However, the requirements under the present Article 19 appears to enhance the likelihood of selecting candidates who are most unlikely to fulfil these objectives.

Article 19(2)(f) tackles the fear of political partisanship by neutralizing the presidential nominee. A member of a political party must resign from the party before contesting the elections. However it appears from the requirements that the presidential aspirant will necessarily be a member of the establishment much attuned and probably sympathetic to the policies and ideology of the ruling party. All the positions mentioned in Article 19(2)(g) are essentially public offices occupied by people who are part of the system. The question is, will such a president who is cut from the same cloth as the rest of the establishment be effective as a check against an errant government?

When executives collide

While the Constitution anticipates possible conflict between the president and the Government, it does not provide for an amicable resolution of the conflict in every instance. For example, under Part XI (Financial Provisions), a conflict could arise if the president refuses to give his assent to any bill or measure which draws on the national reserves. However, only in respect of Supply or Supplementary Supply Bills[110] does the Constitution provide a possible way out. Parliament may overrule the president by a two-third majority vote, but only if his assent was withheld contrary to the recommendation of the CPA.[111] In the absence of such a resolution, Parliament may by resolution authorize expenditure to any amount provided it does not exceed the amount for the preceding financial year.[112] This proviso is necessary if government is not to go into paralysis.

However, similar arrangements have not been provided in other areas where the president exercises his discretion. In the case of appointment of key public officers under Article 22, for example, the

Constitution does not say what would happen if the president continuously thwarts the efforts of the Government to appoint certain officials. It appears that if an errant president decides to sabotage the government of the day, he can do so by simply refusing to assent to anything the government puts before him and which legally requires his assent.

In such an instance, it appears that the only way to solve the problem is either to curtail the president's powers or to have him removed from office. Reducing the president's powers is extremely difficult in view of Article 22H since it provides that the president has discretion to withhold assent to any bill which 'provides, directly or indirectly, for the circumvention or curtailment' of his discretionary powers.[113] Removing the president would attract a host of other problems as we will see below.

In early 1995 a problem arose with respect to Article 22H. In fact, notice of this problem had been served in a speech by Deputy Prime Minister Brigadier General Lee Hsien Loong when he moved the Constitution of the Republic of Singapore (Amendment No. 2) Act 1994.[114] The problem arose from the fact that Article 5(2A) was hitherto not in operation. Concurring with the Select Committee's recommendations, the Government considered it unwise to bring this section into operation until they had a chance to fine-tune the system. In the meantime, Article 22H which refers to Article 5(2A) specifically was operational. The deputy prime minister put the issue thus:

> When the Elected President's amendments were passed in January 1991, the legislative intent was that, firstly, Constitutional amendments which circumvent or curtail the Elected President's discretionary powers should be subject to a referendum, and, secondly, the Elected President's veto over Constitutional changes which affect his powers should not be brought into effect immediately, but only after we have had several years of experience operating and refining the system.
>
> This was to have been achieved by placing the master entrenching mechanism clause in one Article – Article 5(2A), and then delaying bringing Article 5(2A) into effect until we are ready.
>
> This was done. Unfortunately, we overlooked another Article – Article 22H – which was incorrectly drafted, and which has been brought into effect. Article 22H was intended to cover non-Constitutional legislation. If such legislation circumvents or curtails the President's discretionary powers, the President can refuse assent, and if the Courts uphold the President, the matter is final.

Article 22H applied to non-Constitutional legislation does not cause any problem. Such legislation should never circumvent or curtail the President's discretionary powers. These powers are spelt out in the Constitution. If a Constitutional provision is unsatisfactory, the remedy is to amend the Constitution, not to pass other legislation which contradicts it.

But Article 22H, as it stands, has the unintended effect of covering Constitutional amendments other than the core provisions which have already been covered by Article 5(2A).[115]

Two problems arise here. First, the so-called non-core provisions (i.e. those not specifically covered in Article 5(2A)) are protected by 'an inappropriate criterion'.[116] This means that at the present time, if the president vetos any amendment which curtails or circumvents his discretionary power, there is no recourse to a referendum – since Article 5(2A) is not yet operational – and the courts' decision on the narrow question of whether the amendment does or does not circumvent or curtail the president's discretionary powers ends the matter. The courts cannot determine the wider question of whether, as a matter of policy, the president's discretionary powers ought to be curtailed or circumvented, and there is no mechanism to decide this wider question.

The second problem is that 'Article 22H has prematurely conferred upon the president a power to veto non-core Constitutional amendments'.[117] As Brigadier General Lee explains:

This leads to an anomaly: amendments to non-core Constitutional provisions are subject to Presidential veto if they circumvent or curtail the President's discretionary powers, whereas the core provisions setting out these powers have, correctly, not yet been entrenched.[118]

One of the key amendments introduced by the Constitution of the Republic of Singapore (Amendment No. 2) Act is the creation of a Special Tribunal consisting of at least three judges of the Supreme Court to consider any question referred to the Tribunal concerning the interpretation of the Constitution. Clearly the Government was anxious to provide an appropriate forum for the resolution of interpretive problems such as those raised by Article 22H.[119] Under the new Article 100 of the Constitution, the president may refer to the Tribunal 'for its opinion any question as to the effect of any provision of this Constitution which has arisen or appears to him likely to arise'.[120] Once the reference is made, the Tribunal must consider and answer the question within 60 days,[121] and the opinion of the majority of the judges of the Tribunal shall be pronounced in open court[122] and is final.[123]

In early 1995, President Ong Teng Cheong referred a constitutional question to the Special Tribunal under the new Article 100 wherein the Tribunal was asked to consider whether the President could veto a bill to amend Article 5(2A) and Article 22H of the Constitution.[124] The Special Tribunal, in a controversial and puzzling decision, ruled that the President could not.[125]

The removal process

Under Article 22L, the president can be removed if the 'Prime Minister or not less than one-quarter of the total number of the Members of Parliament' gives 'notice of a motion alleging that the President is permanently incapable of discharging his functions of his office by reason of mental or physical infirmity' or that the president has been guilty of either intentional violation of the Constitution, treason, misconduct or corruption involving the abuse of the powers of his office, or any offence involving fraud, dishonesty or moral turpitude.

If the motion has been adopted 'by not less than half of the total number of the Members of Parliament, the Chief Justice shall appoint a tribunal to inquire into the allegations made against the President'.[126] If the Tribunal which consists of at least five Supreme Court judges reports to the Speaker that in its opinion the president is either permanently incapable of discharging his functions of has been guilty of one of the allegations, Parliament 'may by a resolution passed by not less than three-quarters of the total number of the Members of Parliament remove the President from office'.[127]

Two problems arise here. The first problem concerns the constitution of the tribunal to consider the president's alleged 'misconduct'. Article 22L(5) states that the judicial tribunal should be appointed by the Chief Justice and 'shall consist of not less than 5 Judges of the Supreme Court of whom the Chief Justice shall be one, unless he otherwise decides...'. The idea of appointing judges to the Tribunal is that a fair degree of independence may be maintained. Judges are perceived as being independent mainly because of the security of tenure and remuneration provided by the Constitution. However, under Article 94(3), a person

> qualified for appointment as a judge of the Supreme Court or a person who has ceased to hold the office of a judge of the Supreme

Court may be appointed as the Chief Justice... or may sit as a judge of that Court... and such person shall hold office for such period or periods as the President, if the President, acting in his discretion, concurs with the advice of the Prime Minister, shall direct.

This means that a judge of the Supreme Court, who has attained the age of retirement (i.e. 65 years)[128] may in fact have his tenure extended by contract. Such supernumerary judges do not have the same security of tenure as judges below the age of 65 and are appointed by the president 'in his discretion', concurring with the prime minister's advice. There is, of course, nothing to prevent an errant president from threatening a supernumerary judge with a refusal to continue appointing him. And since there is nothing to prevent the Chief Justice from nominating supernumerary judges to sit on the Tribunal, the independence which is much needed in such a Tribunal may be jeopardized.

The second problem involves the question of interpretation. How would the term 'misconduct' be interpreted by the courts? While it is possible to ascertain what does or does not constitute 'misconduct' in the respect of judges or public officials, since their duties and responsibilities are fairly well-defined and established, it becomes far more difficult in the political realm to make a ruling on what constitutes 'misconduct'. Indeed, even with respect to judges, one need only recall the nightmare of the Tun Salleh affair[129] and the removal of the Malaysian judges, to question the workability and objectivity of such an exercise.

There are no hard and fast rules in the political arena. A president's exercise of discretion may appear to political sympathisers to be perfectly sensible and responsible whereas the same action may be viewed by an unsympathetic politician as a disastrous and irresponsible move. It is not possible, nor indeed desirable, to expect a body of judges to pass judgment on matters that are essentially political. This would involve the judiciary in roles which were never contemplated in the original scheme of the Constitution.

PROSPECTS

Following the passing of the Constitution of the Republic of Singapore (Amendment) Act in 1991, the incumbent president became the first elected president of Singapore. No elections were held or needed to be held because of the deeming provisions under Article 163.[130] However, President Wee Kim Wee's second four-year term of office expired in

1993.[131] During the remainder of his term as elected president, he did not invoke any of his vast powers to either veto budgets or refuse his assent to any key appointments.

This may be attributable to two main reasons. First, a president who was not elected by the people was unlikely to want to 'rock the boat' when his term was coming to an end. He carried on with his usual ceremonial functions and duties as in the past, as if nothing had changed, ending his term without any unnecessary controversy or conflict with the executive. Second, even if he had been inclined to object to government legislation or actions within his discretionary purview, he lacked the legitimacy to do so. Being elected by Parliament and not the people, doubts may have been cast on his legitimacy to act on behalf of the general populace.

The success or failure of the elected president scheme rests very much on how the office is filled and run in the first one or two terms. Indeed, proper election of the *first* elected president was crucial. Institutionally, the potential dangers of presidential elections reside in two areas.

First, the fact that under the Presidential Elections Act 1991, the candidate must place a deposit of three times that required of a parliamentary election candidate.[132] At present the deposit for a candidate seeking a parliamentary seat is $6,000. This would mean that a presidential candidate will need to put $18,000 of his own money on the line. This $18,000 will be forfeited if he polls less than one-eighth of the votes.[133] Furthermore, this amount excludes the many thousands of dollars that will be necessary for running the election campaign. Few persons will be wealthy enough to contest the elections, especially since the Constitution precludes a presidential candidate from having any affiliation with political parties. If the candidate finds a wealthy corporate or individual sponsor to underwrite his costs, there is the danger that he would be beholden to sectarian interests and be controlled by forces outside the political arena.

Deposits are necessary to ensure bona fides on the part of candidates. But with the stringent qualifying requirements under the Constitution, I would venture to suggest that a deposit is unnecessary. Otherwise, presidential elections could turn more on the candidate's financial resources than on any other consideration. The first presidential election must be organized in a manner which projects the dignity of the office, rather than reduce it to a question of buck and luck, as was the case in 1993.

The second danger is to be found in Section 15 of the Presidential Elections Act which provides that should only one candidate be nominated, he shall be declared elected to the office of President. This is highly unsatisfactory.[134] The idea of giving a candidate a walkover can generate suspicions that the selection process – no matter how proper and honourable – is nothing more than an eye-wash. Enough credible people must be encouraged to stand for elections, and a real choice must be offered to the people. In addition, a candidate who is elected to the position of president by default will also lack the legitimacy to disagree with the government, even if he is right to do so.

During the first presidential elections in August 1993, the problems of Section 15 were immediately made apparent when NMP Chia Shi Teck literally forced an election contest by offering himself as a candidate.[135] Even after Mr Chua Kim Yeow was urged to contest Mr Ong Teng Cheong, the election methods were very low key and sedate, prompted presumably by the candidates' attempts to uphold the dignity of the contest and to keep costs down.

Now that President Ong has been elected into office, his every move will be scrutinized by everyone. Here, we come to the greatest irony of the scheme. If the first president never refuses his assent to anything done by the government in his six-year term of office, then again, people will begin to think that the President is nothing more than a figure-head, and the scheme will be seen as a failure. It will be seen as a scheme to get one like-minded person to control another; in which case, we might as well not have any controls at all. Yet, if the President exercised his discretion arbitrarily and habitually disagreed with the executive, then government might be thrown into disarray and paralysis. Having the *first* elected president constantly overruled or, worse still, removed from office will do the institution little credit and will ultimately lead to the failure of the scheme.

CONCLUSIONS

In comparison with other constitutional models, Singapore's elected presidency is unique. It is an instance where one executive is made to control the other but where the ambit of control is tightly regulated so as to pre-empt any proactive tendencies of the president. The elected presidency is not the product of any ideology, or conformity with any theoretical model. Like most of the other constitutional changes that have taken place in Singapore, it represents a reaction against the existing Westminster system of government. Yet, as I have argued elsewhere,[136] the elected presidency does not quite fit into any pattern of political action so far undertaken by the Government. Depending on one's perspective, the move may be interpreted in two ways. First, it could simply be viewed as a pragmatic move by the government to safeguard what they perceive to be a fundamental pillar of Singapore's existence. After all, Singapore is a country with no hinterland or natural resources. The fact that she exists as a nation-state is itself miraculous, and the fact that the Government has deemed it necessary to find a constitutional device to safeguard Singapore's monetary reserves indicates the seriousness of the stakes involved. On the other hand, it could be interpreted as another constitutional device to perpetuate PAP dominance on the political stage. However, this 'conspiracy theory' of PAP regime dominance is overly simplistic and wears thin on further scrutiny.

Given the current institutional arrangements, it is not inconceivable that there might come a day when the present government is ousted from power and an errant or spendthrift government might be elected. The current PAP leadership recognizes this danger and seeks to put in place some form of check against a future profligate government. In the search of appropriate institutions to fulfil this function, the Government is faced with two choices:

- to allow things to take their course and hope that a courageous activist judiciary will, as in the American system, stand up against an extravagant or wanton government; or
- to design some other institution or device to deal with this danger.

The first option is unattractive because Singapore's constitutional system and structure, unlike that of the United States, does not encourage such judicial activism.[137] Furthermore, the judiciary is unelected and will find great difficulty dealing with the counter-majoritarian problem.[138] At the same time, the Government is anxious to spare the judiciary the trauma of dealing with political disputes which it deems the Judiciary ill-equipped to do. The second option is rather more attractive, but as I have remarked elsewhere,[139] the transformation of the office of the president into an elected one is not necessarily the best solution to the perceived problems of the future.

Constitutional change in Singapore, has always been dictated by what the Government terms 'pragmatism'. Like governments in many other Third World nations, the Singapore government has tried to be comfortable with the system it inherited. However, when the ruling elites perceived that these institutions and structures fail to satisfy local aspirations and cultural circumstances, they often made seemingly appropriate adjustments. In the past, the Government chose the route of legal evolution as opposed to legal revolution, slowly transforming the inherited parliamentary system of government to suit local circumstances and needs.[140] However, the creation of the elected presidency in Singapore marks a departure from the evolutionary route. While not entirely revolutionary, the elected presidency is a transformative institution which presents an experimental, innovative form of government quite unique and unparallelled anywhere in the world.

That structures and institutions must suit local conditions is a given fact. Legitimacy in the system comes from the people's belief in and loyalty to the system. The efficacy of a system is only one determinant of its desirability, albeit a key determinant. A cruel and harsh law will almost always prove its deterrent worth, but its impact on the population may be negative. Negative feelings towards the legal and constitutional system chip away at its legitimacy. Eventually, a change must come about, either in the system, or in the party who operates and perpetuates the system. The problem with the elected presidency scheme is that while the Government has correctly identified the potential problems of untrammelled parliamentary power, their constitutional solution has been less than convincing. The problems raised by its complicated provisions indicate the lack of thorough examination and discussion on its implications prior to implementation.

To be fair, we really have to wait and see before we pass judgment. Because of the present political climate and environment, it is unlikely that we will see a non-PAP government before the next century. Neither will it be realistic for us to expect a non-establishment character to emerge victorious at the next presidential polls in 1999. Until then, we cannot seriously expect the president to use his veto powers. The problem with this 'wait and see' approach is that when the president's hand is eventually forced, it may well be too late to avoid a constitutional and political crisis. In that sense, we have made the stakes much too high, and on those grounds alone, the scheme must be considered much too volatile for comfort.

NOTES

1   See Kevin Tan, 'Presidentialism in Post-Colonial Societies: a Brief Comparison', unpublished manuscript.
2   When Sir Stamford Raffles claimed Singapore for the British, he placed it under the control of Bencoolen of which he was Lieutenant-Governor. He then appointed Colonel William Farquhar the first Resident of Singapore who reported directly to him. Raffles sacked Farquhar in 1823 and appointed John Crawford as Resident. In 1826, when the East India Company united Singapore, Penang and Malacca to form the Presidency

of the Straits Settlements, Robert Fullerton (then Governor of Penang) became the first Governor of the Straits Settlements. In 1867, when the Straits Settlements came under the control of the Colonial Office in London, Sir Henry St George Ord became its first Governor. See generally, C. M. Turnbull, *A History of Singapore 1819–1988*, 2 ed (Oxford University Press, 1989).

3   See Section 4 of The Singapore (Constitution) Order-in-Council, 1958.
4   See *Ibid.*
5   See *Ibid.*, at Section 107.
6   President Yusof bin Ishak died in office in 1969. He was succeeded by President Benjamin Henry Sheares who also died in office in 1981. Singapore's third president was C. V. Devan Nair who resigned in disgrace in 1985. See *C. V. Devan Nair: Circumstances Relating to Resignation as President of the Republic of Singapore*, Cmd 8 of 1988; see also T. J. Bellows, 'Singapore in 1988: The Transition Moves Forward' (1989) 29 *Asian Survey* 145, 148.
7   Under the new Article 163, the 'person holding the office of the President immediately prior to 30th November 1991 shall continue to hold such office for the remainder of his term of office and shall exercise, perform and discharge all the functions, powers and duties conferred or imposed upon the office of the President by this Constitution as amended by the Constitution of the Republic of Singapore (Amendment) Act 1991 . . . as if he had been elected to the office of President by the citizens of Singapore'.
8   See Prime Minister's National Day Rally Speech, *The Straits Times*, 10 August 1988: 1.
9   See *Constitutional Amendments to Safeguard Financial Assets and the Integrity of the Public Services*, Cmd 10 of 1988 (hereinafter, *First White Paper*).
10 See *Safeguarding Financial Assets and the Integrity of the Public Services: The Constitution of the Republic of Singapore (Amendment No. 3) Bill*, Cmd 11 of 1990 presented to Parliament on 27 August 1990 (hereinafter, *Second White Paper*).
11 Bill No. 23 of 1990.
12 See Report of the Select Committee on the constitution of the Republic of Singapore (Amendment No. 3), Bill No. 23 of 1990, Part 9 of 1990 presented to Parliament on 18 December 1990.
13 Act No. 5 of 1991 assented to by President Wee Kim Wee on 18 January 1991. The amendments to the Constitution under this Act were not brought into force until 30 November 1991 by GN No. S518/91. An exception was made in respect of the entrenchment provisions under the new Art 5(2A). See Kevin Tan Yew Lee, 'The Elected Presidency in Singapore: Constitution of The Republic of Singapore (Amendment) Act 1991' [1991] *Singapore Journal of Legal Studies*: 179–94, and V. S. Winslow, 'Electing the President: The Presidential Elections Act 1991' [1991] *Singapore Journal of Legal Studies*: 476–81.
14 See *First White Paper, supra* note 8, para 5: 1.
15 *Ibid.*, para 6: 1.
16 *Ibid.*, para 11: 2.
17 *Ibid.*, para 12: 2.
18 *Ibid.*, para 18(a)–(e): 4–5.

19   *Ibid.*, para 18: 3–4.
20   Cap 143 Singapore Statutes, 1985 Revised Edition. See *ibid.*, para 26: 7.
21   Act No. 26 of 1991, assented to by the President on 30 November 1990.
      See *First White Paper, supra* note 8, para 27.
21   See *First White Paper, supra* note 8, para 28.
23   The CPA is established under Part VA. Its five members must be
      Singapore citizens of at least 35 years of age, resident in Singapore and not
      subject to the disqualifications under Article 37E (*viz* the candidate must
      not be of unsound mind; insolvent or an undischarged bankrupt; or has
      been convicted of an offence in Singapore or in a foreign country and
      sentenced to imprisonment for not less than one year or a fine of not less
      than $2,000 and has not received a free pardon. The CPA meets in private
      and it possesses the power to 'require any public officer or officer of any
      statutory board or Government company to appear before the Council'.
24   Even though the Bill provided that the CPA was to comprise six members,
      the government appeared to have changed its mind. The final number of
      members in the amended provisions is five – see Article 37B.
25   *Ibid.*, paras 29–30: 8–9.
26   *Ibid.*
27   *Ibid.*, paras 31–5: 9–10.
28   See *Report of the Select Committee on the Constitution of the Republic of
      Singapore (Amendment No. 3), Bill No. 23 of 1990*, Part 9 of 1990
      presented to Parliament on 18 December 1990 [hereinafter, *Select
      Committee Report*].
29   The other members of the Select Committee were: Goh Chok Tong (Prime
      Minister), Lee Hsien Loong (Deputy Prime Minister), S. Jayakumar
      (Minister for Law and Home Affairs), S. Dhanabalan (Minister for
      National Development), George Yeo (Minister for Information and the
      Arts), Abdullah Tarmuggi, S. Chandra Das, Davinder Singh, Ong Chit
      Chung, Ow Chin Hock, and Chiam See Tong (Opposition Singapore
      Democratic Party).
30   Ten representors gave oral evidence before the Committee. They were:
      Shriniwas Rai, Kenneth Chew, Vincent Tay Shian Poh, The National
      University of Singapore Law Club, The Law Society of Singapore, The
      Institute of Certified Public Accountants of Singapore, The National
      University of Singapore Democratic Socialist Club, Walter Woon,
      Valentine Winslow and Wee Han Kim.
31   See *Select Committee Report*: iii.
32   *Ibid.*: vi–vii.
33   *Ibid.*: viii–ix.
34   *Ibid.*: x.
35   *Ibid.*: xii–xiii.
36   *Ibid.*: xiii.
37   *Ibid.*: xiv.
38   *Ibid.*: xv.
39   *Ibid.*: xv–xvi.
40   *Ibid.*: xvi.
41   *Ibid.*: xvii.
42   *Ibid.*: xvii–xviii.
43   *Ibid.*: xviii.

44 *Ibid.*: xx.
45 *Ibid.*: xxii–iii.
46 *Ibid.*: xxiii–iv.
47 *Ibid.*: xxiv.
48 *Ibid.*: xxiv–v.
49 *Ibid.*: xxvii.
50 *Ibid.*
51 *Ibid.*
52 *Ibid.*: xxviii.
53 *Ibid.*: xxix–xxx.
54 *Ibid.*: x.
55 *Ibid.*: x–xi.
56 See *Singapore Parliamentary Debates Official Report*, 3 January 1991, col. 718.
57 *Ibid.*, col. 719.
58 *Ibid.*, cols 721–2.
59 *Ibid.*, col. 720.
60 *Ibid.*
61 *Ibid.*, col. 741.
62 Article 19(2)(a).
63 Article 19(2)(b).
64 Article 19(2)(f).
65 Article 44(2)(c).
66 Article 44(2)(d).
67 Article 45 contains the disqualification criteria for members of parliament, *viz* being of unsound mind; or an undischarged bankrupt; or holding an office of profit; or failure to lodge return of election expenses, or being convicted of an offence in Singapore or Malaysia and imprisoned for not less than one year or fined not less than $2,000; or voluntarily acquired or exercised citizenship rights in a foreign country; or conviction under an election offence.
68 The PEC is established under Article 18 and consists of Chairman of the Public Service Commission, the Chairman of the Public Accountants Board established under the Accountants Act, and a member of the Presidential Council for Minority Rights nominated by the Chairman of the Council. Its main function is to ensure that candidates for the office of president comply with the requirements under Article 19.
69 Article 19(2)(e).
70 Act No. 27 of 1991, passed by Parliament on 29 July 1991 and assented to by the President on 6 August 1991. For a commentary of the Act, see V. S. Winslow, 'Electing the President: The Presidential Elections Act 1991' [1991] *Singapore Journal of Legal Studies* 476–81.
71 Section 6.
72 Section 6(3).
73 Section 7.
74 Article 20(1).
75 Article 21(1).
76 This article relates to the president's discretion to withhold assent 'to any Bill passed by Parliament which provides, directly or indirectly, for

varying, changing or increasing the powers of the Central Provident Fund Board to invest the moneys belonging to the Central Provident Fund'.

77 This article gives the president the discretion to withhold assent to any bill which 'provides, directly or indirectly, for the circumvention or curtailment' of his discretionary powers.

78 Under this article the president may withhold his assent to any bill 'providing, directly or indirectly, for the borrowing of money, the given of any guarantee or the raising of any load by the Government if, in the opinion of the President, the Bill is likely to draw on the reserves of the Government which were not accumulated by the Government during its current term of office'.

79 Assent may be denied if the president is of the opinion that any Supply or Supplementary Supply Bill 'is likely to draw on the reserves which were not accumulated by the Government during its current term of office'.

80 These companies are listed under Part I of Schedule 5 to the Constitution – Board of Commissioners of Currency, Singapore, Central Provident Fund Board, Housing and Development Board, Jurong Town Corporation, Monetary Authority of Singapore, and the Post Office Savings Bank of Singapore.

81 These companies are listed under Part II of Schedule 5 to the Constitution – Government of Singapore Investment Corporation Pte Ltd, MND Holdings Pte Ltd, Singapore Technologies Holdings Pte Ltd and Temasek Holdings Pte Ltd.

82 These provisions require the respective board of directors and government officials to inform the president if their proposed Supply Bills would draw upon the accumulated reserves of the government companies or statutory boards.

83 This article provides: 'Where an advisory board constituted for the purposes of this Article recommends the release of any person under any law or ordinance made or promulgated in pursuance of this Part, the person shall not be detained or further detained without the concurrence of the President if the recommendations of the advisory board are not accepted by the authority on whose advice or order the person is detained'.

84 This provision concerns the making of prohibition orders against religious leaders who violate the Act.

85 Article 22G.

86 Article 22K.

87 Article 22L(3).

88 Article 22L(3)(a).

89 Article 22L(3)(b).

90 Article 22L(3)(c).

91 Article 22L(3)(d).

92 The Act was passed by Parliament on 25 August 1994 and assented to by the president on 14 September 1994.

93 See *The Straits Times*, 26 August 1994: 29.

94 See new Article 37L(1).

95 See new Article 37L(2).

96 See new Article 100(2).

97 See new Articles 100(3) and 100(4).

98 See *Singapore Parliamentary Debates Official Report,* 25 August 1994, col. 428.

99 See new Article 151A(1).

100 See new Article 151A(2).

101 *Ibid.*

102 See *The Straits Times* 26 August 1994: 26.

103 Strictly speaking, most Peranakans are not considered by the Chinese as being pure Chinese. Indeed many of the Peranakan Chinese have, through inter-marriage, some traces of Malay blood in their genetic make-up. They also adopt many Malay customs and habits. Physical manifestations of this unique local culture can be seen in the *kebayas* (a form of Malay traditional dress) of Peranakan women (known as *nonyas*; the males are known as *babas*), and the fact that Peranakan *patois* is essentially Malay with a sprinkling of dialect and English.

104 Whether this is a good thing or not is highly debatable. On the one hand, it may be argued that it is just as well that race no longer becomes a determining factor in filling the state's highest office, but personal merit. On the other hand, the laws of probability weigh heavily against minorities in this respect.

105 Prime Minister Goh Chok Tong agreed to a moratorium of four years to iron out all the difficulties of these new provisions before bringing Article 5(2A) into force. See *Parliamentary Debates, Singapore Official Report*, 3 January 1991, col. 722; see also *Business Times*, 4 January 1991: 1.

106 See *Constitutional Reference No. 1 of 1995* [1995] 2, *Singapore Law Reports*: 201.

107 See *Parliamentary Debates, Singapore Official Reports*, 3 January 1991, col. 746.

108 Article 19(2)(g).

109 See V. S. Winslow, 'Electing the President: The Presidential Elections Act 1991' [1991], *Singapore Journal of Legal Studies* 476: 478.

110 Article 148A.

111 Article 148D.

112 Article 148A(2).

113 Article 22H(2) provides that if there is a dispute as to whether a bill falls within the rubric of Article 22H(1), the prime minister may refer it to the High Court for a determination.

114 No. 17 of 1994.

115 See *Singapore Parliamentary Debates Official Reports*, 25 August 1994, col. 429.

116 *Ibid.*

117 *Ibid.*, col. 430.

118 *Ibid.*

119 *Ibid.*, col. 428.

120 See Article 100(1).

121 Article 100(2).

122 Article 100(3).

123 Article 100(4).

124 See *Constitutional Reference No. 1 of 1995* [1995] 2, *Singapore Law Reports*: 201.

125 For an excellent account of the events leading up to this reference, see Thio Li-ann, 'Working Out the Presidency: The Rites of Passage' [1995], *Singapore Journal of Legal Studies*; and Chan Sek Keong, 'Working Out the Presidency: No Rites of Passage' [1996] *Singapore Journal of legal Studies*: 1.
126 Article 22L(4).
127 Article 22L(7).
128 See Article 98(1).
129 In 1988, the Lord President of Malaysia, Tun Salleh Abas and two other judges of the Supreme Court, Tan Sri Wan Suleiman Pawan Teh and Datuk George Edward Seah, were removed from their offices on grounds of misbehaviour. For further details, see *The Tribunal Report on the Dismissal of Tun Salleh Abas* [1988] 3 MLJ xxxiii, *Report of the Tribunal established under article 125(3) and (4) of the Federal Constitution – Re: Y. A. Tan Sri Wan Suleiman bin Pawan Teh, Supreme Court Judge; Y. A. Datuk George Edward Seah, Supreme Court Judge; Y. A. Tan Sri Dato Haji Mohd Azmi bin Dato Haji Kamaruddin, Supreme Court Judge, Y. A. Tan Sri Dato Seri Eusoffe Abdoolcader, Supreme Court Judge; Y. A. Tan Sri Wan Hamzah bin Haji Mohd Salleh, Supreme Court Judge* [1989] 1 MLJ: lxxxix. For excellent general accounts of the crisis, see Andrew Harding, 'The 1988 Constitutional Crisis in Malaysia' (1990) 39 ICLQ 57 and FA Trindade, 'The Removal of the Malaysian Judges' (1990) 106 LQR 51.
130 Article 163 of the Constitution reads:

The person holding the office of President immediately prior to 30th November 1991 shall continue to hold such office for the remainder of his term of office and shall exercise, perform and discharge all the functions, powers and duties conferred or imposed upon the office of President by this Constitution as amended by the Constitution of the Republic of Singapore (Amendment) Act 1991 (referred to in this Article as the Act), as if he had been elected to the office of the President by the citizens of Singapore, except that if that person vacates the office of President before the expiration of his term of office, a poll shall be conducted for the election of a new President within six months from the date of the office of President became vacant.

131 Under the old Article 17(3), the president shall hold office for a term of four years from the date of his appointment. President Wee was elected by Parliament under the old Article 17(1) in 1985 following the resignation of Mr C. V. Devan Nair.
132 Section 10(1).
133 Section 10(5).
134 See Winslow's criticisms of this provision in *supra* note 63 at 478–9.
135 His personal account is included in this volume as 'Notes from the Margin' in Chapter 8.
136 See Kevin Tan, 'Presidentialism in Post-Colonial Societies: a Brief Comparison' (unpublished manuscript).
137 See the arguments advanced in favour of judicial activism under American constitutional theory and structure in *Bruce Ackerman, We The People: Foundations* (Cambridge MA: Belknap Press, 1991).

138 See *Alexander M. Bickel, The Least Dangerous Branch: The Supreme Court at the Bar of Politics*, 2nd edn (New Haven: Yale University Press, 1962): 16–23.
139 See Kevin Tan Yew Lee, 'The Elected Presidency in Singapore: Constitution of The Republic of Singapore (Amendment) Act 1991' [1991], *Singapore Journal of Legal Studies* 179: 188–9.
140 For an account of the evolution of Singapore's Constitution, see Kevin Tan Yew Lee, 'The Evolution of Singapore's Modern Constitution: Developments from 1945 to the Present Day' (1989) 1, *Singapore Academy of Law Journal*: 1.

4 The election of a president in a parliamentary system

Choosing a pedigree or a hybrid? [1]

Valentine S. Winslow

INTRODUCTION

The two primary methods today of organizing an executive government are the cabinet system (the 'Westminster export model') or the presidential system.[2] Several Asian nations have experimented with both systems – notably Sri Lanka, South Korea and the Philippines – and may not have yet finally settled on one, with modifications or 'revisions'. Whether each of them has chosen the right system for itself is a question that can be answered only after the tests of time and unusual circumstances.

Singapore adopted a system familiar to its colonial administrators and advisers who inevitably recommended it as suitable for the fledgling colony aspiring towards self-government in the 1950s. In 1954, the Rendel Constitutional Commission recommended a constitution with a cabinet system. It attached 'the greatest importance to the principle of collective ministerial responsibility' when it recommended a Council of Ministers, the first 'cabinet', the majority of whom would be elected members of the Legislative Assembly. At the same time, the report 'laid some stress' on the question of the development of a party system, since this was necessary if a ministerial system, with collective responsibility and subject to criticism from a regular opposition, was to be instituted.[3] A new 'constitution', Singapore's first, came into being in 1955 incorporating these proposals.[4]

In 1958, the United Kingdom Government promulgated a new constitution for Singapore by Order-in-Council which provided for Singapore's status of self-government as a state with a fully-elected assembly and a government which had control over most matters except defence and external security. For the first time, Singapore would have, in place of a governor, a Malayan-born constitutional head of state, called the Yang di-Pertuan Negara, appointed by Her Majesty the Queen. He was a Malay journalist, who retained this title when Singapore became part of the Federation of Malaysia in 1963, and became Singapore's first president when Singapore left the Federation on 9 August 1965. Singapore has been a republic with a constitutional head of state, with the appellation of president, ever since. It has also opted for the parliamentary or 'cabinet' system of government. This system has received certain modifications since independence in 1965, but it is my view that the basic system has not been altered in any fundamental way, and the system finds expression in written constitutional provisions which are based on what in Britain remain merely conventions of the constitution.

The focus of this chapter is the qualifications of presidential candidates, the process of selection of suitable candidates, and the process of electing the president, against the backdrop of the Westminster system of government and the democratic process. It will be seen, perhaps, that there are (unique to Singapore) some aberrations from the usual democratic process.

FEATURES OF THE PARLIAMENTARY SYSTEM IN SINGAPORE

Whereas legislative power in the US presidential system is vested in Congress – comprising the Senate and the House of Representatives – in Singapore it is vested in the Legislature which consists of the president and Parliament.[5] The power of the Legislature to make laws is exercisable by bills passed by Parliament and assented to by the president.[6] Article 21 lays down a fundamental principle, that except as provided by the Constitution, the president shall, in the exercise of his functions, *act in accordance with the advice of the Cabinet* or of a minister acting under the general authority of the Cabinet; although executive authority is vested in the president.[7] The existence of this provision underlines the fact that the presidency has not been significantly altered to the extent of becoming an executive presidency, but a modified constitutional presidency with several additional discretionary powers sufficient to justify the president's receiving a mandate from the electorate by being directly elected.

Article 25 provides that the president shall appoint as prime minister a member of parliament 'who in his judgment is likely to command the confidence of the majority' of the members and that he shall appoint 'other ministers from among the members of Parliament in accordance with the advice of the Prime Minister'. British constitutional conventions are relevant in determining who commands the confidence of the majority and which party or parties would form a government. Similarly, the president has discretion to withhold consent to a request for dissolution of Parliament, but it would probably be exercised according to British and Commonweath conventions.

The president also has discretion to declare the office of prime minister vacant if he, in his discretion, 'is satisfied that the Prime Minister has ceased to command the confidence of a majority' of the members of parliament.[8] Finally, the Cabinet can only be summoned by the authority of the prime minister, who presides over meetings of the cabinet (unless he is absent).[9] The Constitution[10] authorizes the Legislature by law to determine and regulate the privileges, immunities or powers of Parliament; and accordingly, the Parliament (Privileges, Immunities and Powers) Act[11] makes such provision. Significantly, Section 3 of the Act provides that in addition to the Act's provisions, the privileges immunities and powers of the speaker, members of parliament and parliamentary committees 'shall be the same as those of the Commons House of Parliament of the United Kingdom and of its Speaker, Members or committees at the establishment of the Republic of Singapore'.

RECENT MODIFICATIONS TO THE PARLIAMENTARY SYSTEM

Since independence, two main modifications have been made to the system which, however, could not be said to have made serious inroads into that system.

First, two types of non-elected members have been introduced into Parliament. One is the Non-Constituency Member of Parliament (NCMP) and the other is the Nominated Member of Parliament (NMP). The NCMP concept was introduced in 1984, to allow for up to three of the losing opposition candidates belonging to political parties polling the highest number of votes, being declared 'elected', so as to provide a voice for opposition voters and provide 'sparring partners' for government members.[12] The NMP concept was introduced in 1990 to bring into Parliament up to six distinguished and talented individuals who could improve the quality of debate, particularly if they had specialized knowledge; and to represent as wide a range of independent and non-partisan views as possible.[13] Since September 1992, six persons have been appointed to the office of NMP and their presence has contributed to a better quality of debate in Parliament.

Another concept introduced was the Group Representation Constituency (GRC) consisting of four MPs, at least one of whom must be from a designated minority group. Some constituencies must have Malay candidates on each party slate, and others must have an Indian or other minority candidate. The party (or group of independents agreeing to stand together) with the most votes, wins all the seats. There are still several single-member constituencies, where candidates of any ethnic group may stand and compete for the electorate's votes, but they account only for about a quarter of the seats in Parliament at present.

The second modification came in the form of recent constitutional amendments to introduce an elected president, a president elected directly by the people *viz* all registered electors who may vote in general elections. These substantial amendments came into force on 30th November 1991,[14] and Singapore held its first presidential election in August 1993. It was a contest between two 'establishment' candidates, both with credentials which automatically qualified them on the basis of relevant experience under Article 19(2)(g) of the Constitution.[15]

The purpose behind the amendment was, according to the first White Paper produced on the subject, to protect certain 'vital national interests'. One of the concerns of the Singapore Government has been to achieve a high degree of political stability in Singapore. This has been done in several ways. One method has been the official attempt to ensure that Singapore remains a multi-cultural society, seeking unity and equality in diversity – avoiding the 'melting-pot' approach to integration – and to assure minority groups that their positions were not in any way being threatened. Two other ways seem to have been found in the *single* concept of a directly elected president with limited veto powers, whose six-year term of office may outlast an elected government's.

WHY AN ELECTED PRESIDENT?

The twin rationales for an elected president have been stated to be:

1 to ensure that no future government will squander financial reserves which have been accumulated by a previous government (regardless of whether they are from the same party); and
2 to preserve the integrity and meritocracy of the public services.

In a nutshell, various provisions have been built into the Constitution to allow a president, with the advice of a Council of Presidential Advisors, to withhold his approval on measures which purport to utilize previously accumulated reserves.[16] These reserves represent Singapore's only asset, since it has no natural resources of any sort. Additionally, the president is empowered to refuse approval of the Cabinet's recommended appointees to key public service positions, constitutional offices, or executive positions in public corporations.[17]

Apart from these two key provisions, which ostensibly grant to the president executive powers over and above those of a constitutional head of state, his other discretionary powers do not appear to detract from his standing as a constitutional head of state. However his 'veto' powers are clearly of a passive kind, like the driving instructor who has one hand poised over the hand-brake to prevent any unsafe moves by the driver. He has no mandate whatsoever to take the initiative, although as with a Westminster system constitutional head of state, he still continues to have the so-called 'three rights – the right to be consulted, the right to encourage, and the right to warn'.[18] Thus it is always open to him to request more information on matters of state. Indeed, the Constitution entitles the president, in the exercise of his functions, to request any information concerning the government which is available to the Cabinet.[19] Moreover, his constitutional neutrality is respected by his constitutional immunity from suit: he is not liable to legal proceedings for anything done or omitted to be done in his official capacity; and he is not liable for acts or omissions in his private capacity during his term of office.[20]

IS DIRECT ELECTION OF A PRESIDENT A RIGHT?

Nowhere in the Constitution is it stated that the people have the right to directly elect a president even though that is the stated intention of the government's two White Papers on the elected presidency. Article 17(2) merely states:

> The president shall be elected by the citizens of Singapore *in accordance with any law made by the Legislature.*[21]

This guarantees neither that the president shall be elected directly nor that he shall be elected freely on the basis of universal franchise and equality in voting. The provision makes reference to legislation to be passed by the Legislature, and even then leaves the form of the election to be determined by the legislation. The 'legislation' in question is now the Presidential Elections Act 1991, an Act of Parliament easily amendable by a simple majority in Parliament.

This Act provides for election on similar principles as parliamentary elections are to be held, with the same electorate. However, if a future amendment were to provide for (say) an electoral college to be elected in order to elect a president, such a transformation of the voting and electoral procedure would be valid. Likewise, different numbers of votes or even types of votes could be granted to (say) people of different age groups, or of different sexes, and that too, would be valid. Indeed, even though direct elections are now in fact provided by the Presidential Elections Act, the Legislature may in future be free to amend that law by a simple majority to provide (say) for indirect election by the citizens of Singapore. On this score, I submit that it is unsatisfactory that we have no entrenched right *in the Constitution* to a direct, free and equal election of the president. Compare our Article 17(2) to the equivalent South Korean Constitution's Article 67(2) which reads:

> The president shall be elected by universal, equal, direct and secret ballot by the people.

Personally, I consider the South Korean provision as a preferable way to convey the essential spirit of the White Papers. Any constitutional amendment would then have to be matched by an equivalent provision for the conduct of parliamentary elections. It is pertinent to note that the Constitutional Commission of 1966 recommended the insertion of a new article in the Constitution to grant Singapore's citizens an inalienable right 'to be governed by a government of their own choice, expressed in periodic and general elections by universal and equal suffrage and held by secret vote'.[22] They recommended that this should be a fundamental right entrenched in the Constitution. The Commission continued:

> With . . . limited experience of elections, we do not consider it safe to assume that a significant proportion of the people of Singapore will be able to realize, until it is too late to prevent it, that any inroads have been made into the democratic system of general elections by a future government intent on undermining first and ultimately destroying the practice of democracy in Singapore.[23]

The parliamentary debate on the Constitutional Commission's recommendations saw the government accepting such a recommendation in principle. Perhaps it is now timely to reconsider the creation and entrenchment of such a provision for both parliamentary and presidential elections to assure voters that this is an inalienable right in a democracy. Such entrenchment will also inform present and future governments that it is a very grave suggestion that voters of greater age and maturity, with children, should have two votes rather than one.

Any change to such an effect would then be seen as tampering with a fundamental right in a democratic system, and should not be taken lightly, without at least a referendum. In this way, voters as a whole will get the opportunity to decide if they are willing to give up this fundamental right – after careful public debate and consideration – as a 'trade off', in the national interest. Given this option, few voters are likely to accede to the suggestion that they may be less significant than other citizens. After all, universal equal suffrage emphasizes the worth of every individual in society. To alter the voting system would be to deny this tenet. As Churchill put it:

> Many forms of government have been tried, and will be tried in this world of sin and woe. No one pretends that democracy is perfect or all-wise. Indeed, it has been said that democracy is the worst form of government except all those other forms that have been tried from time to time.[24]

Indeed, if the democratic system we are used to should ever be altered, we may well echo the words of (again) Churchill: 'What kind of people do they think we are?'.[25]

ELECTING A PRESIDENT: WHO IS QUALIFIED?

There are two qualifications or characteristics of a presidential candidate which make him almost unique in the world of politics. First, the Constitution attempts to 'depoliticize' him by making it compulsory for a candidate not to be a member of any political party on the date of his nomination for election.[26] This appears to have been based on the views of several representors to the select committee meeting on the constitutional amendment proposals, and which were accepted by that committee. The reason, apparently, was that:

> [W]hen the President is elected he must represent, and be seen to represent, the collective interests of all citizens. He must rise above personal interests and the interests of his family, his friends and his political party. He must act according to his own best judgment of what is in the best national interest. On occasions he may have to take strong stands on matters coming within the president's purview against the political parties which supported him.[27]

Admittedly, resignation from a party shortly before nomination could hardly change the internal political convictions of a person, but it was felt that the president must be manifestly seen to be above party politics. If he remained a party member there might be 'lingering doubts that the president is still subject to party discipline and is thus constrained to act in accordance with decisions of his party caucus. It may be more reassuring to the public if the president stood for election in his own right and not on a party platform'.[28] On the other hand, what was important to the public was knowledge of the candidate's personal calibre, qualifications and experience for the tasks expected of him, namely to protect the citizens' vital interests. His identification with a party might distract voters from the real issue of his personal suitability.

The other unique qualification is that a presidential candidate must, apparently, be particularly well-acquainted with matters of a *financial* nature. Thus, in addition to being similarly qualified as members of parliament and being at least 45 years of age, he must fall into one of two main categories. He is automatically qualified by virtue of having held (for at least three years) certain named offices, such as minister, speaker or chief justice, or chairman or chief executive officer of one of several statutory boards (public corporations), or the chairman or chief executive officer of a company with a paid-up capital of at least S$100 million. Alternatively, he must, for at least three years, have held office

> in any other similar or comparable position of seniority and responsibility in any other organization or department of similar size and complexity in the public or private sector *which, in the opinion of the Presidential Elections Committee, has given him such experience and ability in administering and managing financial affairs as to enable him to carry out effectively the functions and duties of the office of President.*[29]
>
> (emphasis mine)

The Select Committee not only wanted candidates to be persons of integrity, good character and reputation, but considered it imperative that they must meet 'the basic criterion of having the experience and ability of managing funds in a large corporation'.[30] As the Select Committee explained, this did not mean that former ambassadors, professors, university vice-chancellors and the like should be excluded, but that they would be eligible if in the opinion of the Presidential Elections Committee (PEC)[31] they have the requisite experience and ability. Under the Presidential Elections Act,[32] the PEC is given the task of certifying

1 that it is satisfied that a candidate is a person of integrity, good character and reputation; and

2 if the candidate does not automatically qualify because he has failed to hold certain named offices, that he has sufficient experience and ability in administering and managing financial affairs to be able to carry out his functions and duties as president.[33]

Their certificate is final and cannot be subject to appeal or review in any court.[34]

Unlike candidates for parliament, who normally know they are qualified by not being disqualified by bankruptcy or a criminal conviction of a designated kind, a presidential candidate, even if he automatically qualifies by having held one of the named offices, may not know whether the PEC is going to accept him as being a person of integrity good character and reputation. This places too much discretionary power in the hands of a small group of persons, with no guarantee that they are qualified to judge others as being of integrity and good character or are unbiased, as there is no provision for any independent election commission. Further, it attempts to place the ruling of the PEC beyond judicial review, however questionable its decision may be. It also creates the embarrassment of uncertainty for a candidate seeking nomination, for he may be rejected as a candidate for reasons completely unclear to him. Men of eminence will not come forward and agree to nomination if they are likely to be humiliated by rejection – and possibly by less qualified mortals.

In this respect, Singapore has perhaps tried too hard to ensure a safe result. Parliament has attempted to write the Constitution like an insurance policy – so much so that the right of electors to choose the president who appeals best to them is diminished. Who is to say that electors will eventually be left with sufficient choice among the candidates certified to be 'qualified'? A scenario where only one candidate is nominated and then returned unopposed as president, is entirely possible since the qualifications already make very few people qualified. This would defeat the purpose of an elected presidency, as the president is supposed to have a mandate from the electorate in order to have the moral authority to disagree with the (also elected) cabinet on matters in which he may act at his discretion. I suggested to the Select Committee that the South Korean Constitution's provision for a minimum receipt of one-third of the total eligible votes by a solitary candidate had merit in it but the Government saw fit to make no provision to prevent anyone being elected unopposed. In fact, the Presidential Elections Act 1991 actually provides that where only one candidate stands nominated, he shall be declared elected to the office of president.[35] It is likely that the government believed that the stringent pre-qualification requirements sufficiently ensured that any candidate would be competent to be president. As the prime minister said in Parliament on the third reading of the Constitution Amendment Bill to introduce the elected presidency:

> Pre-qualifying all presidential candidates removes the nightmare of freak presidential election results because the contest would be between qualified people. Whoever is chosen can do the job.[36]

Has Singapore got its priorities wrong in seeking the perfect president? If it finds a person of true integrity and stature whom it can trust, is his personal ability to administer financial affairs so crucial that a Council of Presidential Advisors is insufficient to provide him with good financial advice? And is there a conflict between our objectives of having an elected president and a government led by elected members of parliament, in not allowing the elected president to head the cabinet but instead allowing him to veto the cabinet on certain issues? Who is to say who has the greater mandate – an elected president or an elected cabinet? Will we have a future president and a prime minister heading together in the same direction or will they face an *impasse* as a two-headed monster struggling to go in two different directions? Is one likely to be an irresistible force and the other an immovable object?

These are some of the questions we must face in Singapore as we come to terms with the concept of a directly elected president, and as we look back on the first election of Singapore's president. It is not comforting to note that by our stringent criteria, perhaps only one of our first four presidents would have met the pre-qualification requirements! On the other hand, Chua Kim Yeow, one of the two candidates in 1993, was by our stringent constitutional criteria, 'over-qualified' being eligible on perhaps three criteria, even though he was not well-known to the public. Ong Teng Cheong, the winning candidate, was a well-known personality and public figure, but was clearly eligible only on one major criterion.

A consequence (not undesirable) of making members of political parties ineligible to be presidential candidates, is that political parties may neither directly nominate candidates, nor finance their election expenses. A candidate must have his nomination papers signed by two persons, being the proposer and seconder, and four registered electors.[37] Also, the candidate's election agent must account to the returning officer for all receipts and promises of moneys and other valuable considerations from any person for the purpose of election expenses.[38] A political party is an association or registered society in Singapore, not a 'person' (including body corporate). There seems to be nothing to prevent party members acting as agents, from canvassing, or making donations for expenses, in their personal capacity as individuals. Also, there seems to be no legal objection to any political party's officially endorsing a candidate and even canvassing for him, without actually incurring the expenditure of money on his behalf.

A candidate may not incur expenses beyond the maximum limit of S$600,000 or an amount equal to 30 cents for each elector on the register, whichever is the greater.[39] It is obvious that without a political party's financial backing, a private candidate will find the expenses onerous as the entire nation will be his constituency. It is strange that no provision was made for a state subsidy of each eligible candidate nominated, as otherwise only the wealthy will be eligible to be candidates. The experience of the presidential election, however, indicates that a high public profile will obviate the need for extensive campaigning; and it seems that television time will in practice be allocated to candidates. Indeed, the public perception appears to be that a low profile campaign is more appropriate to the dignity of such a high office. In other words, if nothing is known of a candidate, perhaps he wasn't worth knowing about in the first place. He would be able to get the job done, but would not have the stature expected of a president.

NOTES

1 This chapter is adapted from a paper read by the author at a Conference on 'Powers and Functions of Executive Government' held in Melbourne, Australia in November 1992.
2 Two other methods which, apparently 'can be discounted' are the Swiss council sytem and the assembly system of the Third French Republic. See B. O. Nwabueze, *Constitutionalism in the Emergent States* (Farleigh Dickinson Press, 1973), Ch. III: 65.
3 Report of the Rendel Commission, Singapore (1954), paras. 60, 70.
4 Singapore Colony Order-in-Council, 1955 [1955], Statutory Instruments No.187
5 Reprint of the Constitution of the Republic of Singapore (1992 edn), Article 38.
6 *Ibid.*, Article 58.
7 *Ibid.*, Article 23.
8 *Ibid.*, Article 26.
9 *Ibid.*, Article 28.
10 *Ibid.*, Article 63.
11 Chapter 217, Singapore Statutes (Rev. Edn 1985)
12 Constitution of the Republic of Singapore, *Supra* note 5, Article 39.

13 *Ibid.*, Article 39, and Fourth Schedule. Under the procedure of the Fourth Schedule, members of the public are invited to submit names of persons, who must have a proposer, seconder, and four registered electors in support. A select committee will then make the nominations to the president, who makes the appointments.

14 Singapore *Government Gazette*, G.N. No. S518/91.

15 Of course, they still needed a certificate of eligibility from the Presidential Elections Committee certifying that it was satisfied that each of them was 'a person of integrity, good character and reputation', as required by Article 19(2)(e).

16 See: Constitution, Articles 21(2) (c)–(f) and the Articles mentioned therein.

17 See: Constitution, Articles 22, 22A, and 22C.

18 Walter Bagehot, *The English Constitution* (1867), Ch. 2.

19 Constitution, Article 22F.

20 *Ibid.*, Article 22K.

21 Words italicized are emphasized by the writer.

22 Report of the Constitutional Commission 1966 (chaired by Chief Justice Wee Chong Jin), para. 43.

23 *Ibid.*

24 Winston S. Churchill, House of Commons, 11 November 1947.

25 Winston S. Churchill, speaking to the US Congress on 24 December 1941 (after the Japanese had made their entry into the Second World War).

26 Constitution of the Republic of Singapore, *Supra*, note 5, Article 19(2)(f).

27 *Report of the Select Committee on the Constitution of the Republic of Singapore (Amendment No. 3) Bill [Bill No. 23/90]*, Part. 9 of 1990: viii, ix.

28 *Ibid.*: ix.

29 Constitution, Article19(2)(g).

30 Report of the Select Committee, *op. cit.*: x, xi.

31 Under Article 18(2) of the Constitution, the PEC consists of three persons, the chairman of the Public Service Commission, the chairman of the Public Accountants Board and a member of the Presidential Council for Minority Rights.

32 Act No. 27 of 1991.

33 *Ibid.*, Section 8.

34 *Ibid.*, Section 8(2).

35 Act No. 27 of 1991, Section 15.

36 Parliamentary Debates Singapore: Official Report, Vol. 56, No. 11, col. 719 (3 January 1991).

37 Section 9, Parliamentary Elections Act 1991 (Act No. 27/91).

38 Section 56, *Ibid.*

39 Section 50, *Ibid.*

5 The elected president and the legal control of government

Quis custodiet ipsos custodes?

Thio Li-ann

INTRODUCTION

The dogged search for a perfect form of government is an elusive one. Any such endeavour must at some stage engage in the task of engineering an orderly form of government which promotes the human aspiration for freedom, while forestalling a descent into anarchy. A free and open government under which human freedoms, restrained by civic responsibility,[1] can meaningfully be exercised, is premised on the co-existence of form and freedom. In ordering government we should recognize that power, in the hands of inherently selfish Man, can corrupt and is therefore susceptible to abuse. James Madison, one of the principal architects of the American Constitution, described the conundrum as being the simultaneous need to empower government (to promote society's values) and restrain it (to prevent it from destroying these values). 'Ambition must be made to counter ambition', and this necessitates the setting up of institutional checks and balances:

> It may be a reflection on human nature, that such devices should be necessary to control the abuses of government. But what is government itself but the greatest of all reflections on human nature? If men were angels, no government would be necessary. If angels were to govern men, neither external nor internal controls on government would be necessary. In framing a government which is to be administered by men over men, the great difficulty lies in this: You must first enable the government to control the governed; and in the next place, oblige it to control itself. A dependence on the people is no doubt the primary control on the government; but experience has taught mankind the necessity of auxiliary precautions.[2]

The need to check government power – which ostensibly forms the basis of the elected president scheme – implicitly acknowledges human fallibility. Caesar could become ambitious[3] and such ambition must be forestalled. The elected president scheme was designed as a pre-emptive strike against an irresponsible government, freakishly elected by the people, who might proceed to squander the nation's hard-earned resources. Besides evincing a marked distrust in the electorate, the scheme constitutes a paradigmatic shift from a tacit trust in the moral virtue and competence of the governors symptomatic in a feudalistic or paternalistic legal culture, to one of distrust. It also seems to acknowledge the possibility, however faint, of the advent of a breed of governors not cut from the old People's Action Party (PAP) mould.

Singapore's elected presidency was presented as an institutional response to curb the untrammelled power of the parliamentary executive.[4] The existence of a *de facto* single-party dominant state in Singapore has, I submit, thrown the checks and balances dynamic into disequilibrium. While the ruling PAP has constantly maintained that parliamentary democracy can exist under the *status quo*, they have nevertheless initiated a series of constitutional reforms which are meant, *inter alia*, to fill the 'parliamentary gap'. This chapter argues that the need to fill the parliamentary gap arises from the lack of effective constitutional opposition[5] in Parliament, which is a prerequisite for operating our Westminster system of government. The elected presidency is the latest in a long line of constitutional experiments, and is certainly the most revolutionary.

In the first section of this chapter, I will examine the assumptions and premises upon which our Westminster heritage is based. The second section considers how and to what extent the Westminster system of government has been retained and how it operates in the context of Singapore. In the third section, the nature and *modus operandi* of the elected presidency, its powers, and how it checks and is counter-checked by other government institutions is discussed. Finally, I will assess the institution's efficacy, in respect of that age-old question, *quis custodiet ipsos custodes*? (Who will bind the ruler?) and specifically, whether it achieves the prescription behind the separation of powers doctrine. I will also consider whether criticisms and suspicions that this scheme is no more than another attempt to stultify the growth of a bipartisan system and to perpetuate the PAP's stranglehold on power are well founded.

THE LEGACY OF THE WESTMINSTER MODEL OF GOVERNMENT

The prime ideology moulding Singapore's post-independence constitutional history has been 'pragmatism'. The imperative of nation-building and economic development drowned subtler, intangible nationalistic concerns. Retaining the Westminster model of parliamentary democracy already in place[6] was favoured over any experimentation with a more autochthonous system. Unemployment, housing shortages, and the communist insurgency had to be dealt with. Power was centralized in the executive to mobilize the nation's limited resources and individual liberties were overridden by the communitarian imperative. Within a generation, Singapore has progressed from economic poverty to prosperity. This economic success is largely attributable to the authoritarian style of government which rests on the base of economic legitimacy.[7] At present, cries for 'intangibles' like a more free and open society and a better quality of life are becoming more and more audible.

Between 1965 and 1979, the constitutional amendment procedure required a simple majority. Among the main amendments made during this period was the creation of the Presidential Council for Minority Rights. After 1979, when the constitutional amendment procedure was restored to a special two-thirds majority, constitutional amendments continued apace. Indeed the period after 1979 may be considered the 'renaissance' of constitutional experimentation. Chronologically, changes to constitutional government began with the introduction of the Non-Constituency Member of Parliament in 1984, Group Representative Constituencies in 1988, and the Nominated Member of Parliament Scheme debuted in 1990. To crown it all, the ceremonial office of the presidency was transformed into an elected one with real executive power in 1991.[8] The introduction of the elected presidency sparked comments that this constituted the definitive *quietus est* to Singapore's inherited system of parliamentary government. After the opposition Barisan Sosialis walked out of Parliament in 1968, the PAP inhibited the growth of the political opposition through a variety of techniques including the use of the Internal Security Act to indefinitely detain political opponents, the strict control of the media, establishing close links with the important National Trade Union Congress, and developing extensive grass-roots links.[9] Up till now, it has succeeded in preserving its hegemonic status in what was, after 1968, essentially a *de facto* one-party state.

Constitution-making in post-colonial times has been characterized by written constitutions based on the notion of a higher law which departs from the English model since Britain remains virtually the only country in the world without a written constitution.[10] From the outset, this so-called Westminster model as imported was modified *vis-à-vis* its prototype, even though the original intention was to substantially reproduce a British form of parliamentary democracy.

Among the characteristic features of modern Commonwealth countries are the limitations of parliamentary sovereignty, guarantee of fundamental human rights, judicial review of the constitutionality of legislation, the transfer of responsibility for terminating a superior judge's tenure of office from a legislative to a judicial forum, and the vesting of full control over the public service and the conduct of elections in the hands of independent commissions. The aim of these provisions is to capture the spirit and practice of British institutions; the methods of approach involve the rejection of British devices and the imposition of un-British fetters on legislative and executive discretion.[11]

Rather anomalously, a form of government which developed in the context of parliamentary supremacy was transplanted as a system espousing constitutional supremacy, with Parliament being a limited, rather than illimitable body. By delineating the extent of parliamentary powers, a written constitution – which rests on the apex of the legal norm hierarchy[12] – curbs what Parliament may do. The constitutional principle of separation of powers prevents transgression of institutional limits by any of the three branches of government. Where Parliament is supreme, trust is primarily reposed in the efficacy of political checks while a supreme Basic Law itself represents a legal check. The judicial branch of government is tasked with determining whether institutional limits are exceeded. Despite the presence of a supremacy clause, the Singapore constitution like the American one contains no express judicial review provision, although such a power is implicit in an independent judiciary[13] as argued by Alexander Hamilton in *The Federalist*.

The elements of the Westminster system may be summarized as follows:[14]

1 at minimum, a unicameral legislative chamber freely elected by the adult citizens by secret ballot;
2 political pluralism: electors are to have a real choice between two or more political parties;
3 executive power (vested in the head of state) but largely exercised by a cabinet of ministers headed by a prime minister as *primus inter pares*

who is chosen from the party commanding majority support in the elected chamber and answerable to that chamber;

4   a recognized opposition (akin to Her Majesty's Loyal Opposition with the Leader of the Opposition being a constitutional office receiving a salary paid out of the Consolidated Funds); and

5   a set of constitutional conventions (which may be directly incorporated into the constitution proper).

Optimal growth conditions require 'a vigorous press, powerful interest groups and an alert public opinion' which serve to restrain the prime minister and his cabinet. Singapore clearly lacks these conditions, having instead a pro-establishment press,[15] no interest group infrastructure[16] and a muted public opinion galvanized primarily by economic considerations. In sum, the legal culture is one of hierarchy and control.[17] Benevolent authoritarianism, which produces a very high standard of living, does not seem too bitter a pill to swallow.

MAKING PROVISION FOR THE PARLIAMENTARY GAP

The Westminster system was transplanted to Singapore's soil, a terrain which did not produce a reproduction of the original. This particular political system had a 'propensity to become transformed into a dictatorship when transplanted in societies without political cultures which support its operative conventions'.[18] The functioning of constitutional government cannot be seen *in vacuo* but must be set in its political and cultural context. However, 'culture' as defined by rulers, can sometimes serve as a justification for perpetuating a hegemonic form of government. The government believes that a bipartisan and adversarial system of government is unsuitable in an 'Asian democracy'[19] which prizes consensus above contention. Neo-Confucianists who stress a submissive attitude towards government leadership are quick to celebrate their version of Confucianism as the cause of Singapore's economic boom,[20] asserting the dubious proposition that economic growth and democracy are incompatible.[21] Culture, however is not immutable,[22] particularly with the growth of a middle class and the influence of an apparently universal motivating factor for human beings: the profit motive. Economic growth tends to precipitate demands for political liberalization, for a more open, accountable and participatory form of government. The more restrained a government is, the more authoritarianism is diluted. Against this backdrop, we must evaluate the elected presidency's contribution to the political control of the rulers by the populace indirectly through their choice of guardian-president.

The fusion of powers

Walter Bagehot stressed that the 'latent essence and effectual secret' of the British Constitution, in contrast to its presidential competitor, was the fusion of the legislative and executive functions:

> The independence of the legislative and executive powers is the specific quality of presidential government, just as their fusion and combination is the precise principle of the (British) Constitution.[23]

Singapore inherited this fusion of powers between the executive and legislative branches of government, bridged through the medium of the Cabinet which heads both the executive and legislature. Cabinet keeps Parliament[24] under control through party discipline, rendering the doctrine of ministerial responsibility mythical. Where the ruling political party commands a solid parliamentary majority, Parliament is impotent when it comes to blocking the Government. This fusion of powers does not contradict the separation of powers doctrine,[25] provided the Constitution establishes a substantial degree of judicial independence.[26]

Professor Jennings pointed out in *Cabinet Government*[27] that no democracy can exist without the presence of the opposition. The opposition functions as a check to government and a focus of discontent of the people. This function is all the more significant in polities without a second chamber, since the opposition plays a crucial role in parliamentary debate and overseeing the government. As such, it may also influence the formulation and execution of government policy. In a polity bereft of a viable opposition, parliamentary democracy is severely impaired by the loss of this check.

Creating a parliamentary 'opposition'

Certain techniques of political control[28] and a political culture lacking the concept of a 'loyal opposition' inhibit the healthy growth of an opposition. As Lucian Pye has observed:

> Confucianism has a heavy emphasis on harmony. It never developed the art of the adversarial relationship. How do you disagree without being disagreeable? Does the leadership protect itself and prevent any opposition from emerging? That's where the danger comes.[29]

PAP backbenchers attempted to 'play' the role of the opposition but this was obviously unsatisfactory given its inherent limitations. Even if PAP backbenchers were to disagree with a minister during parliamentary debate, the party whip ensures that critics within the PAP will abide by the party line when the vote is cast. In 1981, the PAP's monopoly on parliamentary seats was breached by the highly symbolic conquest of the Anson constituency by a lone opposition candidate. Thus the constituency opted for real opposition rather than the pseudo opposition provided by PAP backbenchers. More worrying for the ruling party, the percentage of votes was steadily declining, with a stunning 12.6 per cent anti-PAP swing in the 1984 elections. With all its Orwellian connotations, 1984 was the year the constitutional renaissance[30] commenced.

Alternative voice instruments

Since 1984, two new species of parliamentarians have been created. The Non-Constituency Member of Parliament (NCMP)[31] was introduced in 1984, and designed to guarantee an opposition element in Parliament. The top three opposition losers who secure at least 15 per cent of their constituencies' votes would be offered NCMP seats. NCMPs are decidedly inferior to directly elected MPs, particularly since their voting powers are severely restricted e.g. they did not extend to supply or constitutional amendment bills. As watchdogs, they are toothless, and the opposition charged that this new institution was created to lull the electorate into thinking that they need not vote in opposition MPs since there would always be NCMPs in Parliament. The NCMPs however appear equipped to do no more than serve as debating foils for the younger PAP MPs not yet versed in the intricacies of verbal fencing in Parliament. Lacking a power base, NCMPS have no standing to speak in Parliament. With the election of four opposition MPs in the 1991 general election,[32] the scheme has fallen into desuetude. It remains in the Constitution, but is not invoked when opposition is directly voted in.

In 1990, a second type of parliamentarian, the Nominated Member of Parliament (NMP),[33] was introduced. Selected by a Special Select Committee, potential NMPs had to satisfy fairly stringent qualifications showing themselves to be candidates who had distinguished themselves in the fields of public service, arts, sciences, etc.[34] Their main function was to provide constructive, non-partisan alternative views and the House would benefit from the special expertise of the NMPs. Since an NMP would have no need to play up to the gallery, unlike an

Opposition MP, he was unlikely to introduce an overtly adversarial spirit into Parliament. The introduction of non-elected parliamentarians drew sharp criticisms in and out of the House. It was a retrograde step, reminiscent of the colonial days where 'suitable natives' were appointed to the Legislative Council. At the same time, NMPs lacked the legitimacy to speak in Parliament since they represented no one but themselves. Finally, there was a fear that the PAP would use the NMP scheme as a backdoor to sneak in its own supporters.

Despite these fears and criticisms, the lively, informed and independent participation of NMPs has certainly raised the level of debate in Parliament. While the scheme may prove useful as an interim measure, or as a prelude to fuller democracy, critics suspect that the government is actually creating an approved channel of dissent in a further attempt to stultify the growth of the opposition. An 'opposition' created and approved by the government will never be as threatening as one possessing grassroots support. The NCMP and NMP will certainly serve as a safe outlet for some acceptable non-party voices, but this could also entail the dulling of the electorate's democratic instinct for greater choice.

Entrenching multi-racial representation

The Group Representative Constituency (GRC)[35] was introduced in 1988 with the express purpose of entrenching a multi-racial element in Parliament as voters were apparently not returning a racially balanced slate of candidates. The problem of minority rights under-representation had to be addressed. Under this scheme, three former single member constituencies are grouped together to form one mega constituency or Group Representation Constituency. A team of three MPs run for each GRC, one of whom must be of a stated minority race. By a further amendment in 1991, for not entirely clear reasons, the scheme was modified to arranging groups on the basis 'of not less than three but not more than four candidates'.[36] This scheme entails an implicit rejection of the non-racial approach to government advocated by the 1954 Rendel and 1966 Wee Chong Jin Constitutional Commissions which stated that racial factors should be downplayed and that Singaporeans should be encouraged to think in terms of one collective Singaporean entity.

The GRC scheme makes it harder for the opposition parties with strained resources to compete in elections. Attracting a single credible candidate is difficult enough, ever more so the need to assemble a team of four, with one member being of the stipulated racial group. On paper, the GRC scheme is a politically neutral institution and can serve as a double-edged sword; if the opposition wins just one GRC ward, four opposition MPs ride into Parliament in one fell swoop. In the meantime, it is interesting to note that the PAP won all 13 GRC wards in the 1988 general election and all 15 GRC wards in the 1991 election, although some of the closest results were registered in the GRCs.

It is reasonable to argue that the NMP, NCMP and GRC schemes share a common thread in that, directly or indirectly, they may contribute towards the centralization of power in one political party. By supporting the hegemonic status quo, the evolution towards bi-partisanism is retarded. Implicitly, the growth of a democratic ethos is suppressed. The question, is whether this same thread extends to the elected presidency scheme?

THE ELECTED PRESIDENT: AN EXECUTIVE DIVIDED?

The executive in a parliamentary system of government is bifurcated: the head of state, who is the monarch or the president in a republic, appoints the prime minister as the head of government. Historically, the British monarch as executive was once the singular repository of all sovereign power under the doctrine of the Divine Right of Kings which King James I preached in the seventeenth century. The Glorious Revolution of 1688 changed all that. The doctrine was rejected and the assembly of men who challenged the monarch's hegemony assumed, as Parliament, some responsibility of government, especially over matters of the purse. Increasingly, the monarch's role diminished to the extent that the monarch became increasingly dependent on the goodwill of the legislature. Eventually, government passed to 'His' Majesty's ministers, who were responsible to the legislature. Since these ministers were both members of the executive and the legislature, the system became fused and the executive became divided. Conversely, a presidential[37] system of government was revolutionary in the application of a rigid separation of powers between the trinity of government branches. The holder of the presidential office is both head of state and government.

Lord Diplock, in commenting upon the nature of Westminster Constitutions, has noted in *Hinds v. The Queen* that

> The new constitutions, particularly in the case of unitary states were evolutionary and not revolutionary. They provided for continuity of government through successor institution, legislative, executive and judicial, of which the members were to be selected in a different way,

but each institution was to exercise powers which, although enlarged, remained of a similar character to those that had been exercised by the corresponding institution that it had replaced.[38]

The introduction of the elected president in Singapore has taken the development of the Singapore variant of the Westminster model further along the evolutionary process. Perhaps the term 'revolutionary' might be more apt since the final product is a unique intermediate hybrid form of government treading the middle ground between the two prototypes: British parliamentarianism and US presidentialism.

The rationale for the elected presidency

The overwhelming impetus behind the elected presidency idea is fiscal prudence. When it was mooted in 1988, the proposal stated the desirability of having a safeguard or 'second key' over the financial reserves just in case the electorate chose an irresponsible wastrel government. The solution lay in creating an institutional check over a potentially imprudent executive which would have enjoyed untrammelled power. Clearly, government recognized the basic fallibility and fragility of Man, whom Senior Minister Lee Kuan Yew described as 'inherently vicious'.[39] The fallibility may lie either in the electorate's immature choice of bad government or in the deficiencies of a future government itself.

The fear of the electorate choosing a bad government is addressed by requiring potential candidates to clear the barrier of stringent pre-selection criteria. This severely limits the pool of potential candidates to an estimated 400 persons. The second fear is dealt with by setting up a 'countervailing power' to check the executive's broad powers. In a nutshell, as befits the *raison d'être* of the changed presidency, the president has veto powers over the spending of national reserves and public appointments. The original rationale was extended to carve out a watchdog role for the president to check against the abuse of powers under the Internal Security Act, the Maintenance of Religious Harmony Act[40] and investigations by the Corrupt Practices Investigation Bureau.

The status quo: ante- and post-amendment

The president was previously elected by Parliament. By a 1991 constitution amendment,[41] Article 17(2) now provides:

The president shall be elected by the citizens of Singapore in accordance with any law made by the Legislature.

This implies that the president, in receiving some sort of mandate from the electorate, is directly accountable to it. Article 20 stipulates that the president shall hold office for a six-year term, independent of the life of Parliament and can only be removed in accordance with the procedure set down in Article 22L. Previously the term of office lasted for four years and removal could be effected by a parliamentary resolution supported by two-thirds of the total number of the members present.[42] Prima facie, there is democratic value in a popularly elected rather than an endorsed president though this is based on the pre-supposition that the playing field for potential presidential candidates is level, though this is not the case. Ironically, it is easier to satisfy the requirements for prime ministership than for the presidency in Singapore, especially since the prime minister as head of the cabinet and government holds effective executive power. Indeed, the Singaporean presidential candidate is probably the most stringently qualified in the world. On a comparative note, the US Constitution requires that a candidate for the American presidency – arguably the most powerful political executive in the world today – merely be a US citizen resident in the United States for a minimum of 14 years and be at least 35 years of age.

The pre-selection criteria

From a purely theoretical perspective democratic principles are compromised if candidates have to meet a pre-selection test. It not only smacks of extreme elitism but also limits the people's freedom of choice and political participation. It also begs the question as to who is qualified to decide on this criteria and to apply it accordingly. On a practical level, it may be argued that the use of eligibility criteria sifts out incompetent, weak and flawed candidates (as defined by the criteria). The argument for setting special qualifications for the presidency – characterized in the Select Committee Report as a post of 'highest honour and responsibility' – is that the president needs to have a degree of financial expertise so that he can determine whether the reserves are being wisely spent. A candidate's expertise and administrative skills are gleaned either from his having held certain public offices[43] or being the CEO of a major company. Naturally, from the electorate's point of view, the institution of pre-selection criteria assumes that they are not sophisticated enough to tell the sheep from the goats.

The criteria were drafted by cabinet and endorsed by Parliament, rather unsurprisingly. Article 19 provides, *inter alia*, that the candidate must have held certain stipulated offices for a period of three years, e.g. that of Minister, Chief Justice, Speaker, Attorney General, Accountant-General or certain private sector posts like CEO of a company incorporated under the Companies Act with a $100 million paid up capital or the catch-all 'other similar or comparable position of seniority and responsibility'.[44] Suggestions to include within the automatic qualification category the Solicitor General, ambassadors and heads of professional bodies were rejected. Furthermore, the candidate must be 'a person of integrity, good character and reputation'.

What should perhaps be noted at this point is that the body which lays down the criteria effectively determines who may run for the post. By implication, that body can also exclude any person considered 'undesirable'. It was decided that the suitability of a candidate should be determined by a Presidential Elections Committee (PEC) which is composed of the Chairman of the Public Service Commission, a member of the Presidential Council for Minority Rights and the Chairman of the Public Accountants Board. Two of its members are government appointees and are likely to hold pro-establishment views; the appearance of non-partisanship in this regard is marred. While it is easy to understand the idea of having an accountant determine whether the candidate has the requisite financial expertise, it is difficult to see how the accountant can possibly possess superior judgment in assessing the candidate in respect of politically sensitive matters in which the president is likely to engage. Furthermore, the subjectivity of the criteria means that the PEC is imbued with considerable discretion in ascertaining what is, in their conception, 'suitable'. Their decision is not subject to judicial review[45] nor does the PEC appear to be accountable to anybody for their decision. Certainly this cannot bode well for an increasing demand for participatory democracy and increased transparency in decision-making and accountability of government. For example, out of four applicants, the PEC deemed only two fit to stand for election; applications from J. B. Jeyaretnam and Tan Soon Phuan, both members of the Workers' Party, were rejected and no reasons were given other than a lack of satisfaction about their financial capability and moral character.[46]

Moreover, it is hard to perceive a reasonable link between the pre-selection criteria in relation to the president's expanded role as a venue of appeal in politically sensitive matters concerning internal security, religious sensitivity or even in ensuring corruption-free government.

This watchdog role requires a degree of political judgment, a feel for the temper of the grassroots, assets which are not the sole prerogative of the financially adept. Bearing in mind the original conception of a strengthened presidency to promote fiscal prudence, enlarging the president's powers to include these matters has a distinct *ex post facto* tagged-on quality to it.

Barring minimal qualifications pertaining to age and sound state of mind, for example, the logic of democracy demands that a broad selection of people should be able to stand. Equal rights of candidature is an aspect of equality under the law and it is precisely this which confers political and moral legitimacy on the eventual victor of freely contested elections. Elections are the most concrete form of political participation and the means by which the ruled 'control' their rulers. An aspect of such 'control' requires the electorate to have a genuine choice between a variety of candidates as wide as the number of persons offering themselves for public service, instead of an artificially constrained choice.

Enlargement of presidential powers

Prior to the constitutional amendment, the presidency was a largely ceremonial appointed post, bearing great semiotic significance.[47] The office transcended parochial race issues since the person filling the office was a national figure, and his bailiwick was the entire nation. As a symbol of national unity and continuity, the president stood aloof from the clash of race, class and ideology which constitute politics. Past presidents have been Malay, Eurasian, Indian and Chinese. As the constitutional head of state, his discretionary powers were limited to the power of appointing as prime minister the person who commanded the confidence of a parliamentary majority, and the power to refuse to dissolve Parliament, both powers being necessary for a smooth transition between governments. In one fell swoop, the office lost its ability to be a symbol of multi-racial harmony. The pool of qualified persons is estimated to be about 400. Proportionally, this must significantly reduce the chance of a person belonging to a minority group from ever satisfying the onerous pre-selection criteria.

The office has also been transformed into that of a Westminster-styled ceremonial head of state with additional powers. It is essentially non-executive or reactive in nature, although the office carries with it significant 'negative' custodial powers over certain bills, which can be used with considerable discretion. This extends to vetoing the spending of reserves accumulated by past governments, key statutory boards and government companies. The veto power also extends to key senior government and military appointments where the president deems potential candidates unsuitable, thereby maintaining the image of honest and good government, untainted by nepotism or incompetence. Furthermore, the president can check potential government abuse of power under the Internal Security Act which authorizes preventive detention, and the Maintenance of Religious Harmony Act which can curb propagation of extremist or dangerous religious views. Generally, the president is an overseer of government in these limited aspects.

Outside of the clearly defined 'may act in his discretion' powers which include veto powers over budgets, key appointments and the like laid out in Articles 21(2)(a)–(i), the convention incorporated in Article 21(1) is operative despite executive authority being vested in the president:

> Except as provided by this Constitution, the president shall, in the exercise of his functions under this Constitution or any other written law, act in accordance with the advice of the Cabinet or a Minister acting under the general authority of the Cabinet.

The wording 'may act in his discretion' is objective and relates to the actual exercise of discretion by the president. That is, the president himself must personally apply his mind to the matter at hand and it may be argued that not to do so would constitute an abdication of his responsibility and, borrowing an administrative law analogy, an act *ultra vires* the Constitution.[48] It has been argued that Article 21(1) only means that the president has no discretion, for example, when granting presidential pardons such as partially granting the clemency plea in the recent politically sensitive case of Michael Peter Fay, the American convicted of vandalism. When assenting to bills (other than supply bills or supplementary supply bills and constitution amendment bills) passed by Parliament, the president simply rubber stamps the Cabinet's decisions.

It is, however, unclear whether the elected president may, without consulting the prime minister, freely choose which functions to attend. His presence at functions with political overtones may be construed as endorsement of a particular cause. Furthermore, an activist president may make political speeches calling for review of present government policies or even influence civil servants against their political masters, competing for their loyalty through the use or the threat of using his veto power in civil servant appointments. The president's power of patronage, his easy and ready access to the mass media, could make the office the object of desired capture by interest groups.

The president, if he has the predisposition of a de Gaulle, can treat the Constitution's silence as *carte blanche* for rewriting the conventions shaping the role of the presidency in a parliamentary system. He can even carve out a significant policy-making role for himself in the future, being unconstrained by precedent in his unique office. For example, the president can attend and address Parliament, conceivably influencing the law-making process. Article 22F provides that in the exercise of presidential functions, the president upon request is entitled to any information concerning government which is available to Cabinet or any statutory board or government company. The Constitution imposes a mandatory duty upon any minister, senior ministry officer or CEO of a statutory board or government company to furnish any information concerning the reserves or budget, upon presidential request. Access to such information is crucial to developing an overall perspective on the financial state of the nation and the best financial policy to adopt. It allows the president to take a more active interest in the workings of government as well.

The president as watchdog

Over finances   The president is empowered to veto the government's spending for the year if it is likely to draw on the reserves accumulated by a previous government. The government is then obliged to abide by the previous year's budget. The president is likely to exercise this financial veto where the government of the day has a tenuous majority in Parliament and resorts to costly electorate-pleasing tactics to curry short-term political gains but which are, in the long term, deleterious to the nation's interests. The institution embodies fiscal conservatism which entails not living beyond means, postponing immediate gratification in favour of planned saving with a view to the long term. Whether one regards this as Confucian values – which the government is eager to do – or the Protestant work ethic – as Weber characterized it, the president's mandate in this regard is quite clear: to be conservative.

Guarding against corruption in government   The president now has a role in ensuring good and honest government and safeguarding against high-level corruption. Under Article 22G, the Director of the Corrupt Practices Investigation Bureau may proceed with investigations even if the prime minister refused authorization, provided the president concurs therewith. In the appointment of certain public officers, the president has discretion to refuse an appointment, although he is obliged to consult the Council of Presidential Advisors. The final decision rests solely with him.

Over fundamental liberties Where the vindication of fundamental liberties is concerned, one might expect the president to adopt a more robust attitude, since he is cast as the guardian of these liberties, in lieu of the judiciary. If the elected president's political ideology is in complete unity with that of the government, he can hardly be expected to provide much of a safeguard. There are differences in political outlook spanning the entire individualism–communitarianism spectrum. As the jealous guardian of individual liberties, it is hoped that the president will veer towards individualism.[49]

The president has the final say in the issuing of detention orders under the Internal Security Act and prohibition orders under the Maintenance of Religious Harmony Act, as provided for in Article 21(2)(g)–(h). There is no need to consult the Council of Presidential Advisors as in these cases the president already has the advice of the Advisory Board or the Presidential Council for Religious Harmony.

Over constitutional changes The 1991 Constitutional Amendment which created the elected presidency also modified the amendment procedure for certain parts of the Constitution. Article 5(A) reads:

> Unless the President, acting in his discretion, otherwise directs the Speaker in writing, a Bill seeking to amend this clause, Articles 17 – 22, 22A to 22O, 35, 65, 66, 69, 70, 93A, 95, 105, 107, 110A, 110B, 151 or any provision in Part IV (Fundamental Liberties) or XI (Financial Provisions) shall not be passed by Parliament unless it has been supported at a national referendum by not less than two-thirds of the total number of votes cast by the electors registered under the Parliamentary Elections Act.

This amendment entrenches certain provisions including, rather salubriously, those relating to fundamental liberties.[50] Other notable provisions enjoying entrenchment are the provisions governing the elected presidency itself,[51] and those governing the prorogation and dissolution of Parliament. If ever an unscrupulous government desires to amend the Constitution to stay in power without calling elections, it will have to take this issue to the people. Building on this latter scenario, the wording of this article unfortunately suggests that if the president was in collusion with an unscrupulous government, he would be in a position to prevent the issue being put via referendum to the people! This would prevent the people from serving as a check on their representatives, which would be most undesirable.

Separating the powers or perpetuating the status quo?

An essential condition of free government, that is, a government under law, is reflected in the constitutional idea of the separation of powers. The essence of this doctrine is that abuse of power is less likely when power is not concentrated in the same hands. Pains must always be taken to ensure that the proposition *Lex Rex*[52] does not becomes the inverted *Rex Lex*.

A preliminary issue which must be addressed is the fact that parliamentary government, as established by the Constitution, has been transformed without so much as a reference to the People of Singapore. In a democratic state, the people are the ultimate repositories of sovereign power. Abraham Lincoln, in his seminal speech at Gettysburg, encapsulated the spirit of democracy by describing it as 'government of the people, by the people, for the people'. This sets democracy apart from hereditary rulership and absolutism. Governors, being trustees of the power they wield, are accountable to the people from whence they derive their powers.

The nature of a constitution depends on the source of its authority (whether or not it is an original act of the people) and whether it is justiciable and enforceable as law (as opposed to a political document not susceptible to judicial enforcement). A written constitution has been conceptualized thus:

> The instrument in which a constitution is embodied proceeds from a source different from that whence spring other laws, is regulated in a different way, and exerts a sovereign force. It is enacted not by the ordinary legislative authority but by some higher and specially empowered body. When any of its provisions conflict with the provisions of the ordinary law, it prevails and the ordinary law must give way.[53]

The institutions and procedures for formal judicial review of the constitutionality of acts exist in Singapore, borrowing the reasoning in *Marbury v. Madison*.[54] It is emphatically the province and duty of the judicial department to say what the law is. Those who apply the rule to particular cases, must necessarily expound and interpret that rule. If two rules conflict with each other, the courts must decide on the operation of each. Chief Justice John Marshall elaborated the basis upon which a written constitution is a fundamental law. He argued that those who rejected this premise would be reduced to the position of having to assert that 'the courts must close their eyes on the constitution and see only the law' when the constitution and the law were in conflict. Such doctrinal heresy subverts the very foundation of all written constitutions.

The Singapore Constitution, it will be remembered,[55] cannot be considered an act of the people in the sense of being adopted via referendum nor is it a creation of a constituent assembly. Nevertheless, the philosophy behind a written constitution is that it creates and therefore limits the institutions it creates; a creature cannot presume to be superior to its creator. If not, a written constitution is simply an absurd attempt 'to limit a power in its nature illimitable'. If we pursue the logic of popular sovereignty, a state and its organs are the creation of the people through a written document called the constitution. A constitution is supreme not only because it is logically prior in time but hierarchically superior,[56] since it rests on the superior authority of the people as the source and donor of all political power in the state. Constitution supremacy[57] is not sustained merely by a supremacy clause but must proceed from the consciousness of the people that the constitution is *theirs* and not something imposed from above, thereby highlighting their responsibility to observe its rules. This is where the legitimacy of the constitution stems from. Without this consciousness, a constitution is not worth more than the proverbial piece of paper it is written on.

A government has a limited mandate to govern according to the constitution under which it took office. Thus, when the government wishes to effect so fundamental a change as to drastically alter the nature of the constitutionally established institutional allocation of power, the issue should be submitted to the people for their endorsement or rejection. The people are, after all, the ultimate donors of political power. Indeed, there is a moral responsibility that such a proposed change be put to the people in the form of a referendum. As the parties to the social contract wherein they organized themselves into a state, only they can vary the terms of the contract. Holding a referendum is a means of allowing the people to decide in pursuance of their sovereign power.

It is most regrettable that the government refused to hold a referendum on this significant constitutional reform. By so doing, it effectively cut off what would have been a very healthy debate on the merits of the proposed institution and on possible alternative forms of control on the executive. The government's assertion that it does not govern by referendum or that its victory in the 1988 elections (where it secured less then 61 per cent of the votes) remains unconvincing.[58] One can infer that the PAP was not keen to leave it to the people to decide on the desirability of this new institution since it remains unclear whether they could have secured the requisite 66 per cent vote in a referendum. Indeed, the disconcerting speed with which this change was effected creates a distinct impression of a *fait accompli* completely inappropriate for such a momentous reform.

In examining the institution proper, two interrelated issues must be conceptually differentiated. First, whether the institution of the elected president will be an effective check against fiscal waste or government abuse of powers in specified instances; and second, whether there are sufficient safeguards against the president's abuse of power.

WHO GUARDS THE GUARDIANS?

The elected president versus the government: effective bilateral checks?

The elected president is not an executive president in the Gaullist sense,[59] yet in its altered form, the presidency is a far cry from the traditional Westminster-model ceremonial head. Although the president's 'negative' custodial powers over the financial reserves, integrity of the public service and some potential abuse of government powers do not envisage an active policy-making role, the employment of the veto power could well constitute a thorn in the government's flesh. In this section, we consider the nature of the president's veto powers, the constitutional provisions for conflict resolution between the president and the Cabinet, and the role of the Council of Presidential Advisors.

The limited nature of the veto

The operating principle of the president's veto power is that where, for example, the president disapproves of a budget which is likely to eat into the reserves not accumulated by the present government, the government must present a revised budget within a specified time. Pending the president's decision, spending is limited to 25 per cent of the preceding year's budget. If the revised budget is rejected as well, the approved budget for the preceding financial year comes into effect.

However, the presidential veto is not absolute and cannot be utilized with impunity. An overriding mechanism is built into the *modus operandi* of the veto, which dulls its efficacy and is a safeguard against presidential abuse of the veto power. Parliament is only able to override a presidential decision to withhold assent to a supply bill when the president is acting against the recommendation of the Council of Presidential Advisors. Article 148D provides that it may do so by passing a parliamentary resolution supported by at least two-thirds of the total number of MPs. We can see that the Council of Presidential Advisors represents a significant check over presidential decisions in this matter and can effectively render his decision inconsequential, thereby lowering his ability to use his veto power either constructively or destructively.

Whenever the president exercises his discretion in approving or disapproving a budget, he is required publish his reasons in the *Gazette*.[60] The imposition of this duty to give a reasoned decision represents a check on the president, guarding against careless use of his power and ensuring that he actually addresses his mind to the issue at hand.

Recourse in the event of conflict

It is unlikely that frictional situations will arise in the immediate future which will force the president to exercise his veto power, especially given the close working relationship between the prime minister and the president, who was his former deputy prime minister. Indeed, had retired civil servant Chua Kim Yeow won the election, this assessment would remain unchanged. As the *Jakarta Post* accurately characterized it, the first presidential election was a 'contest between pro-Government candidates'.[61] Whatever the outcome of the election, the government would have rested easy.[62] None the less, it is envisaged that a possibility of conflict between the president and prime minister may occur sometime in the future, for example, if the Council of Presidential Advisors agrees with a presidential veto. Would that effectively thwart cabinet policy?

There is a school of thought that subscribes to the notion that the Constitution only empowers the president to act reactively and never in an initiatory fashion. This assumes that an adversarial relationship between the president and prime minister will not materialize. A presidential–prime ministerial clash may nevertheless arise if the president takes advantage of the 'grey areas' where the Constitution is silent on the nature of his powers. The Cabinet may argue that such arrogation of power is *ultra vires* the spirit if not the letter of the Constitution. Parliament can then initiate the Article 22L removal provisions on grounds that the president's action constitutes 'an intentional violation of the Constitution'.

Gridlock: going to the polls   A gridlock may arise where no *ultra vires* issues are present or where general recourse to Article 22L is unavailable. If the prime minister is unable to prevail through the use of the override mechanism – especially where support from the Council of Presidential Advisors is not forthcoming – the alternative courses of action are quite drastic. A frustrated government may seek to curtail the president's powers but this cannot be effected by either a simple or special parliamentary majority alone, as Article 22H[63] safeguards undue incursion into the president's sphere of power:

> The president may, acting in his discretion, in writing withhold his assent to any Bill passed by Parliament (other than a Bill to which Article 5(2A) applies) if the Bill provides, directly or indirectly, for the circumvention or curtailment of the discretionary powers conferred upon him by this Constitution.

The only way to curtail the president's power is to go to the polls and seek a referendum.[64] Indeed, the entire office of the elected president is entrenched under Article 5(2A). The logic behind conferring a Rubicon-like quality to this new office with its untested and untried provisions is not easily grasped. Changing these provisions is extremely difficult, time-consuming and costly. Indeed, how the enlarged role of the president is to function has not been worked out in detail. As the first elected president himself said:

> As we accumulate experience with the new system, we can refine the arrangements and define through practice and precedent how the EP will function. In time, the presidency should grow into an institution (which) strengthens our political stability, guarantees high standards of government and assures Singaporeans of a secure and prosperous future.[65]

Obviously, this infant institution has a lot of growing up to do, and this makes the short-sightedness of the entrenchment provisions all the more baffling.[66] Even fine-tuning the system requires drastic recourse to a referendum, which is immensely impractical. It is ironic that while no referendum was held to create the institution, a referendum for its modification, let alone dismantling, is required.

Removal provisions   The initiative for setting in motion the procedure to remove the president remains with the legislature but the responsibility for deciding the motion of unfitness or incapacity falls on the judiciary's, and not the legislature's shoulders.[67] Article 22L governs the removal process. The legislature's role is cast in two stages:

first, it may issue a motion alleging that the president is permanently incapable of discharging the functions of the office by reason of mental or physical infirmity. Alternatively, the motion may allege that the president committed one of the following:

- intentional violation of the Constitution;
- treason;
- misconduct or corruption involving the abuse of the powers of his office; or
- any offence involving fraud, dishonesty or moral turpitude.

Article 22L(5) provides that where a motion alleging unfitness of the incumbent to serve is issued by Parliament and adopted by half the members of Parliament, the Chief Justice is to assign five Supreme Judges to compose a tribunal to ascertain whether the allegations are borne out. The president cannot retaliate by dissolving Parliament while being investigated, save in limited specified instances.[68] If the tribunal report finds the allegations affirmative, the second stage of Parliament's involvement is to issue a parliamentary resolution supported by at least three-quarters of the total membership of the House to remove the president from office.

An instance of possible conflict of interest arises from the provisions governing the temporary discharge of presidential functions when the office is vacant: Article 22N provides that where the office is prematurely vacated, either the Chairman of the Council of Presidential Advisors or the Speaker, in that order, may temporarily serve in a presidential capacity. Failing this, it falls on Parliament to appoint a person to exercise the presidential functions provided the said person is qualified to be elected as president, under Article 19.

Potentially, the Chief Justice, whose office is expressly stipulated in Article 19(2)(g)(i), may act temporarily as president. Perceived bias may arise where the vacancy is attributable to a parliamentary motion alleging incompetence or unfitness, with the Chief Justice cum acting-president appointing the tribunal, which may include himself, to investigate the motion. The awkwardness of the situation is reminiscent of the situation in which Chief Justice John Marshall must have found himself, in the seminal American case of *Marbury v. Madison* where the suit arose directly and immediately out of an error committed by Marshall himself when he was Secretary of State!

The first two grounds of removal are self-explanatory: the first relates to breaching the letter of the Constitution, and treason is plainly understood as an act amounting to a denial of allegiance to the state. The remaining grounds, however, merit further examination. The latter two contain nebulous terms like 'misconduct' and 'moral turpitude'. Conceptually, a principled base upon which to proceed is absent owing to the large degree of subjective discretion involved. Since no guidelines are given in terms of defining instances where 'misconduct' might occur, there is a grave danger of arbitrariness since 'misconduct' can be broadly or as narrowly construed, according to taste.

The removal provisions for Supreme Court Judges include a finding of 'misbehaviour'. Like 'misconduct', the meaning of 'misbehaviour' is about as clear as mud. The 1988 Malaysian constitutional crisis precipitated by the removal, *inter alia*, of the Lord President Tun Salleh Abas on the basis of a highly controversial finding of 'misbehaviour' is instructive. The Malaysian provisions in this respect are *in pari materia* with Singapore's. Critics, besides being appalled at the conduct of tribunal proceedings, have charged the removal with being politically motivated and legally unjustified.[69] Furthermore, the investigating tribunal was vested with full procedural discretion and adopted a startling 'make it up as we go along' approach which surely breaches every rule of natural justice or fairness conceivable. In fact, Tun Salleh Abas was removed without being heard, which the tribunal considered 'regrettable'. He had in fact objected to the biased composition of the tribunal whose head was next in line for Tun Salleh's post. A clearer prospect of bias could not be found![70] It would be wiser to define the grounds of removal in Article 22L which is unclear and to specify minimum standards of procedural fairness in advance.

Role of the Council of Presidential Advisors

The 1991 Constitutional Amendment also created the Council of Presidential Advisors (CPA). Article 37B(1) states that this Council shall comprise:

- two members appointed by the president acting in his discretion;
- two members appointed by the president on the advice of the prime minister; and
- one member appointed by the president on the advice of the Chairman of the Public Service Commission.

The president appoints a Council member to be Chairman, who shall vacate his seat when a newly elected president assumes office during the Chairman's term of appointment. Article 37I states that the Council's function is to make recommendations to the president on any matter referred to the Council by the president pursuant to Articles 21(3) or 21(4). Article 21 which governs the president's discretionary powers requires him to consult the Council in some cases before exercising his discretion. Examples of this mandatory requirement include the appointment of statutory board members, and concurrence with loan-raising or disapproving transactions drawing on accumulated reserves. In other cases, such as withholding concurrence in relation to the detention of any person, the reference to consulting the Council is merely directory. The Council is duty bound to state reasons for advising the president to withhold his assent to supply bills and is given the power to order the appearance of public officers to give information concerning matters the president has referred to the Council. The Council regulates its own *in camera* proceedings, subject to presidential approval. Precluding public participation in Council deliberations is unfortunate as it removes a sense of accountability, which publicity stirs, and which the non-elected Council might otherwise feel. This contributes to the impression that the efficacy of the president as a bilateral check *vis-à-vis* the government is not what it was lauded to be.

Implications for the separation of powers

By providing for separate presidential and parliamentary elections, the formal institutional[71] separation of powers is secured. This asserts that in general the organization, personnel and tasks of the three different government branches ought to be kept entirely separate. The president's six-year term thus runs independently of Parliament's usual five-year life span. Having a direct mandate from the people, the president's tenure is not subject to the whim of the legislature. The organic separation is buttressed by Article 19(3)(a) and (d) which require that the president shall 'not hold any office created or recognized by this Constitution' and that 'if he is a Member of Parliament, vacate his seat in Parliament'. The president cannot be both a member of the executive and a member of the legislature[72] in the way a Cabinet member can straddle these two government branches in a Westminster-model based system of government. However, as the president and Cabinet executive both share the same genre of power in an overlapping fashion, there is no functional separation of powers.[73]

The Philosopher King v. 'a few good men': nature of the institution

Without a vision, people perish. Not to be caught wrong-footed, the government identified a problem as a potential future scenario: that of an irresponsible government with untrammelled power financially mismanaging the nation's hard-earned reserves. After identifying this problem, a quantum leap was made to the proposition that a man was needed to stand in the gap and check fiscal waste, and that man should be the president. The logic of having one man for this job, and that man the president, is not immediately apparent.[74] As President Ong himself put it, it is 'just one man against the entire government machinery'.[75]

In the context of a society where the prime minister has declared his intention of conducting government in a more open, consultative style, it seems incongruous to confer such significant powers on one person instead of seeking safety in numbers. It would be more consonant with the goals of participatory democracy and the idea of separation of powers to subject important decisions to the collective wisdom of several good men rather than defer to the judgment of a single individual. There is a natural check and balance dynamic in working in a group.

On closer examination, it appears that the president does not have a free hand in exercising his important veto powers. In the case of supply bills, his decision can be overridden by Parliament where the Council of Presidential Advisors disagrees with that decision. The Council is a very effective, if not over-effective, check on the president. Whether or not such a bill may be vetoed will in some cases be contingent upon the Council's recommendation. Hence, the CPA effectively 'shares' the veto power with the president in this regard. Pronouncements have been made to the effect that the Council is in fact serving as a *de facto* Senate. If this is so, one wonders whether the elected presidency is the best institutional response to the perceived problems of potential fiscal misuse. Might not the alternative of a *de jure* wholly elected Senate at least provide the added benefit of a body of persons directly accountable to the electorate in their wielding of a potentially important power?

The final list of problems to be solved by the elected presidency was extended to include other varied and distinct objectives like protecting individual liberties in the area of personal liberty and religious freedom. This latter role bears a distinctly tagged-on quality. Why should the lone president bravely face the wrath of the Cabinet? Why cannot he be bolstered by the support and moral courage that numbers bring? There appears no ostensible problem of delay and inefficiency that too many cooks may bring. Rather than having one Philosopher King, we could, through an elected senate or some independent watchdog commission, have several guardians with the dual benefits of collective wisdom and accountability through election.

Human rights watchdog: ousting the judiciary

As President Ong noted, his office entails more than 'adding up numbers'.[76] In certain specified instances, the elected president replaces the judiciary's traditional constitutional role as the guardian of individual liberties stipulated in Part IV of the Constitution. The inclusion of a Bill of Rights in the Singapore Constitution represents a counter-majoritarian check against legislative majorities and executive decisions. Its purpose is to withdraw certain matters from the vicissitudes of political controversy. Nevertheless, none of the rights are couched in absolute terms and may be derogated from in limited instances. Such derogation is determined by delicately balancing competing individual and collective interests, a role traditionally undertaken by the judiciary as the impartial arbiter between state and individual.

Conceptually, a Bill of Rights constitutes a recognition of the centrality of man's humanity. Nwabueze expresses it well:

> Man is first and foremost a *human* being and only secondly a *social* being, that his individuality comes before his social instincts, and that the attributes of his humanity are more basic and fundamental to his existence than the material benefits of social life. The latter are meaningless to him if he is no longer able to breathe, think or feel. The material conditions of a good decent life are meant to complement his humanity, to enable him fully to realize his human personality. It would be a contradiction if the pursuit of social security and social well-being were to override man's humanity. Neither of course should override the other. It is important, however, that the opposition between them should be recognized and efforts made to balance them.[77]

Translated into the constitutional context, this envisages a presumption in favour of the individual liberty at stake, which is the approach adopted by the Privy Council in the seminal case of *Ong Ah Chuan v. Public Prosecutor*.[78] From a reading of Singapore constitutional case law, human rights protection and, indeed, the value of the individual, is consistently rendered subservient to the collective interest. For example, in the area of free speech which is constitutionally entrenched in Article 14, speech which is critical of the conduct of public officials is not considered important despite its central role in preserving the accountability of such officials in a democracy. No attention whatsoever was given to the need to alter the weights in the balancing exercise between individual and collective interests where a common law offence comes up against the constitutional liberty of free speech.

In *Attorney General v. Wain*,[79] it was stated that there existed no inconsistency between the right of free speech and the common law offence of scandalizing the court. The latter offence is designed to guard against unwonted injury to the Court's reputation which would prejudice the administration of justice. The doctrine developed in the context of England where common law liberties are merely residual. Surely when a liberty such as free speech is elevated into a constitutional liberty, the balance struck at common law governing contempt of court must be reconsidered. Greater protection should be afforded a constitutional liberty whose enhanced value is reflected by its inclusion in the highest law of the land. The present law on contempt of court in Singapore is so broad as to render *any* criticism of the judiciary potentially contemptuous! Who then, will guard the Guardians?[80]

Similarly, in the case of *Jeyaretnam Joshua Benjamin v. Lee Kuan Yew*,[81] which involved a defamation suit for statements criticizing a public official, the judiciary was extraordinarily restrained in according paramountcy to a public official's reputation, almost completely ignoring the value of speech critical of that official. Once again, it was stated that free speech was subject to the common law tort of defamation without any re-consideration of the balance of interests struck by that tort, which developed in the absence of any notion of a constitutional liberty. The American case of *New York Times v. Sullivan*[82] and the European Court case of *Lingens v Austria*,[83] which accept that the limits of acceptable criticism for public officials should be wider than for private individuals (the thicker skin argument), were rejected. Great emphasis was placed on the need to protect the reputation of public officials to avoid the fear of deterring 'sensitive and honourable men from seeking public positions of trust and responsibility'.[84] There was no thick skinned 'public figures' exception, as developed in American jurisprudence[85] – presumably, Singapore politicians are too delicate to tolerate much criticism.

This is supremely ironical in the light of the recent English case of *Derbyshire City Council v. Times Newspapers Ltd*[86] where the House of Lords concluded that it was more important to allow uninhibited freedom of political speech than to protect a public authority's reputation. Libel law, of course, entails a judicious balancing of free speech interests and an individual's right to reputation, but insofar as public authorities are concerned, the value of political speech has been elevated, which paves the way for wide immunity to be accorded to libel suits against public officials. Free speech lacks positive status in Britain, being but a residual liberty which law can circumscribe. Yet political speech has been accorded greater weight in the balancing process in the absence of a written constitution and bill of rights. Certainly, more adjustment is required in Singapore where free speech has constitutional status!

This cursory examination of free speech and public official reputation in Singapore is representative of the generally deferential attitude adopted by the Singapore judiciary with respect to individual rights. It has certainly not developed a robust approach to protecting constitutional liberty. Bearing this in mind, it was thought desirable that in certain areas where legislation derogates from human rights protection, the elected president would be better placed to serve as a political check against executive power, rather than involve the judiciary in providing legal checks. Political judgment is certainly involved in the decision, for example, to cancel, confirm or vary a restraining order issued by the minister under the Maintenance of Religious Harmony Act[87] or in disapproving detention orders under the Internal Security Act.

It is submitted that in dealing with sensitive issues such as determining when religious propagation amounts to religious extremism or defining what constitutes subversion, requires an impartial arbiter, traditionally represented by the judiciary. If the president assumes this aspect of the judicial function as co-guardian of certain fundamental liberties, we must examine the effectiveness of this political check, especially since there is a lack of vigorous judicial approach in the protection of human rights. Central to this role is the assurance that the president is politically independent of the Cabinet and that he is imbued with the notion that his office must maintain an activist eagle eye against human rights abuses. This will achieve the constitutional ideal of limited government which, one can surmise, must have been the *raison d'être* for according the president a role in protecting individual liberty in the first place.

The elected president serves as a check within a divided executive by replacing the judiciary as the avenue of appeal in security-related areas. How effective is this intra-branch separated powers rationale? As it stands, the judiciary's power of judicial review pertaining to ISA detentions was severely curtailed by an amendment to Article149(3)[88] of the Constitution, thereby allowing amendments to be made to the ISA[89] itself. One of the reasons proffered for the amendment was that

> Singapore judges (would) in effect become responsible for and answerable to decisions affecting (the) national security of Singapore because they would then have the final say.[90]

This school of thought asserts that the matter is non-justiciable, and that it is unacceptable to transfer the political issue of issuing detention orders to unelected judges. It rejects the counter-majoritarian argument which asserts that judicial review by an independent judiciary is the only way to safeguard and enforce liberties. This latter argument is premised on the fact that since judicial review is concerned with the manner in which a decision-making process is made, rather than the merits of the decision itself, it does not unduly intrude into the political realm. Owing to the vagueness and multi-faceted nature of tests like '*Wednesbury* reasonableness', 'relevancy' and 'purpose', it may feasibly be argued that these terms can become tools for judicial activism and judicial legislation since they are broad enough to mask a judicial policy-choice. It is true that the merits/legality dichotomy is often paper-thin, but considering the staid conservatism of Singapore's judiciary and its deference to the executive, it is highly unlikely that the judiciary will exploit the malleability of these tests to annex more subjects for its supervisory empire. In the absence of judicial review, the elected president can serve admirably as a political check to fill in the vacuum. However, the safeguard this office provides appears minimal, and this may result in the perpetuation of the executive cabinet's untrammelled power.

Appeals in the national security area are made to essentially government-appointed advisory boards which hold their proceedings *in camera* although Article 22(f) provides that the president may refuse to appoint the chairman and members[91] of an advisory board constituted for the purposes of Article 151. Article 151(4) provides that when the advisory board recommends the release of any detainee, the person shall not be detained without the concurrence of the president if the relevant minister rejects the advisory board's recommendations. Hence, without presidential concurrence, the minister is bound by the advisory board's recommendation. However, the president is precluded from any role when the advisory board recommends detention or continuation of detention. This means that there is effectively no appeal when minister and board agree on detention. The deliberations of the non-elected advisory board in this scenario determine whether the president's concurrence is even required.

The judiciary is precluded by section 17 of the Maintenance of Religious Harmony Act (MRHA) from taking cognizance of any offence under this act save where the Public Prosecutor consents. Section 8 of the MRHA empowers the minister to issue a restraining order to a religious leader or member of a religious institution where he is satisfied that an act has been committed which:

- causes feelings of enmity, hatred, ill-will or hostility between different religious groups;
- carries out activities to promote a political cause, or a cause of any political party while, or under the guise of, propagating or practising any religious belief;
- carries out subversive activities under the guise of propagating or practising any religious belief; or
- excites disaffection against the president or the Government of Singapore while, or under the guise of, propagating or practising any religious belief.

A restraining order of up to two years (subject to renewal) can be used to prohibit in written or oral form the addressing of a particular topic or theme; prohibit the occupation of certain editorial posts or publication of material without the prior permission of the minister. These wide powers potentially intrude not only on the liberty of religious expression, but of freedom of speech and expression protected under Articles 15 and 14 respectively. This is especially so as the line between 'religion' and 'politics', is nowhere defined in the Act and, judicially or politically, is notoriously difficult to draw. Section 18 is an ouster clause which excludes any judicial participation in this matter:

> All orders and decisions of the president and the Minister and recommendations of the Council made pursuant to this Act shall be final and shall not be called in question in any court.

The expanded presidency is expected to check such wide powers. Section 12 MRHA read with Article 22I provides that every restraining order shall cease to have effect unless it is confirmed by the president within 30 days from the date the Presidential Council for Religious Harmony's recommendations are received by the president. The president is obliged to consider these recommendations and is empowered to cancel, confirm or vary the order. He is expected to act in his discretion where the advice of the Cabinet goes contrary to the Council's recommendation. Thus when Cabinet and Council are *ad idem*, the president provides no individual safeguard. Again, much depends on the independence of the Council which is established under Part II of the MRHA. The Council must have a minimum of six and not more than 15 other members and one chairman. All Council members are appointed by the president on the advice of the Presidential Council for Minority Rights for three-year terms. Section 3(2) provides

> Not less than two-thirds of the members of the Council shall be representatives of the major religions in Singapore and the other members shall be persons who, in the opinion of the Presidential Council for Minority Rights, have distinguished themselves in public service or community relations in Singapore.

This is an important provision. Singapore citizens professing various religions are directly involved in some decision-making in this important area. The power to issue restraining orders could possibly be transferred from the Cabinet to the Council. Such a move would symbolize trust in the maturity of the religious leaders of the people, and consequently, participation from the 'bottom' of the system. At the same time, this would encourage a spirit of co-operation among the various religious leaders and create a climate conducive to the peaceful co-existence among the different faiths and belief systems, promote a better understanding of the particular religious sensitivities of each group. At a macro-level, the Council may emerge as a potential tension diffusion mechanism. The role of the president in this area, in any case, appears superfluous. The best way to combat religious extremism is to reconsider and enlarge the role of the Presidential Council for Minority Rights, especially since the president is insufficient as a political check over undue incursion of religious liberties. In any case, it is unclear what ideological stance the president will adopt *vis-à-vis* Cabinet.

Judicial review as a tool for enforcing human rights is derived from the structure of the US Constitution since such power is implicit in the notion of an independent judiciary. The preference for a political check as opposed to a judicial check is more in keeping with the English constitutional tradition which is essentially anti-judicial and inclined towards political checks which ultimately reside in the people as possessors of sovereign power. Even so, even within the common law method,[92] there is potential for according a priority to fundamental rights comparable to their entrenchment in a set of written norms. The English judiciary has not been slack in its protection of the famous civil liberties of Englishmen, nowhere more evident than in the development of English administrative law. In the case of *Derbyshire* discussed above, aside from giving quasi-constitutional status to political free speech, it also accepted the legitimacy of deploying the substantive content of the European Convention of Human Rights (to which Britain is party) as a tool to further develop the common law.

This approach does not turn the High Court into a court of merits or primary decision-maker, which would upset the constitutional balance between elected decision-makers and the unelected judiciary. As the judiciary has traditionally been tasked with ascertaining the principles on which the people will be protected from the arbitrary exercise of power, it is well-placed to articulate certain axioms as basic rights by building on existing common law principles.[93] It is noteworthy that the Australian High Court adopted an activist approach in two fairly recent cases[94] by implying fundamental guarantees even though the Commonwealth constitution does not contain a American-styled Bill of Rights. The important underlying principle is that both the American and, increasingly, the British courts, ultimately perceive themselves as defenders of the people's rights. No such bias on the part of the Singaporean judiciary appears apparent.

A final subsidiary point should be made about the president as a sort of constitutional guardian over certain fundamental liberties. Article 5(2A) provides that a bill seeking to amend any provision in Part IV of the Constitution – which contains the fundamental liberties provisions – must be supported at a referendum by at least two-thirds of the total number of electors and passed by a two-thirds parliamentary resolution. Rather curiously, Article 5(2A) provides that in such a situation, if the president acting in his discretion so directs the Speaker in writing, no referendum has to be held. The burning question is: Why should any person or institution potentially stand in the way of the people themselves deciding something which so crucially pertains to them? It cannot conduce to the healthy growth of a democratic ethos if someone is always there to make fundamentally important decisions on behalf of the people in a top-down fashion. The price of liberty is eternal vigilance and the beneficiaries of fundamental liberties should be given the fullest measure of responsibility in securing and protecting *their* liberties.

The judiciary's failure to develop a robust approach towards protecting individual rights leave a gap between what the Constitution *prima facie* promises and the liberties actually enjoyed in real life. To justify the judiciary's deference to the executive, recourse to culturally relativistic arguments that 'Asian' society is group oriented, preferring harmony over contention and valuing the collective over the individual, have been employed. From the above analysis, the less than happy state of affairs in respect of the president's role in security matters is not alleviated by his concurrent role as co-guardian over human rights. As the provisions stand, there is no guarantee that the president will be truly independent of the cabinet. Neither is it certain that the president, supposedly a conservative and reactive office, will adopt an active, pro-individual role in safeguarding constitutional liberties. There is nothing to prevent the president from sharing the same dismissive ideology towards human rights that the government of the day might hold.

GUARDING THE GUARDIAN: THE IMPERATIVE OF INDEPENDENCE

Much of the institution's efficacy – perceived or otherwise – is contingent on it being truly independent from executive influence. The need for an independent check to effectively counter the concentration of power in the Singapore system is paramount. The need for independence is recognized in Article 19(3)(c) and (d) which require that the president 'not be a member of any political party' and 'if he is a Member of Parliament, (to) vacate his seat in Parliament'. Article 19(2)(f) further requires that for a person to qualify as a presidential candidate, he must not be 'a member of any political party on the date of his nomination for election'.

An office which involves the exercise of political judgment must be a political office. As such, the president cannot be totally apolitical (despite the media portrayal of Chua Kim Yeow as a 'credible apolitical alternative'). At the same time, he must be perceived to be above partisan politics. Indeed, Chua finally struck a chord among many voters when he asked, in his second televised speech, whether the people wanted to have the PAP 'extend their political dominance into the presidency'. Since actual or perceived objectivity is so crucial, regardless of the personal integrity of any particular president, there must be safeguards against the possibility of partisanship. During the Select Committee hearing,[95] it was suggested that former ministers and politicians be ruled out entirely – there being no surer way of severing the ties that bind – thereby enhancing public perception of the presidency as an independent institution. A less drastic recommendation was that former Cabinet members be disqualified from running for president for five years after leaving the Cabinet, five years being the normal life of a Parliament. This would provide a 'cooling off' period and considerably lessen the perception of bias, allowing the distancing of personal ties. Such a safeguard would protect a member of government moving directly from Cabinet to the presidency.[96] Unfortunately, this proposal was disregarded and the first elected president did move directly from his senior Cabinet post to become the first elected head of state.

It is submitted that the present criterion requiring non-party membership does not go far enough to ensure that the office of the president remains completely partisan. In the absence of an effective parliamentary opposition to scrutinize and censure government action and ultimately threaten to replace the present day government at the next polls, what measures can be adopted to perform the functions of the missing opposition? Obviously, an independent human rights commission or financial watchdog body composed perhaps of members of the public, elected and frequently rotated, is a possibility. But working with what we have, certain modifications are in order. A five-year 'cooling-off' period will ensure that a presidential candidate maintains some detachment from current politics. The pre-selection criteria could also be dispensed with, broadening the pool of potential candidates and allowing the electorate to do the job of filtering through the wheat and weeds. Why should an accountant who sits on the Presidential Elections Committee have any particular expertise in deciding who is fit to make politically sensitive judgments? As it stands, the possibility of collusion or the appearance of collusion is a problem which has not been eradicated despite the overt severance of party ties. Formal independence is a mockery in the absence of substantive content.

CONCLUDING OBSERVATIONS

It has often been stated that constitutions are not sacrosanct documents and must be changed in accordance with the changing needs of the nation. Even so, every mature democratic system has an immutable prerequisite: that of preserving a limited government beyond the trappings of formality. The essence of constitutionalism is the taming of naked power by law. Constitutional wisdom aspires to this by advocating the separation of powers in different hands, through the establishment of a system of checks and balances. This need is particularly pressing in the Singapore context where the restraint and *not* the empowerment of government, has been the problem.

The development of a one-party dominant state in a parliamentary system with the Cabinet as the sole locus of centralized power has underscored the need for an opposing power to check the untrammelled power of the parliamentary executive. In the years after independence, the Constitution has been modified by amendments which have created unique innovations such as the NCMPS, NMPs and GRCs, ostensibly to serve as checks and balances in some way. The declared rationale for these innovations was to create a more equitable system of parliamentary representation which would safeguard minority interests and to guarantee some form of 'institutionalized' opposition. Laudable as these objectives appear, the underlying suspicion that these new creations can be manipulated to inhibit the growth of a grassroots genuine opposition, capable of forming an alternative government, has yet to be dispelled. What they have in common are the functions which would otherwise be performed by an effective parliamentary minority.

The elected president is the latest in a line of constitutional changes designed to strengthen the structure of government by providing a 'countervailing' check in certain areas. Certainly, it is the most revolutionary alteration to Singapore's present system of government which stands as a hybrid between presidentialism and parliamentarianism. While the underlying rationale of the scheme, that of checking government power, is certainly sound, it is by no means clear that the problem of over-centralized power has been satisfactorily resolved. Further, whether this institution is the best means to achieve such a purpose is open to serious doubt. These include the dubious 'one man for the job' rationale, the doubtful autonomy of the institutions, in particular the CPA and the PEC, the makeshift quality of certain provisions, the less than serious consideration of alternative proposals mentioned in the White Paper, the hastiness surrounding the passing of this amendment. Cumulatively, these factors have aroused suspicions which are not entirely addressed. Stated simply, in the guise of separating powers, the institution provides merely the semblance of an additional safeguard, a further addition to the plethora of already existing 'safeguards' designed apparently to check government power. However, like Hamlet, who discovered that one could smile and smile and yet be a villain, we must go beyond what seems; we must determine the effectiveness or otherwise of this institution. The elective element confers an apparent legitimacy on the office, but this aura of legitimacy masks the concentration of power and the perpetuation of the political status quo.

NOTES

1 'The freedom then of man, and liberty of acting according to his own will, is grounded on his having reason which is able to instruct him in that law he is to govern himself by, and make him know how far he is left to the freedom of his own will. To turn him loose is not the allowing him the privilege of his nature to be free, but to thrust him out amongst brutes and abandon him to a state as wretched and as much beneath that of a man as theirs.'

John Locke was asserting that integral to the government of man was man's ability to govern himself based on a firm ethical foundation from which the sense of moral or civic responsibility flows. See Russell Kirk in *The Conservative Constitution: The Rights of Man vs the Bill of Rights*, (Regency Gateway, 1991): 376.

2 'The Federalist No. 51', in Alexander Hamilton, James Madison and John Jay *The Federalist Papers*, (Bantam Classic edn, 1982): 262.

3 It is interesting to note that Senior Minister Lee Kuan Yew, in an interview in *Foreign Affairs*, rejected the liberal humanistic intellectual tradition which claimed that 'human beings had arrived at this perfect state where everybody would be better off if they were allowed to do their own thing and flourish'. A utilitarian relativism in ethics does not provide a firm moral base or consensus which is ultimately founded on religious truth and without which no society in recorded history has ever survived. Senior Minister Lee correctly asserted that

certain basics about human nature do not change. Man needs a certain moral sense of right and wrong. There is such a thing called evil, and it is not the result of being a victim of society. You are just an evil man, prone to do evil things, and you have to be stopped from doing them. Westerners have abandoned an ethical basis for society, believing that all problems are solvable by good government, which we in the East have never believed possible.

It follows that a government which prides itself on its moral legitimacy is itself staffed by ultimately imperfect people. In the last analysis, moral legitimacy must flow from a higher source whether this be God, an abstract first principle or popular sovereignty, for example.

(*Foreign Affairs* 1993, 73: 112)

4 *Constitutional Amendments to Safeguard Financial Assets and the Integrity of the Public Service*, Cmd 10 of 1988, para 12.

5 An 'effective' opposition should not only competently discharge its functions of parliamentary scrutiny and censure or articulate alternative views but should also make political turnover a real, viable possibility.

6 In 1959, Singapore enjoyed internal self-government and received a new constitution from the United Kingdom providing for a wholly elected legislature with the UK remaining responsible for defence and external affairs. In 1963, Singapore became subject to the Malaysian federal constitution on joining the Federation and also received a new state constitution. This 1963 Constitution was later amended and continues to be the Republic's Constitution. It was expelled from the Federation in 1965 and four months after separation, Parliament enacted the Republic of Singapore Independence Act 1965 (RSIA) to provide 'that all existing laws

shall continue in force on or after Singapore Day'. Subject to 'modifications, adaptations, qualifications and exceptions as may be necessary to bring them into conformity with this Act and with the independent status of Singapore upon separation from Malaysia'. Certain provisions of the Constitution of Malaysia were selectively made applicable to Singapore as section 6 RSIA. For a succinct constitutional history of Singapore, see Kevin Tan, 'The Evolution of Singapore's Modern Constitution: Developments from 1945 to the Present Day', *Singapore Academy of Law Journal* (1989) 1: 6–17.

7   East Asian democracy which retains a tight rein on social control seems supported or mandated by economic prosperity. Economic legitimacy, which incorporates a Machiavellian justification of the means by the end has a dangerous Achilles heel: it is vulnerable to the situation where growth falters and the economic goods no longer can be delivered. It is argued that orderly succession is nowhere as satisfactorily guaranteed as in Western parliamentary democracies. See Eric Jones, 'Asia's Fate', *The National Interest* (1994) 18: 22–3 where he points out the defects of authoritarianism.

8   At the time of writing, Senior Minister Lee Kuan Yew's proposal to change the voting system by giving those aged 35 to 60 years double votes because they are more responsible is fermenting in the mind of the constitutional changers. Suffice to comment at this incipient stage that this does not appear to bode well for democracy as 'theoretically, any government can stay in power in perpetuity as long as it can take care of the interests of a group it gives the two votes to'. See *Straits Times*, 12 May 1994: 24.

9   See Thio Li-ann, 'The Post Colonial Constitutional Evolution of the Singapore Legislature: A Case Study', [1993] *Singapore Journal of Legal Studies* 80: 93–6.

10   For an assessment of the successes and failures of Commonwealth constitution-making during the past 40 years or more, see William Dale, 'The Making and Remaking of Commonwealth Constitutions', *International and Comparative Law Quarterly* 1993, 42: 67–83.

11   S. A. de Smith, *The New Commonwealth and its Constitution*, London: Stevens & Sons, 1964: 77.

12   Andrew Harding has argued that the true *grundnorm* of Singapore is not the Constitution but the Legislature because at the time of independence Parliament exercised legislative powers in a manner which makes the Legislature supreme. For a discussion of this issue, see Kevin Tan, 'The Evolution of Singapore's Modern Constitution: Developments from 1946 to the Present Day', *Singapore Academy of Law Journal* (1989) 1: 17–23. Apart from the interesting nature of this jurisprudential analysis, it is submitted that the adoption of a system of government as described and delimited in a Basic Law or Constitution gives effect to the logic or philosophy behind the instrument of a constitution as a higher law or standard against which government enactments and actions are to be evaluated. This reflects in part a concern that the conduct of governance should be in accordance with principle (which presupposes a clear articulation of a constitutional theory) which is not to be sacrificed upon the altar of expediency or pragmatism. The latter cannot provide a sure basis for ordered liberty. If there are no absolutes by which to judge society,

than society is absolute. See C. Perry Patterson, 'The Evolution of Constitutionalism', *Minnesota Law Review* (1948): 427–57.

13 It may be argued that serious incursions have been made into judicial power by ouster clauses expressly precluding judicial review in instances where fundamental liberties may be derogated from certain preventive detention matters under the Internal Security Act (Cap 143) and the Maintenance of Religious Harmony Act (Cap 167A). Part of the court's traditional role as guardian of the Constitution and the liberties it contains has been relegated to the elected president as a political rather than a legal check was considered more appropriate. The efficacy of this alternative safeguard is at best, in doubt.

14 This list is modified from Dale's list. See *Ibid.*

15 See Tan Teng Lang, *The Singapore Press: Freedom, Responsibility and Creditability*, Singapore: Institute of Policy Studies, Occasional Paper No. 3, 1990; and Roger Mitton, 'What Role for the Press?: Singapore's Answers', *Asiaweek* September 1992: 44–55.

16 See generally *The Decline of the Rule of Law in Malaysia and Singapore Part II*, Record of the Committee on International Human Rights of the Association of the Bar of the City of New York; and *The Rule of Law and Human Rights In Malaysia and Singapore*, A Report of the Conference held at the European Parliament (March 1989), KEHMAS.

17 See generally Lucian Pye, *Asian Power and Politics: The Cultural Dimensions of Authority*, Cambridge, MA: Harvard University Press, 1985.

18 See Dale *supra* note 25 citing the 1972 Wooding Commission set up to review the Trinidad and Tobago Constitution.

19 The concept of democracy must have a core of fixed values to be meaningful. One cannot hijack the term for the legitimacy it confers by prefixing it with 'Asian' or 'African' or 'Pacific' or 'Western'. In his re-conceptualization of democratic criteria designed to apply to non-liberal, multi-ethnic and multi-cultural societies in the post-colonial African context, Professor Carew usefully stipulated five standard democratic criteria:

1 a democracy should include all adults who are subject to the binding collective control of the association;
2 effective participation;
3 voting equality;
4 control of agenda; and
5 enlightened understanding.

See George Munda Carew, 'Development Theory and The Promise of Democracy: The Future of Post-colonial African States', 1993, Vol. 40, No. 4 *Africa Today* 31: 45.

20 See Fareed Zakaria, 'Culture is Destiny: A Conversation with Lee Kuan Yew', *Foreign Affairs* (March/April 1994): 125. He points out that if Confucianism explains the economic boom today, it should also explain the region's economic stagnation for four centuries. It has been suggested that the circumstances of the post-war world may have more to do with the modern economic success than does an old style of government which involves the suppression of freedoms and an absence of impartial law.

21 See for example, 'Asia's Different Drum', *Time Magazine* 14 June 1993: 16; 'The Common Good', *Asiaweek* 15 February 1994: 18; 'Asia's Fate: A Response to the Singapore School', *The National Interest* (1994) Spring: 18; 'Culture is Destiny: A Conversation with Lee Kuan Yew', *Foreign Affairs* (1994) March/April; and 'Asia's Soft Authoritarianism Alternative', *New Perspectives Quarterly* (1992) Spring: 60.

22 Senior Minister Lee has pointed out that there is one remarkable phenomenon common to the fastest growing countries in East Asia which entails to a significant extent the rejection of age old customs and culture: the growth of religion in Korea, Thailand, Hong Kong, Singapore and Japan. Korea was singled out as being remarkable as it was never colonized by a Christian nation and yet about some 25 per cent of the population have taken to Christianity, which entails a fundamental shift from its traditions. 'Culture is Destiny: A Conversation with Lee Kuan Yew', *Foreign Affairs* (March/April 1994): 118.

23 Walter Bagehot, *The English Constitution*, The Fontana Library, 1963: 69.

24 For a revision of the roles Parliament can play, see generally Thio, *supra*, note 9 especially at 88–92 and 113–16.

25 Lord Diplock in the 1977 Privy Council appeal case of *Hinds v. R* [1977] Appeal Cases 195: 212 seems to assert that the separation of powers was a feature of the British constitution despite academic views to the contrary by referring to some Commonwealth constitutions as having been drafted by persons 'familiar... with the basic concept of separation of legislative, executive and judicial power as it had been developed in the unwritten constitution of the United Kingdom'. He seems to be speaking of a functional separation of powers, that is, a person exercising one kind of governmental function should not exercise another.

26 Much may be said about inroads made into the independence of the judiciary, though suffice it to say that it has not developed a robust jurisprudence that is oriented towards the safeguarding of fundamental liberties as advocated by the Privy Council in the seminal case of *Ong Ah Chuan* [1981] Appeal Cases 648; as evidenced in cases dealing with the rights of the accused (*Mazlan v. PP* [1993] 1 SLR 512) and freedom of speech and contempt of court laws (*A. G. v. Barry Wain, Malayan Law Journal* (1991) 2: 525); and preventive detention cases in general where the Courts adopt a deferential posture *vis-à-vis* executive judgment. The sole exception notably is that of *Chng Suan Tze v. Home Affairs and Ors, Malayan Law Journal* (1989) 2: 449, where in a bold and well reasoned judgment, the Court of Appeal found a detention order invalid on a technicality. This decision so earned the government's displeasure that within two weeks of the judgment being issued, it was legislatively overruled by the Constitution of the Republic of Singapore (Amendment) Act 1989 (No. 1 of 1989) which came into effect on 27 January 1989, amending Article 149 which paved the way for an amendment of the Internal Security Act with the insertion of an ouster clause limiting judicial review severely and barring ISA detention appeals to the Judicial Committee of the Privy Council: see Yee, Ho, and Seng, 'Judicial Review of Preventive Detention under the ISA', *Singapore Law Review* (1989): 10, for a comprehensive account of ISA developments. More politically sensitive matters concerning fundamental liberties, particularly in the realm of religion and politics, have

been declared non-justiciable matters and the traditional legal check the judiciary provides has given way to a political check in none other than the elected president. The efficacy of the latter is at best untested. These developments in general do not bode well for the independence of the judiciary conscious of its checking role in the scheme of separated powers so crucial to preserving the rule of law. It has been said that the judiciary at times appears more executive-minded than the executive! See generally Tham Chee Ho, 'Judiciary Under Siege' and Yong Seng Sieu, 'Clarity or Controversy – The Meaning of Judicial Independence in Singapore and Malaysia', both in *Singapore Law Review* (1992) 13: 60 and 85 respectively.

27 Ivor Jennings, *Cabinet Government*, 3rd edn (1959): 15–16.

28 This might include keeping a tight rein on the granting of licences needed for holding political rallies, the lack of a free press, perceived victimization (see *Straits Times*, 17 April 1993: 32 for an examination of issues arising from the allegedly politically motivated sacking of lecturer Dr Chee Soon Juan from the National University of Singapore), the threat of libel suits and the background fear of preventive detention a government has no qualms in invoking.

29 'Asia's Different Drum', *Time Magazine*, 14 June 1993, 16:18.

30 The latter day modifications to the Singapore legislature have been dealt with in detail by Thio, *supra* note 9 at 97–108.

31 For a detailed examination of this creature, see Valentine Winslow, 'Creating a Utopian Parliament', *Malaya Law Review* (1984) 28: 268.

32 For an account of the pessimistic reaction of the PAP in losing four seats out of a then 81-seat House, see 'No more Mr Nice Goh?', *Time Magazine*, 16 September 1991.

33 See Thio, *supra,* note 9.

34 Fourth Schedule, Republic of Singapore Constitution.

35 *Supra*, note 36: 104–8.

36 It is to be noted that multi-racialism could be entrenched by having a two member GRC. This might well be a more equitable modification to the system.

37 For a comparison of parliamentary and presidential systems of government, see generally Douglas V. Verney, 'Parliamentarianism and Presidentialism', in Arend Lipjhart (ed.) *Parliamentary versus Presidential Government*, (Oxford University Press,1992).

38 [1977] Appeal Cases 195 (Privy Council on Appeal from Jamaica).

39 *Straits Times*, 17 May 1994: 28.

40 Cap 167a, Singapore Statutes, 1990 Edition.

41 It is important to reiterate that a government proposal to initiate a constitutional amendment is still a foregone conclusion in Singapore despite the formally onerous two-thirds parliamentary majority requirement laid out in Article 5(2) as the ruling PAP party holds a clear majority, having 77 out of the 81 elected MPs seats. At present, there are 87 Members of Parliament, six of whom are non-voting Nominated MPs. Since the government can change the constitution at will (excepting the parts protected by further safeguards in Article 5(2A), it would appear that while lip service is paid to the notion of constitutional supremacy *de jure, de facto* parliamentary supremacy is the order of the day.

42 Article 17(3).

43 It is not immediately apparent how, for example, the office of Chief Justice, under which one is automatically deemed to have the requisite financial experience, is able to provide for the acquisition of such financial expertise to deal with the nation's estimated US$43 billion in reserves.

44 See Article 19(2)(*f*)(iv).

45 See Article 18(9).

46 See *Straits Times*, 17 August 1993: 3.

47 Kevin Tan, *supra*, note 6.

48 Unlike the administrative law context, there might not be a remedy equivalent to mandamus, etc. available to redress this omission to exercise discretion by the president, as Article 22K provides that save for certain exceptions, 'the president shall not be liable to any proceedings whatsoever in any court in respect of anything done or omitted to be done by him in his official capacity'.

49 A distinction must be drawn between the word 'individual' which suggests individual dignity and worth and 'individualism' which suggests an egotistic mentality that exalts individual interests above everything else. The use of the term individualism in this respect is meant to refer to a philosophy of human rights which vindicates the paramount importance of protecting individual worth and dignity, bearing in mind that rights are to be exercised and thought of in the framework of responsibility. For example, the right to free speech cannot be abused to slander someone's reputation.

50 In fact the Wee Chong Jin Constitutional Commission recommended that fundamental liberties be entrenched. A quarter of a century later, they finally are! See paras 10–12.

51 It is to be noted that amendments to Article 150(5)*(b)* are such that the Government is prevented from resorting to using emergency powers to circumvent the safeguard roles of the president.

52 Samuel Rutherford (1600–61) was a Scottish Presbyterian commissioner at the Westminster Assembly in London and later Rector at St Andrew's University, Scotland. He wrote *lex rex* in a society of landed classes and monarchy and unsurprisingly, this stirred immediate controversy. The concept of *lex rex* is simply that the law is king and that the king too is under the law. If the king and his government disobeyed the law, they were to be disobeyed. The book was outlawed in both England and Scotland and Rutherford was declared a civil rebel for his views.

53 Bryce 1901, Vol. 1: 151.

54 (1802) 1 Cranch 137.

55 *Supra*, note 27.

56 Its superiority is reflected by the general provision in Article 5(2) requiring, save where stipulated, a parliamentary resolution supported by two-thirds of the total number of MPs as opposed to merely a simple majority for ordinary legislation: this is expressed as the need for the constitution to be 'rigid', that is, not susceptible to change without due deliberation. If the procedure for Constitutional amendment is not sufficiently rigid and is too easily amendable, the constitution, by being deprived of its sanctity, will lose its status as bedrock of constitutionalism. It is to be noted that in Singapore where dominant party politics is practised, a special legislative majority *per se* will not in and of itself secure the rigidity or longevity of the Constitution since attaining it is a foregone conclusion.

57 Article 4 states: 'The Constitution is the supreme law of the Republic of Singapore and any law enacted by the Legislature after the commencement of this Constitution which is inconsistent with this Constitution shall, to the extent of the inconsistency, be void'. The supremacy clause does not in and of itself give the Constitution its supremacy but is a reflection of the understanding that in the hierarchy of laws, the Constitution sits at the top of the ladder.

58 See Kevin Tan, *The Elected Presidency in Singapore: Legislation Comment and List, Singapore Journal of Legal Studies* (1991) 179: 191–3.

59 Such a system features a powerful and independent policy-making president who is elected by the people on the basis of elections distinct from parliamentary elections. Parliament is continued but in an attenuated and subordinate capacity. As head of the cabinet executive, the president is more powerful than the prime minister and his term of office is independent of the legislature's whim. For a study of the Gaullist system in Asia, see H. M. Zafrullah, *Sri Lanka's Hybrid Presidential and Parliamentary System and the Separation of Powers*, University of Malaya Press (1981); and A. N. Wilson, 'The Gaullist System in Asia: The Constitution of Sri Lanka', in *Parliamentary versus Presidential Government*, Oxford University Press (1992): 152–7.

60 See Article 22B(2).

61 As reported in the *Straits Times*, 23 August 1993: 27.

62 See the *Straits Times*, 2 September 1993: 2, where it was reported that Senior Minister Lee had said to the *Nanyang Siang Pau* (Chinese language newspaper) that the Government had endorsed Chua and would have been equally happy if he had won since Chua was a 'credible apolitical alternative'. This is unsurprising, particularly in the light of the fact that Chua was coaxed out of retirement to run for the post by former PAP stalwart Dr Goh Keng Swee and present Finance Minister Richard Hu, as admitted by Chua himself in his first television broadcast. The full text of this was reported in the *Straits Times*, 28 August 1993: 22.

63 It may be noted that pursuant to the newly inserted Article 100 (Constitutional Amendment No. 17 of 1994), the question as to whether Article 22H can be amended without presidential consent has been referred to a Supreme Court Tribunal for a ruling. The proposed amendment seeks to provide that even where the president refuses to consent to a bill which reduces his powers, the ultimate choice as to whether such a bill should become law should lie in the hands of the electorate in the form of a referendum. I find it highly ironical that while the creation of this institution was itself not put to a referendum, the decision whether to reduce the powers of said institution should be placed in the electorate's hands. See *Straits Times*, 26 August 1994: 1.

64 This is on the assumption that a two-third parliamentary resolution can be obtained. If not, the government may have to resign, make the modification of presidential powers an election issue and win the elections by at least a two-thirds majority. A two-thirds majority in Parliament is needed to propose an amendment which still has to be subject to a national referendum. Alternatively, the prime minister may bide his time until the next presidential elections and then call upon the electorate to vote another man into office who will support government policies.

65 *Straits Times*, 2 September 1993: 1.

66 It is important to note that the provisions of Article 5(2A) do not come into actual operation until the lapse of a four-year moratorium from its inception in June 1991. The scope of Article 22H in relation to a 'suspended' Article 5 (2A) was the subject of the first constitutional reference heard in 1995: see [1995] 2 SLR 201. For a discussion of issues pertaining to the Reference, see Thio Li-ann, 'Working out the Presidency: The Rites of Passage' [1995] Singapore Journal of Legal Studies 509; and Chan Sek Keong 'Working out the Presidency: No Passage of Rites' [1996] Singapore Journal of Legal Studies 1.

67 Article 17(3), Constitution of the Republic of Singapore, Revised Edition 1985.

68 Article 65(3A).

69 See, for example, Andrew Harding, 'The 1988 Constitutional Crisis in Malaysia', *International and Comparative Law Quarterly* (1990) 39: 57; and F. A. Trindade, 'The Removal of the Malaysian Judges', *International and Comparative Law Quarterly* (1990) 106: 51 where he concludes that the charges of misconduct were not borne out.

70 The Tribunal Report on the Dismissal of Tun Salleh Abas is found in *Malayan Law Journal* (1988) 3: xxxiii.

71 Finnis, 'Separation of Powers in the Australian Constitution', *Adelaide Law Review* (1967–70) 3, 159: 162.

72 Article 38 does provide that: 'The Legislature of Singapore shall consist of the president and Parliament' but the president's role by convention is formal and limited to assenting to bills generally on the advice of the Cabinet and dissolving Parliament.

73 Finnis has characterized the functional separation of powers thus: 'One may postulate a conceptual system of governmental functions, and require that these functions be exercised so entirely separately that no institution of government should exercise more than one of them. For example, one might conceive a Constitution in which there would be three functions or powers of government: legislative, executive and judicial. Then there might be any number of institutions set up to exercise these powers or functions, but all of them subject to the overriding requirement that no person or body should exercise more than one function'. *Supra* note 71, at p.168.

74 See Kevin Tan, *op. cit.*

75 *Straits Times*, 21 August 1993: 1.

76 *Straits Times*, 3 September 1993: 32.

77 Ben O. Nwabueze, *The Presidential Council of Nigeria* (London: C. Hurst & Company, 1981): 24.

78 [1981] Appeal Cases 648. Lord Diplock stated that a generous interpretation was to be accorded individual liberty, to avoid the 'austerity of tabulated legalism', thereby given full measure to the right at stake.

79 *Malayan Law Journal* (1991) 2: 525.

80 An alternative instructive view towards contempt of court, one which gives full weight to the importance of free speech in this context, was adopted in the American case of *Bridges v. California* (1941) 314 US 252. The Court stated:

The assumption that respect for the judiciary can be won by shielding judges from published criticism wrongly appraises of American public opinion. For an enforced silence, however limited, solely in the name of preserving the dignity of the bench, would probably engender resentment, suspicion and contempt more than it would enhance respect.

81 *Singapore Law Review* (1992) 2: 310. For a case comment, see Michael Hor, 'The Freedom of Speech and Defamation' *Singapore Journal of Legal Studies* (1992): 542.
82 (1964) 376 US 254. This case posited a requirement of actual malice for a defamation suit against a public official to succeed.
83 *European Human Rights Review* (1986) 8: 407. The Court stated that since a public official knowingly opened his actions and speech to public scrutiny, he had to display a greater degree of tolerance to criticism, in the interests of the open discussion of political issues.
84 This passage from *Gatley on Libel and Slander* (8th edn) was cited with approval in the pre-Canadian Charter case of *The Globe and Mail Ltd v. John Boland*, (1960) Supreme Court Review 208 which was in turned quoted approvingly by Justice Thean in this present case.
85 *Gertz v. Robert Welch*, 418 US 323.
86 [1993] AC 534. For a case comment, see Barendt, 'Libel and Freedom of Speech in English Law', *Public Law* (1993): 449.
87 Cap 167A *Singapore Statutes*, 1990 Revised Edition.
88 The Constitution of the Republic of Singapore (Amendment) Act 1989, Act 1 of 1989, s3(c).
89 Four new sections were inserted by amendment. Section 8A defined 'judicial review', Section 8B effectively was a legislative overruling of the reasoning behind the case of *Chng Suan Tze v. Minister of Home Affairs*, (1989) 1 Malayan Law Journal 69 which applied an 'objective' test to the understanding of presidential satisfaction, by providing that the law in this area would be that of 13 July 1971 (the day after the case of *Lee Mau Seng* was decided, which adopted a 'subjective' approach). Furthermore, only judicial review of the procedural requirements of the Act was allowed; substantive grounds of review were hence precluded. Section 8C abolished appeals to the Privy Council in this area and Section 8D in effect provided for the retrospective operation of the amendments.
90 See *Singapore Parliamentary Debates Official Report*, Vol. 52, 25 January 1989, col. 469.
91 See Article 151(2).
92 This may be described as the process by which principles are developed through incremental decision-making in which apparently new principles belong to a continuum whose starting point is uncontentious and well established. See Sir John Laws, 'Is the High Court the Guardian of Fundamental Constitutional Rights?', *Public Law* (1993): 59.
93 Lord Browne-Wilkinson, 'The Infiltration of a Bill of Rights', *Public Law* (1992): 397.
94 See H. P. Lee, 'The Australian High Court and Implied Fundamental Guarantees', *Public Law* (1993): 606.
95 See the Report of the Select Committee on the Constitution of the Republic of Singapore (Amendment No. 3) Bill, Part 9 of 1990 at C52–C66.
96 *Ibid.*, B37–8.

6 Chaining the Leviathan

A public choice interpretation of Singapore's elected presidency

Tilak Doshi[1]

What is personal liberty, if it does not draw after it the right to enjoy the fruits of our own industry? What is political liberty, if it imparts only perpetual poverty to us and all our posterity? What is the privilege of a vote, if the majority of the hour may sweep away the earnings of our whole lives?

Justice Joseph Story[2]

The possibility of a weak or bad government ruining Singapore for good is not a theoretical one. It can happen. . . . Let us, while we have assets and reserves to safeguard, institutionalize a system of checks and balances, even if it means curtailing our own powers.

Prime Minister Goh Chok Tong[3]

The initiation of the gradual transfer of power from the first generation PAP leaders to the second in the early 1980s by the then Prime Minister Lee Kuan Yew and his senior associates was accompanied by much explicit concern over the 'succession problem'. The prospect of the passing of a tough and dominant leader from the political stage brought critical attention to the fact that, under Singapore's unicameral parliamentary system, any future government – PAP-led or otherwise and with however a slender majority – had unlimited powers of the purse, powers to spend the state's funds or sell assets which the state managed in its fiduciary capacity. In the process of the generational transfer of power, Premier Lee – by then one of the longest-serving prime ministers in the world – and his closest colleagues were fully aware of the importance of a durable constitutional basis required for sustainable and high rates of economic growth in an international system of competing nation states. Senior PAP leaders, including Premier Lee, were preoccupied by the question of how best to establish institutional and procedural safeguards for protecting the nation's largesse against human folly or frailty.

A range of constitutional safeguards were considered. The chief one focused on expanded powers of the position of president, the titular head of state, first mooted by Prime Minister Lee when he spoke at the 1984 National Day Rally. The debate over the position of an elected president, with veto powers over the use of the nation's financial reserves and over the appointment of key civil servants, was conducted by the PAP leadership with its usual pragmatism and alacrity. In July 1988, the government published a White Paper on 'Constitutional Amendments to Safeguard Financial Assets and the Integrity of the Public Service' in support of the proposed bill. On 3 January 1991, Parliament passed the constitutional amendment bill for an elected president with custodial powers over Singapore's reserves and over key appointments in the public services.

What can economics contribute towards an understanding of the elected presidency amendment? Clearly some of the most fundamental questions raised by the passing of the amendment lie within the provinces of constitutional law, political science and public administration. Can economics, understood as a discipline primarily concerned with the objective measurement of relative costs and benefits, go beyond the rather obvious and bald conclusion that if the costs of implementing a constitutional amendment are exceeded by the benefits of the exercise, then it should be carried out? Such a statement would indeed be vacuous, given that the real problem in assessing the worth of the constitutional amendment is precisely in the differing perceptions, expressed by supporters and critics of the constitutional change, in the measure of costs and benefits. Critics of the bill emphasize 'costs' while, quite naturally, its supporters emphasize 'benefits'. Economists' judgments on what are 'costs' and 'benefits' may well be sensible, taking into account wider and more relevant considerations than the average man on the street, but such judgments remain their subjective preferences against those of others. Before proceeding with the task at hand, it is therefore imperative to define clearly, from a positive economics standpoint, the domain of analysis.

Mainstream economics explains choices made by economic agents, their interactions, and the collective outcomes of such interactions *within* the given legal and institutional structures of polities. In practising their profession, economists pre-suppose a political process which elicits, albeit imperfectly, constituents' preferences with regard to matters such as authority over public finances and over key appointments to the civil service. In keeping with the strictures of positive economics, economists cannot feign to place a value on the relative costs and benefits of institutional or legal changes. While economics has contributed much to our understanding and measure of the efficacy of different possible means or 'policy options' employed to given ends, the standard test of mainstream economics for improvement in welfare – whether a given set of tastes are better satisfied – goes out of commission when the legal and institutional structure within which those tastes are expressed and pursued, alters.

The public choice literature, by providing insights into what likely consequences a particular institutional set-up might have on public finances, provides us with a basis for an informed judgment of the efficacy of Singapore's elected presidency amendment. Unlike orthodox economics which seeks to explain choices of economic agents within given institutional constraints, public choice theory – most closely associated with the pioneering work of James Buchanan – attempts to explain the working properties of alternative sets of institutional rules that constrain the choices of economic agents. As opposed to the economists' traditional study of *choice within constraints*, public choice theory focuses on the *choice of constraints*. It examines political decision rules that exist in order to yield plausible hypotheses about just what sort of fiscal outcomes will tend to emerge.[4]

Before we proceed with the question of how political constitutions might affect the economic prospects of nations, it is convenient to set the context by assessing the critical role that public-sector savings played in Singapore's rapid economic growth. The elected presidency amendment to the Constitution gathers full significance once the role of public savings in Singapore's remarkable growth experience is established.

THE ROLE OF PUBLIC SAVINGS IN SINGAPORE'S ECONOMIC GROWTH

Singapore's experience of economic growth has been exceptional, even by the standards of the other high-performing East Asian economies. The economy grew on average a remarkable 8.5 per cent between 1966 and 1990, with a doubling of per capita income every decade. In just the two decades over 1970–90, real per capita GDP more than tripled. The rapid growth in output was achieved with an exemplary low-inflation record. Despite high world inflation rates and Singapore's open economy, domestic inflation as measured by the GDP deflator exceeded 5 per cent only in seven years since 1961; and it has been less than 3 per cent for more than two-thirds of that period. The remarkable rates of economic growth of Singapore, along with that of the other East Asian economies, has been noted by observers since the late 1970s, and an extensive literature has developed around the issue of what lies behind these successes.

The dominant view among economists in explaining the growth experience of these economies[5] is based on the theory of comparative advantage derived from factor endowments. International trade based on comparative advantage allows countries to expand their production and consumption possibilities, to exploit scale economies, and utilize the forces of international competition to prevent domestic price distortions and the development of inefficient industries. The export-orientated policy regimes in these countries, in this view, have on the whole minimized market distortions and relied on the price mechanism for efficient resource allocation. The major policy prescriptions are the adoption of a realistic exchange rate and real interest rates, the liberalization of imports and export promotion. The corresponding view of the appropriate role of the state is to provide public goods required for the efficient functioning of the market system, most important of which are law and order, price stability and infrastructural investments. Relatively free markets, open economies and a minimalist state, it is argued, constitute the basic parameters of economic success.

More recently, revisionist studies of East Asian economic development argue that rapid economic growth was promoted by active government intervention and appropriate industrial policy which went beyond the strictures of mainstream economic theory as inspired by Adam Smith. Indeed, it has now become commonplace to argue in some influential circles that the East Asian success in economic growth has demonstrated the fallacy of the mainstream minimalist approach to economic policy and supports the case of sophisticated governmental intervention in 'picking winners'.[6] In this argument, East Asia's 'strong' governments took an active role in economic management and promoted economic growth by 'channelling' market processes in line with long run developmental goals.[7] Detailed studies of South Korea and Taiwan indicate discretionary policies which include industry-specific import restrictions, financial subsidies, fiscal incentives and credit rationing.[8] In the case of Singapore, the role of government is both varied and pervasive. The government intervenes in the labour and domestic savings markets through wage guidelines and mandatory contributions to the Central Provident Fund. It has influenced private-sector investment decisions through sector- and industry-specific discretionary incentives. In major socio-economic sectors with public goods characteristics such as public housing, utilities, urban development and infrastructure, large statutory authorities have been given broad mandates to carry out government policy. The state also has wide interests in directly productive activity via government-owned enterprise.[9]

Studies on government intervention in East Asia, however, do not prove that such intervention which accompanied economic growth actually promoted it. Nor do they disprove the counter that had there not been such interventions, economic growth was likelier to be even more rapid. A positive analysis of Singapore's economic growth experience cannot resolve the differences between those who see in the example of Singapore a convincing model of strong government – one that is able to limit individual liberties in the interests of the common good, take charge of directing economic development, and sacrifice short run consumer interests for the sake of long run growth – and others who hold more conventional and circumspect views of the economic growth process.

Quantitative studies on the sources of economic growth, while unable to resolve the debate between mainstream economists and their revisionist detractors, point to the inordinate levels of savings and investments in the growth experience of the East Asian countries. By emphasizing the extraordinary mobilization of resources in these countries as the basis of their success, applied growth accounting puts a focus on the importance of Singapore's accumulated savings and therefore on its proper management by a popularly elected government.

Growth accounting studies are based on a tautology: economic growth is made up of growth in supplies of 'inputs' and growth in the efficacy (or 'productivity') with which each unit of input is utilized. As a result, sustained growth can only occur if there is a rise in output per unit of input, i.e. there is an increase in the productivity of all inputs used. Increased use of inputs must face diminishing returns if it is unaccompanied by productivity increases. Accounting for growth, then, is a question of measuring how much of the growth is due to increases in the quantity and quality of inputs such as labour and capital, and how much is due to increased efficiency. Among economists, the latter is essentially a residual unexplained by increases in the labour force, by the better education of workers in the labour force, and by the stock and vintage of physical capital. This residual is generally believed to arise from a number of factors such as better management and entrepreneurship in the use of inputs and, in the long run, the growth of knowledge and technological progress.

Empirical studies of East Asia come up with a result rather unsurprising within received growth accounting theory but at odds with conventional wisdom. Studies of industrial countries have established that after increases in factor inputs are accounted for, there is a component of incremental growth attributable to 'total factor productivity', essentially a residual measuring technological progress. This does not seem to be the case in Singapore or in a number of other East Asian countries.[10] One authoritative study of the sources of growth in the East Asian NICs found it impossible to reject the hypothesis that there was no technical progress (i.e. improvements in the ways inputs are combined) in the four Asian tigers during the post-war period.[11] In his summary of growth-accounting studies in Asia, Paul Krugman observes that 'Asian growth, like that of the Soviet Union in its high growth era, seems to be driven by extraordinary growth in inputs like labour and capital rather than by gains in efficiency'.[12] In the most rigorous study to date of Singapore growth experience, economic growth in Singapore, in contrast with the experience of the developed countries, is fully explained by increases in inputs.[13]

Consistent with these growth accounting studies, the most important statistical ratios that stand out in Singapore's economic time series data are the extremely high savings and investment ratios. Gross savings as a proportion of GDP grew from 16 per cent in 1966 to a remarkable 42 per cent by 1985; similarly, investments grew from 22 per cent of GDP in 1966 to 43 per cent in 1985.[14] These rates of savings and investment are unmatched by any other market economy. Also without match in comparable market economies, though typical of the command economies, is the high share of public-sector savings as a proportion of national savings. As a mobilizer of savings, the Singapore government's achievements share important similarities with the socialist economies.[15] It needs to be emphasized that the determination of Singapore's gross national savings was largely a policy choice, not one based on the market outcome of individual savings behaviour.

The driving force in Singapore's savings performance has been the public sector. Public-sector savings include surpluses on the consolidated government budget and surpluses realized by the statutory boards. In the decade 1975–85, the share of public-sector savings in gross domestic savings increased from 21 per cent to over 70 per cent.[16] The private sector's contribution to the high savings rate was effected through mandatory contributions to the Central Provident Fund (CPF). The share of private-sector savings in the form of mandatory CPF holdings was extremely high by the standards of provident fund schemes in other market economies. The CPF share of total private savings almost doubled in the space of a decade, from 27 per cent in

1974 to 46 per cent in 1984, reducing the importance of voluntary private savings.

Upon gaining office with the end of colonial rule, the PAP leadership was fully cognizant of the imperative faced by the newly emerged democracies: to create capital based on voluntary abstinence along the model of Victorian England or on compulsory abstinence emulating the Stalinist example. Inheriting a low savings rate typical of a colonial entrepot – populated by immigrants consisting largely of radical labour unions and a highly politicized China-orientated group of entrepreneurs – the latter option was seen as the only feasible one by the incoming PAP government after independence in 1965. Singapore's high post-independence savings rate cannot be understood as an attempt by government to maximize the total expected utility of its citizens over some given time horizon, the approach most familiar to economists' models. On the contrary, the Singapore government seems to have had economic growth as its maxim and not utility. Convinced of the paramount need for high savings and high investments, the PAP government enforced abstinence with the clear objective of maximizing growth.[17]

It is, however, not often noted by observers of the Singapore experience that, quite unlike the socialist example, Singapore's public sector never constituted the major source of domestic investment despite accounting for the predominant share of domestic savings. Although the country's high rate of savings could increasingly finance capital formation within the country, by the late 1980s when gross national savings regularly exceeded gross fixed capital formation, the investment picture remained dominated by private (foreign and local) investments. Thus over the period 1970–90, while the public sector accounted for 70 per cent of national savings, it contributed to only about 30 per cent of capital formation. In essence, the government opted to invest a high proportion of public-sector savings and CPF assets abroad in equities, bonds, foreign exchange, real estate and short-term financial assets, exchanging an outflow of national savings for an inflow of direct foreign investments. The critical nature of foreign enterprise in introducing international markets and modern technology to the domestic economy was explicitly recognized in the trade-off between an outflow of domestic savings and inflows of foreign investments. Apart from the provision of a world-class infrastructure and a large stock of public housing, the government's two most important priorities (the former economic and the latter socio-political), the high level of public-sector savings and mandatory CPF contributions allowed the Singapore government to build up one of the world's largest holdings of foreign reserves. It is in this context, then, that one can appreciate the critical importance attached by the PAP leadership to the prudent management of Singapore's accumulated reserves.

Evidently, the critical role of savings and investment to economic growth is not something recognized only by academic studies of growth accounting; the architects of Singapore's economic modernity were fully aware of these imperatives early on.[18] Thus it is not surprising that, by the early 1980s, Singapore's political leaders were contemplating constitutional safeguards for protecting the country's financial reserves, most favoured of which was the enactment of the elected president amendment.

ELECTED PRESIDENT: PROVISIONS AND RATIONALE

In many countries, irresponsible free-spending governments have mismanaged the national finances and irreversibly ruined their economies. When a government sets out to spend money on generous subsidies, dispenses largesse in order to bribe the electorate, it has to do so by raiding the country's financial reserves or by raising large international loans for consumption rather than investment. Before long the country, no matter how rich or well endowed, approaches bankruptcy and economic growth comes to a halt.

Government White Paper[19]

In his role as a fiduciary guardian of the state's assets, the elected president has the right to veto the annual budgets of the Government, statutory boards and key government-owned companies, if they draw down reserves accumulated during the terms of previous governments (Clause 8 of the Amendment Bill No. 3). The president's concurrence must be obtained for the disposal of the assets and reserves, including land and immovables belonging to and managed by

1 the Government and key financial institutions, namely the Monetary Authority of Singapore (the Treasury), the Government Investment Corporation of Singapore (responsible for managing Singapore's foreign reserves) and the Currency Board;

2 the Statutory Boards, namely the Public Utilities Board, the Jurong Town Corporation, the Port of Singapore Authority, Telecoms, the CPF Board, the Post Office Savings Bank, Singapore Broadcasting Corporation, Civil Aviation Authority of Singapore; and

3 Government-owned companies, the most important of which are the holding companies Temasek Holdings, Sheng-Li Holdings, MND Holdings.

The president's concurrence is also required for any extraordinary measures for raising loans in the local and international markets on pledges of Singapore's reserves or assets.

To ensure that the powers of the elected president are not obviated by corrupt or otherwise incompetent personnel in charge of key institutions, the president has the right of assent to key appointments in the most important agencies which manage public-sector assets, including the Attorney-General, the Auditor-General and the Accountant-General, chairmen and members of statutory authorities, the Board of Commissioners of Currency, the GIC. An advisory committee has the power to give advice and recommendations on matters referred to it by the president. While the president must seek the committee's advice and recommendations before the exercise of veto over the drawing down of assets or over key appointments in the civil service, he has discretion to accept or reject such advice. The president can also refuse to assent to legislation which is deemed to circumvent or curtail the powers of the president to exercise a custodial role over financial assets and his role in assenting to appointments in the public service and statutory boards. Any further amendments to the entrenched powers of the president must be endorsed by a referendum if the president so requires it.

In supporting the amendment bill, the White Paper argued that the CPF savings of citizens, which constituted a large part of the nation's wealth, is held in trust by the government and has to be protected from default or debasement of currency caused by a future government. It asserted that no future government should be allowed to gain short term popularity at the expense of the country's long-run interests and that it could not be assumed that such a government would not take office in Singapore. It concluded that entrenched constitutional safeguards were therefore necessary, particularly in the light of the fact that the existing constitution provided untrammelled power to the prime minister and Cabinet – 'even of a temporary coalition which comes into power by a majority of only one seat' – over financial assets and reserves managed by the state.

The public choice model

The convenient notion of the state held implicitly by the economist as policy advisor is that of a platonic guardian obligingly imposing taxes and subsidies to correct market distortions for the common good. Some early work among economists began to query policy issues with the more plausible premise that governments often formulate policies to win elections rather than win elections in order to increase social welfare.[20] This work was formally developed by prominent economists such as Anne Krueger, George Stigler and Gary Becker who helped form the basis of later models of 'neo-classical political economy'. This has now burgeoned into the very large literature on rent seeking and public choice theory. In brief, this literature is all about the processes by which governments restrict entry into a market and create special privileges through administrative rules, licences, tariffs, taxes, legal monopolies and the like, thereby generating 'rents' or artificial scarcities and higher prices for particular resources. The state is not viewed as a maximizer of social welfare but as provider of political favours to pressure groups. This results in 'directly unproductive activity' which yields pecuniary returns to parties competing for these rents but which does not produce goods and services; in so far as this activity absorbs real resources, it represents a net welfare loss to society.[21]

In its enquiry into the relationship between constraints on political choice and patterns of budgetary outcomes, perhaps the most significant insight of public choice theory lies in its recognition of the 'tragic flaw in Keynesian inspired macroeconomics'.[22] Keynes presumed that economic policy is made by a small group of wise and enlightened people who acted in accordance with the public interest even when this might run foul of sectional interests. Shorn of its historical context, it can be argued that the Keynesian model is purely symmetric: budget deficits are incurred during recessions and surpluses during inflation to smooth out the peaks and troughs of the business cycle. Yet, in encouraging the belief that a small group of enlightened policy-makers would defy sectional and vested interests for the public good, the Keynesian consensus failed to foresee the emergence of populism and powerful lobbies as prime factors in the policy-making process in the modern world.

It is now well recognized that popular Keynesian policy presumptions, set in modern political settings, have led to the inherent bias in public finances towards budget deficits and inflation. Allowing politicians to increase spending without having to raise taxes, government proclivity towards profligacy to win elections and favour powerful constituencies has been given full play in liberal democracies. In its application to public finance, the tenets of popular Keynesianism were directly opposed to the classical world of Adam Smith where frugality was the cardinal virtue of the state and where this norm assumed shape 'in the widely shared principle that public budgets should be in balance, if not in surplus, and that deficits were to be tolerated only in extraordinary circumstance'.[23] Buchanan argues that when the Victorian constraints of virtue lost their hold on political agents, formal rules limiting deficit financing became necessary to ensure responsible fiscal behaviour.[24] Like the authors of the White Paper, some of the most notable commentators on economic policy and public finance have observed the processes by which governments have become bound to serve the several interests of a conglomerate of special constituencies and lobbies, to the detriment of society and the economy at large.[25] The miscarriage of the democratic ideal – when policies become the hireling of vested interests and populist politics hold sway – has become increasingly apparent to students of modern political economy.

In the extant public choice models, two broad sources of political support determine the probability that the incumbent ruler retains office. First is the 'median voter' whose political support for the ruler is proportional to the level of economic welfare that he (or she) enjoys under the current regime.[26] The median voter tends to behave in a collectively suboptimal way by underinvesting in favour of immediate consumption. The argument that 'mob' democracy threatens private property as newly enfranchised classes use their political weight to redress the initial endowment of wealth by a populist levelling down is well established in classical political economy.[27] In its modern liberal democratic setting, the populist bias towards inflation has been noted not only by economists such as James Buchanan[28] but also by eminent political theorists such as Samuel Huntington[29] who argued that democracy undermines growth by unleashing pressures for immediate consumption at the expense of investment and, hence, economic growth.

The second type of political support, what can be termed 'particularism' as distinguished from a general populism, underlies the 'rent-seeking' model put forth by Olson[30] and Becker[31] among others. Citizens tend to behave in a collectively sub-optimal way by organizing into lobbies and pressure groups that pressure governments to transfer incomes in their own favour. In this model of particularistic politics, interest groups compete for rents, each maximizing the difference between the costs of lobbying and the eventual benefits from policies that are induced by such lobbying. The outcome is inefficient both because lobbying wastes resources that could otherwise have been put to productive use, and because it creates market distortions which impose further costs, the latter often being a multiple of the direct costs of lobbying. When government policy agencies becoming permeated by such particularistic pressures, policies lose their internal coherence and generate a high level of discretionary redistribution at the expense of policies which promote economic growth.[32]

How does one prevent a sovereign and unlimited representative assembly, like the Singapore legislature, within an inherited unicameral Westminster parliamentary system, from being progressively driven into steady and unlimited extensions of governmental intervention, often invoked in the name of social welfare? The answers to this question given by those committed to democratic principles yet cognizant of its inherent bias towards inflation and fiscal profligacy inevitably point to constitutional limitations on the power of representative legislatures. For Hayek, the road to serfdom could only be prevented by dividing supreme power between two distinct, democratically elected bodies. It was, to him, 'at least conceivable though unlikely that an autocratic government will exercise self-restraint; but an omnipotent democracy simply cannot do so'.[33]

Unlike Hayek, Buchanan prefers written rules entrenched in the constitution. He proposes a 'fiscal constitution', essentially a combination of fixed monetary growth and a rule for balanced budgets.[34] A constitutional rule, based on the principle of balanced budget, would eradicate governmental authority to manipulate the fiscal system – to print money and to run sustained budget deficits – for short run political returns. A waiver clause in the case of emergencies, wars or financial crises, could be invoked under a two-third majority rule. This would also require an adjustment rule forcing budgets back into balance over a period of time, which would automatically be triggered when the threshold in the difference between revenues and expenses is crossed. Inflationary financing by governments would be ruled out by statutory independence of the Central Bank whose role would be restricted to the avoidance of inflation (and devaluation).[35] It is evident that the Singapore experiment of constitutional change with an elected president can be best viewed as a response of a government that is acutely aware of the profound challenges facing liberal democracies, issues that have been posed by constitutional theorists such as Hayek and Buchanan.

In the elected presidency amendment to the Constitution, the PAP leadership opted for an elected body – a solution closer to Hayek – rather than a set of fairly detailed written constitutional rules favoured by Buchanan. A greater dependence is cast on the person of a fiduciary elected president – on his competence in seeking appropriate advice and on his moral probity – than on the interpretation of written constitutional rules of decision-making. In the light of modern political economy, particularly as interpreted by Hayek and Buchanan, the PAP government's decree to constitutionally entrench the role of a custodial, elected president, can be seen as an important move towards institutionalizing required limits on a popularly elected legislature. By imposing requirements to make their fiscal actions apparent to the public via an independently elected president, the amendment to the Constitution of Singapore raises the domestic political costs of fiscal irresponsibility. While ultimate sanctions are now provided by international capital markets, particularly in the case of open economies such as Singapore, the greater transparency and predictability afforded by the amendment improves the market's ability to quickly judge the quality of the fiscal environment.

Yet, no law can impose fiscal discipline on politicians determined to evade it in their own self-interests. Unlike monetary policy, where the clear target of price stability can be subject to an independent central bank statutorily bound to the sole aim of avoiding inflation, optimal fiscal policy and a 'prudent' budget balance are a function of a number of parameters not easily measured. The balance between private investment, public investment and consumption expenditure, the stage of the economic cycle, the level of public debt, changes in the net worth of state assets and other attributes of the fiscal environment are at best 'moving targets'. Statutory limits can be obviated with appropriately fudged definitions in accounting and audit statements. Unlike an inflation target, the budget cannot be completely delegated to unelected officials making decisions on purely technical criteria. In the absence of unambiguous rules over budget decisions, the Singapore constitutional amendment can be seen as a practical 'second-best' attempt at over-coming the inherent fiscal propensities of democratic government, similar to contemporary efforts in the US and New Zealand.[36]

THE MANAGEMENT OF PUBLIC-SECTOR SAVINGS

It is clear that the newly industrializing countries in East Asia have received rewards – in remarkable rates of economic growth and industrial development – for their extraordinary mobilization of resources. Yet, if it is true that the 'secret' to Asian growth is no more than 'simply deferred gratification, the willingness to sacrifice current satisfaction for future gain',[37] the question immediately arises as to whether Singapore is over-saving. This question, though distinct from, would be at least as important as, if not prior to, the question of whether a nation's savings are constitutionally safe from the dangers of a government which is populist or corrupt (or both). If it was in fact the case that Singapore was 'over-saving', then an elected president might well oppose some future government compelled by the ballot box to reflect contemporary constituents' preferences for current consumption over investment (for future consumption). The president would thereby be working to the detriment of the nation's economic welfare as perceived by its citizens. Reflecting on such a conundrum, the Nobel Laureate Franco Modigliani, invited to Singapore as Lee Kuan Yew speaker, noted that 'Singapore is accumulating assets on a massive scale...you wonder what is the point; do you want your kids much wealthier than you are?'[38]

Professor Modigliani's question is not answerable on positive grounds. A high level of savings can be justified on a number of normative arguments. Singapore's large holdings of national savings in short-term foreign financial assets could be cast as a requirement of an optimal insurance plan for external security challenges. In a modern highly competitive arena of nation-states, awareness of geo-political realities may well be the preserve of great statesmen and quite out of reach of the average man-in-the-street. The greater the probability decision-makers attach to pessimistic expectations, the lower would be the weight given to current consumption relative to the future and the more would be invested for economic growth and its associated industrial and military capabilities.

There is a widespread belief that governments, as trustees to the general public, have a special responsibility for the future over and above that expressed by private actors in the current market. It could also be argued that if governments hold special ethical responsibilities to future generations which cannot take part in current decisions and if they are the only institution that can be relied upon to protect posterity, it may well be optimal that public savings exceed levels that would have prevailed if private choice dominated the outcome. Investments, as a provision for the future through postponed consumption, may be termed a public good since 'a better future' cannot be restricted to any particular individual, much like national defence or public health. As private investment decisions do not take into account the social benefits of providing for future generations, the level of private investment undertaken will fall short of its optimum. The public sector should therefore make up for the shortfall by adopting an interest rate below that of the private sector, reflecting society's 'true' collective preference to provide for posterity.

One strand of modern economic theory suggests that there are plausible reasons for believing that private savings behaviour may not even be representative of an individual's own time preference. The empirical observation that many people would like to save more, but when they have money the urge to spend overwhelms them, has been explained in rational choice theory as a class of principal–agent problem: the 'principal', representing that part of someone's personality concerned with 'strategic' long-term planning may not be able to delegate the task of saving to the 'agent', representing that part of the personality that acts for the 'tactical' short run. Thus it may well be rational choice to rely on compulsory savings if people know that they are easily tempted.[39]

These normative arguments proposed for higher savings are, however, not matters of consensus in contemporary societies (or among economists for that matter). The impossibility of operationally aggregating people's choices into a universally acceptable measure of 'an intertemporal social welfare function' is well known to economists. Many people, often because of their experience or knowledge of the costly failures of governmental intervention in human history, would be wary of accepting the notion that governments in general know better than individuals about investment choices in inter-generational welfare. It is also by no means clear whether the level of bequests in democratic countries, pecuniary and otherwise, made by individuals to their children and grandchildren, exhibit the current generation's lack of empathy for 'posterity'. For those in relatively wealthy countries, one could ask whether the current generation would really want their much poorer forefathers to have tightened their belts further just so that they could have been richer today, a Robin Hood activity stood on its head as it were.

Eschewing normative judgments, economists tend in general to hold onto the mainstream doctrine that, short of very clear and measurable exceptions of market failure, such as in the well-established case of public goods, the return to public investment should match the private competitive return.[40] Indeed, to the extent that public-sector activities absorb investment opportunities available to the private sector, there exists a social opportunity cost measured by the difference between (higher) private-sector rates of return and those of the public sector. In this view, the social opportunity costs of public investment are measured by the private spending that is displaced by taxes, public borrowing or inflation (the last merely being an implicit tax). Whether the social benefits of public-sector investments match these opportunity costs at the margin would then be an empirical question requiring careful study.

Whatever side one takes in putting a normative value to public-sector investments, it is not possible to fully measure the costs and benefits of Singapore's public investments. The information required to quantify the totality of public assets and their rates of return is not published, and no data is available to outside observers on rates of return to capital managed by statutory authorities (including the Central Provident Fund (CPF)), government-owned enterprises or the Government Investment Corporation in charge of the huge portfolio of Singapore's cash and short-term assets. Singapore's officially published foreign reserves of US $31 thousand million do not account for all of the country's foreign assets, according to the country's Finance Minister Richard Hu; furthermore, these reserves are not similar to, nor fully accounted by, CPF funds which also amounted to some $31 thousand million in 1988.[41] The October 1995 issue of the American financial magazine *Institutional Investor* pointed out that the top three institutional investors in Singapore were, in order of portfolio size: the CPF Board, holding assets of US$40.75 billion (S$57.86 billion), the Government Investment Corporation (US$38.5 billion or S$54.7 billion), and Post Office Savings Bank of Singapore (US$15.02 billion or S$21.3 billion).

It is nevertheless clear to non-governmental economists and financial commentators in the market that government-owned or controlled entities in Singapore do not generally make sustained losses or depend on subsidies to cover such losses. While observing that, given the excellent economic performance of the republic since independence, Singapore has demonstrably avoided the pitfalls of financial mismanagement that have been characteristic of the public sector in many developing countries, recent studies of public-sector performance have focused on key issues of institutional and procedural challenges facing the country's financial decision-makers.[42] It has been pointed out that with very concentrated decision-making power over large amounts of financial resources, Singapore's civil or statutory authorities increasingly face the dangers of 'information overload' and diseconomies of scale in the complex problems of co-ordination and direction.[43]

It should be pointed out that these challenges to the successful management of large financial assets are not unique to Singapore. As the large literature on corporate management attests, they are of perennial concern to the chief executive officers of the modern global conglomerates in key industries with large economies of scale. In this context, one benchmark test to measure efficient management of financial resources would be to ask whether fund managers employed by the state compete, notionally if not directly, with their private-sector counterparts who invest private savings on behalf of private beneficiaries. Are civil servants in charge of the prudential management of the nation's reserves facing an incentive structure similar to that existing in competitive capital markets? In Singapore, as elsewhere, there is always the tendency of performance evaluation in public-sector bureaucracies to value loss-avoidance (via routine work procedures) over gain-making by initiative. When the errors of commission are more rigorously proscribed than those of omission, risk-averseness might be higher than optimally dictated by market expectations. Indeed, there is a very real danger that civil servants, under great pressure to succeed, might display a lack of initiative and imagination.

The elected presidency amendment, while being an important institutional response to the inherent problems of populism and expedient politics in modern democracies, does not (and in all fairness, cannot be expected to) resolve the problem of good governance. There remain major challenges, both intellectually as well as in the practical sense, to the efficient management of resources by the state. The economic issues discussed in these paper are only some of the more obvious and apparent to public debate on the subject. The elected presidency amendment, by provoking commentary on the subject, among those who claim to speak as professionals as well as those casting opinions as citizens, helped raise some of these questions in sharp relief on the political map for the first time since the country's independence.

By raising the level of public consciousness of the fundamental challenges facing contemporary liberal democracies, the constitutional amendment has already provided a crucial social benefit in educating the domestic populace of the obligations of responsible citizenship. Subjecting the fiscal behaviour of a hitherto all-powerful, popularly elected majority in the legislature to veto in some aspects of the constitution's financial rules of the game by a separately constituted and elected authority in the person of the president, and by making transparent at least some aspects of fiscal accountability, the PAP government has raised the stakes facing would-be challengers to party incumbents. If only in the negative sense of the veto, the constitutional amendment has raised the domestic political costs of fiscal irresponsibility.[44] However, the recent decision by the Special Tribunal to disallow the president from calling a referendum to block the incumbent government's ability to amend the constitution with respect to the president's powers, would seem to lessen the authority of the president in the ultimate instance.

CONCLUSION: CHAINING THE LEVIATHAN

In a modern democratic setting, where citizens' proclivities towards the politics of democratic populism and special-interests lobbying are inherent, what concrete measures may be taken to counter the political bias towards budget deficits and policies which favour particular constituencies at the expense of overall economic welfare? Reflecting this question, Premier Lee Kuan Yew said to an audience in the Philippines, 'I believe that what a country needs to develop is discipline more than democracy. The exuberance of democracy leads to indiscipline and disorderly conduct which are inimical to development'.[45] The economic rise of Japan and the East Asian economies, now including China, has been seen by influential leaders in these countries, as well as by many opinion leaders in the West, as demonstrating the fallacy of the traditional laissez-faire approach to economic policy based on the individualist tradition of liberal democracy. In this view, the success of these countries is seen as the result of strong governments which place limits on individual liberties for the public good, take charge of promoting economic development, and sacrifice short-run consumer interests for long-run economic growth.

To Western economists on both sides of the Atlantic, familiar with the results of governmental intervention, the model of a 'strong government' takes the debate full circle back to the Fabian fallacy, that 'error of monumental proportions'. Thus, for Buchanan, '[to] call for further helmsmanship from the pilots who have exacerbated our troubles in the first place... is not a remedy that many of us would anticipate with much enthusiasm'.[46] For Robert Bartley, presenting an American perspective on democracy and development, entrusting decision-making power over economic policy to a small group of technocrats wholly free from political interference puts enormous burdens of courage, wisdom and rectitude on national leaders and, '[a] nation seeking out to follow this [Asian] model might be lucky enough to draw a MacArthur, a Pinochet or a Lee Kuan Yew. But it is at least as likely to draw a Marcos, a Peron, or a Mobutu'.[47]

An assessment of the economic efficiency of alternative sets of institutional arrangements, putting aside the irresolvable normative issues of aggregating individual preferences, inevitably leads to human civilization's age-old questions of political virtue, for no decree or legal principle can ensure a moral leadership. Ultimately, the predicted fiscal properties of alternative sets of institutional and legal rules depend on the assumed model of individual behaviour of political or bureaucratic decision-makers. Some critics of the government may well object to the PAP's hard-headed rationale for the constitutional amendment on the grounds that the altruistic public servant not only makes restrictive or market-orientated rules redundant but also counter-productive by not appropriately recognizing the virtues of a public-spirited civil service. To some citizens, it may seem morally correct to believe that, to the extent that the constitutional amendment casts politicians as likely opportunists, government leaders who supported the amendment assume models of individual behaviour that reflect more narrowly defined self-interest on the part of politicians and public servants than, in all fairness, may be warranted.

Yet, as pointed out by James Buchanan, there is a 'strong presupposition' that individuals do not undergo behavioural changes when they shift from being actors in the market place to being bureaucrats or politicians.[48] *Homo economicus* has always taken a central role in classical political economy. David Hume thought that

> political writers have established it as maxim that in contriving any system of government, and fixing several checks and controls of the constitution, every man ought to be supposed a knave, and to have no other end, in all his actions, than private interest.[49]

And John Stuart Mill believed that

> the very principle of constitutional government requires it to be assumed that political power will be abused to promote the particular purpose of the holder, not because its always so, but because such is the natural tendency of things...[50]

In recognizing that moral leadership and fiscal prudence are not assured by institutional and legal rules, however well thought-out, the PAP leadership found it imperative to vest veto powers – albeit limited to some areas and ultimately subject to a two-thirds majority in Parliament which can amend the Constitution and the powers of the elected president – over a sovereign, popularly elected legislature in the person of a separately constituted custodial president. In acting so dramatically against the inherited tradition of Westminster, and in holding an unfashionable (even cynical, some would say) view of the political and bureaucratic creatures of contemporary democracies, surely the Singapore government deserves to be credited, even by its most convinced critics, for the courage of its political convictions and intellectual honesty. In curtailing the great powers of his own government, prime minister Goh Chok Tong and his Cabinet have, none too soon, credibly begun the process of chaining the Leviathan.

NOTES

1 I would like to thank the editors of this volume for their inordinate patience and their support in ensuring the completion of this article. I would also like to thank Subbiah Gunasekaran, Kenneth James, K. U. Menon and Tan Kim Song for reading the manuscript and suggesting improvements. The usual disclaimers, of course, apply, and the remaining errors of fact or interpretation are purely my own.

2 Cited in M. Conant, *The Constitution and the Economy* (University of Oklahoma Press, 1991): 73.

3 Speech during Second Reading of the Constitution of the Republic of Singapore (Amendment No. 3) Bill, *Reports of the Singapore Parliamentary Debates.*

4 See James Buchanan, *Explorations Into Constitutional Economics* (Texas A&M University Press, 1989): 65.

5 See, for example, Ann O. Krueger, *Liberalization Attempts and Consequences* (Cambridge, MA: Sallinger Publishing Company, 1978) and B. Balassa, *The Newly Industrializing Countries in the World Economy* (New York: Pergamon Press, 1981).

6 It is instructive to note here, despite the current intellectual credibility of the 'Asian model' of economic development, Dr Goh Keng Swee, the architect of Singapore's economic success, had no hesitation in pointing out in an address to the Malayan Economic Society in 1957 the severe limitations of government in issues of enterprise:

> The economists who have been trained in the liberal tradition will have no hesitation in saying the policy of inducing, by special protective measures, the growth of entrepreneurship, is self-defeating in a free enterprise system. It will neither create captains of industry nor will enterprise remain free much longer.... No official selection board or public service commission can possibly spot potential captains of industry by whatever techniques of selection that it may devise.
>
> (Goh Keng Swee, 'Entrepreneurship in a Plural Society', *The Malayan Economic Review* (1957) Vol. III No. 1: 5)

7 See, for example, Robert Wade, *Governing the Market: Economic Theory and the Role of Government in East Asian Industrialization* (Princeton, NJ: Princeton University Press, 1990).

8 See Colin I. Bradford and William H. Branson (eds) *Trade and Structural Change in Pacific Asia* (Chicago: Chicago University Press, 1986).

9 See Peter Chen, 'Singapore's Development Strategies: a Model for Rapid Growth', in Peter Chen (ed.) *Singapore Development Policies and Trends,* (Singapore: Oxford University Press, 1983); see also Lawrence Krause, Koh Ai Tee and Lee Tsao Yuan (eds) *The Singapore Economy Reconsidered* (Singapore: Institute of Southeast Asian Studies, 1987).

10 See, for example, Lee Tsao Yuan, 'Sources of Growth Accounting for the Singapore Economy', in Lim Chong Yah and P. Lloyd (eds) *Singapore: Resources and Growth,* (Singapore: Oxford University Press, 1986); Lin Kuan-Pin, '*Productivity in ASEAN Manufacturing* (Singapore: Institute of

Southeast Asian Studies, 1986); and A. Sanchez, *Capital Measurement and Total Factor Productivity Analysis* (unpublished PhD Dissertation, University of the Philippines, 1983).

11 L. Lau and Kim Jong-Il, 'The Sources of Growth of the East Asian Newly Industrialized Countries', *Journal of Japanese and International Economies* (1994).

12 See Paul Krugman, 'The Myth of Asia's Miracle', *Foreign Affairs* (1994) 73: 70.

13 See Alwyn Young, 'A Tale of Two Cities: Factor Accumultation and Technical Change in HongKong and Singapore' *NBER Macroeconomic Annual 1992*.

14 See Koh Ai Tee, in Lawrence Krause, Koh Ai Tee and Lee Tsao Yuan (eds) *The Singapore Economy Reconsidered* (Singapore: Institute of Southeast Asian Studies, 1987): 83.

15 See, for instance, W. Huff, *The Economic Growth of Singapore: Trade and Development in the Twentieth Century* (Cambridge: Cambridge University Press, 1994).

16 *Ibid.*: 84.

17 *Ibid.*: 332–50.

18 *Ibid.*

19 'The Constitutional Amendments to Safeguard Financial Assets and the Integrity of the Public Services' (1988), Para. 5.

20 For instance, see G. Tullock, *Towards a Mathematics of Politics* (Ann Arbor, Mich.: University of Michigan Press, 1967); W Niskanen, *Bureaucracy and Representative Government* (Chicago: Aldine-Atherton, 1971); and A. Downs, *An Economic Theory of Democracy* (New York: Harper & Brothers, 1957).

21 See J. Bhagwati, 'Directly Unproductive Profit-Seeking (DUP) Activities', *Journal of Political Economy* (1982): 90.

22 James Buchanan, *The Economics and Ethics of the Constitutional Order* (Ann Arbor, Mich.: University of Michigan Press, 1991): 34.

23 For instance, 'What is prudence in the conduct of every private family can scarce be folly in that of a great kingdom'. (Smith, cited in Buchanan, *Ibid.*: 91.)

24 See James Buchanan, *Explorations into Constitutional Economies* (Texas A&M University Press, 1989): 65.

25 See F. A. Hayek, *The Constitution of Liberty* (Chicago: University of Chicago Press, 1960).

26 Since the voting constituency includes the large mass of individuals, high organization costs and the free rider problem lead members of this group to behave atomistically. We can thus aggregate the group into the representative or 'median' voter. This assumes that citizens' *perceptions* of the consequences of the incumbent government's actions (which determine whether they extend political support) are generally accurate. While this is an analytic convenience, the assumption can be supported on the grounds that such perceptions will tend to be positively correlated with actual consequences since more favourable consequences are more likely to be perceived as such by a greater number of people.

27 Thus, Thomas Macaulay thought universal suffrage would bring 'the end of property and thus all civilization', and David Ricardo could only argue to

extend suffrage 'to that part of them [the people] which cannot be supposed to have an interest in overturning the right to property' (both cited in Adam Przeworski and F. Limongi, 'Political Regimes and Economic Growth', *The Journal of Economic Growth* (1993): 752.

28 See James Buchanan, *The Demand and Supply of Public Goods* (Chicago: Rand McNally, 1968).

29 Samuel P. Huntington, *Political Order in Changing Societies* (New Haven, Conn.: Yale University Press, 1968).

30 Mancur Olson, *The Logic of Collective Action: Public Goods and the Theory of Groups* (Cambridge, MA.: Harvard University Press, 1965).

31 Gary Becker, 'A Theory of Competition Among Pressure Groups for Political Influence', *Quarterly Journal of Economics* (1983) 98: 371–400.

32 See Stephen P. Magee, William A. Brock and Leslie Young, *Black Hole Tariffs and Endogenous Policy Theory* (Cambridge: Cambridge University Press, 1989).

33 See F. A. Hayek, *The Road to Serfdom* (Chicago: Chicago University Press, 1944): 99.

34 See James Buchanan, *The Economics and Ethics of the Constitutional Order* (Ann Arbor, Mich.: University of Michigan Press, 1991).

35 The adoption of the independent charter for the Central Bank in New Zealand is a recent example of constitutional safeguard for monetary policy.

36 In early March, the latest attempt in the US Congress to enact one version of a balanced budget programme was defeated. In New Zealand, the government recently passed the Fiscal Responsibility Act which requires the government to publish accounts similar to private companies with a statement of income and expenditure and a balance sheet of assets and liabilities, to publish explicit targets for net debt, and to identify prudent fiscal policy in terms of the budget balance, debt, and public sector net worth.

37 See Paul Krugman, 'The Myth of Asia's Miracle', *Foreign Affairs* (1994) 73, 62: 78.

38 See Salil T. Tripathi, 'Singapore Savings Rate excessive wages could be raised' *Business Times,* 17 July 1992.

39 See, for instance, the survey of recent economic literature on rationality in *homo economicus* in *The Economist* (24 December–6 January 1994–5 issue).

40 It should also be noted that Frank Knight and Ronald Coase both established the case that market failure does not necessarily imply government intervention if costs of the latter are also taken into account.

41 'Liquid assets per head among the highest in the world', *Straits Times*, 13 August 1988.

42 See, for instance, contributions in Lawrence Krause, Koh Ai Tee and Tsao Yuan (eds) *The Singapore Economy Reconsidered* (Singapore: Institute of Southeast Asian Studies, 1987); also the government-chaired Economic Committee report 'The Singapore Economy: New Directions' Report (1986) which investigated the causes of the country's unexpected recession in 1985–6.

43 See Krause in Lawrence Krause, Koh Ai Tee and Tsao Yuan (eds) *The Singapore Economy Reconsidered* (Singapore: Institute of Southeast Asian Studies, 1987): 121.

44 [Editors' note] See *Constitutional Reference No.1 of 1995, Singapore Law Reports* (1995) 1: 201.
45 *The Economist*, 27 August 1994: 15.
46 See James Buchanan, *The Economics and Ethics of the Constitutional Order* (Ann Arbor, Mich.: University of Michigan Press, 1991): 104.
47 See Robert Bartley, 'Capitalism, the Market Mechanism and the State in Economic Development: An American Perspective', in Robert Bartley, Chan Heng Chee and Samuel Huntington and Shijuro Ogata (eds) *Democracy and Capitalism: Asian and American Perspectives* (Singapore: Institutute of Southeast Asian Studies, 1993): 62.
48 See James Buchanan, *Explorations Into Constitutional Economics* (Texas A&M University Press, 1989): 63.
49 *Ibid.*: 64.
50 *Ibid.*

7 Singapore's first elected presidency

The political motivations

Hussin Mutalib

Although hailed as the most radical change to Singapore's Constitution since independence, the impact of introducing the elected presidency (EP) scheme was minimal. A random survey conducted by the *Straits Times* during the run-up to the presidential election indicated that most Singaporeans were either apathetic, viewing it as a 'non-event'[1] – perhaps because the government's candidate was expected to win anyway – or knew very little of the new powers of the elected presidency. The general lukewarm reaction corresponded to the newspaper's earlier observation that it received only five letters on the subject, compared to some 40 letters when the nesting place of some herons was disturbed.[2]

Even the presidential 'contest' in August 1993 which was expected to enthuse the electorate, failed to do so. This can be attributed to the fact that the electorate was confronted with a choice of two establishment candidates both of whom had served the government for more than 30 years each. Of the estimated 300–400 people considered qualified for the post,[3] only former Accountant-General Chua Kim Yeow agreed to stand against Ong Teng Cheong. Even so, his candidature was a reluctant one, and Chua only agreed to stand after much persuasion. His decision not to campaign for the post or distribute banners, and initially not even to speak to the media, drew only derision from many Singaporeans. In the end, 'in a civilized if somewhat sterile process, Singapore elected a new President'.[4] The contest for Singapore's top public office, was based almost solely on two short televised speeches by each candidate.

This lukewarm reception belies the importance of the EP scheme. Its significance lies in several domains. First, it represented the latest in a series of moves to strengthen the stranglehold of the ruling People's Action Party (PAP) on political power; another quest for regime dominance as it were. Second, it signalled the ruling regime's increasing concern for preserving Singapore's prosperity and more importantly, their vision of good government for Singapore through the constitutional process. The need to establish a process by which generational political change and leadership succession could be achieved provided the main impetus for the establishment of the EP scheme.

In this chapter, I will begin by exploring the matrices within which political parties and actors operate in Singapore, and contextualizing the EP scheme within this paradigm. I will then consider the overriding values, ideals and system espoused by the ruling PAP elite, and how they have used various constitutional devices, including the EP, not only to secure political hegemony but to perpetuate these values, ideals and systems. In the third part of this essay, I will consider the various scenarios within which the EP scheme can or cannot work.

THE EP WITHIN SINGAPORE'S POLITICAL CONTEXT

To assess the significance of the EP initiative, we need to place it within the wider political dynamic. I shall argue that the regime's overpowering motivation was mainly political but also economic. The PAP's perennial quest for power and dominance over all spheres of life stems from the need to make sure that its ideas and values are sustained for the long-term stability of this country. Further to this objective was the need, particularly since the early 1980s, to find a way to respond and manage the new political aspirations and demands of the electorate.

These political imperatives stem from the PAP's general distrust of parliamentary opposition and the fear that populist pressures may unexpectedly result in the overthrow of the government. The PAP government's bitter experiences with the Barisan Sosialis in the early 1960s may explain its lack of faith in the opposition and in a parliamentary system which allows the opposition to galvanize public opinion by playing on popular sentiments and leads to the abandonment of long-held values and governing principles which are detrimental to the country's future progress and prosperity. So while Lee Kuan Yew and his comrades are still in charge, new institutions are introduced to ensure that their vision of the good life and good government, *their* Singapore, will remain intact after their departure.

Given Singapore's huge foreign reserves and the need to ensure integrity, credibility and efficiency in the state bureaucracy – especially in its top managers – it may be argued that the EP proposal was conceived in good faith. However, it should also be pointed out that the proposal can actually further perpetuate the PAP's control of Parliament and the state machinery. This has been the line taken by the opposition and other 'conspiracy theorists'. Indeed, the timing of its introduction, the stringency of its candidate qualification criteria and other political developments gave much credence to this theory.

The opposition charge that the introduction of the EP clearly manifested the regime's troubled position. Besieged, it had to devise new mechanisms and strategies to reverse the post-1981 electoral downslide. The opposition further argued that this shrewd political move was designed to prevent it from forming the next government. Even if the opposition won control of the government in an election, the EP, being a former PAP stalwart, would be empowered to impede the new government's effectiveness through the use of his veto powers.

All ruling parties seek regime dominance and influence over various facets of the state and society. The same can be said of the PAP and this makes the 'conspiracy theory' unremarkable as such. The key difference between Singapore and other polities is the PAP's ability actually to manifest this objective. In Singapore, the PAP government already dominates Parliament and other key institutions of the state. None the less, regime dominance is not pursued solely for its own sake but is used to promote the PAP's vision of the good state and society.

A superficial examination of Singaporean politics highlights the PAP's overwhelming concern with seeking and perpetuating its political dominance. Closer examination, however, reveals the PAP's more holistic and long-range plan to ensure that Singapore continues to retain the tested principles of governance and *modus operandi*, established by the party's and nation's founding fathers. To ward off the ill-effects of an increasingly demanding electorate, the PAP has decided to put in place new institutions which are expected to last the test of time. The EP initiative is thus one of the many institutions and policies which have been introduced to contain and channel a better-educated and more demanding electorate from pressuring the government to purchase political goodwill by dipping into the financial reserves. In the process, the EP scheme would also presumably better preserve Singapore's prosperity and further consolidate its wealth in the years ahead.

The PAP has dominated Singapore politically since 5 June 1959. Such an impressive record is due to many factors. First, the regime's success in delivering the economic goods; second, its strong leadership and organizational structures; third, the weakness of the opposition; and fourth, the regime's effective strategic political initiatives and socialization measures. While these four legitimizing factors explain the PAP's current strength, new factors such as the external environment (e.g. global democratization) and especially political-demographic changes (via a more educated, younger and discerning population) have begun to exert an increasing strain on the regime's control over the body politic. Faced with such challenges, and against the backdrop of its conspicuous electoral decline since the December 1984 general election, the regime has to find new ways and means to manage the new political realities, bolster its popular mandate and recoup its sliding political support.

The PAP's perennial quest for regime dominance and preservation of 'national' values

Prime Minister Goh Chok Tong is unconvinced that democracy can only function if there is a credible opposition.[5] To him, 'you have to have stability before you can talk about democracy'.[6] The PAP government, especially under Lee Kuan Yew's stewardship, had summarily dismissed any role for the opposition by unabashedly adopting and pursuing a platform which demonstrates its lack of faith in what the opposition can offer to Singapore. The party believed that it alone knew the best answer to the myriad problems and challenges confronting Singapore, and that the growth of a genuine and democratically-elected parliamentary opposition was inimical to national unity and stability. In the words of Milne and Mauzy:

> To the PAP leaders, 'representative' government is less important than 'responsible' government, in which electors are not simply given what they want but are led by elites along the lines most appropriate for Singapore's long-term development. This is not to say that people's opinions and feedback are ignored. But the government believes that it alone should be responsible for laying down the broad lines of policy.[7]

As recently as in 1991, in a widely publicized interview, Lee remarked that 'Asian countries must evolve their own styles of representative government to suit their cultures and circumstances'.[8] He repeated this sentiment in November 1993, when he lambasted the Americans for pressing democracy and human rights upon Asian societies.[9]

Through the long years of PAP's rule, its threshold of tolerance in respect of the opposition has been very low. The party tolerates the existence of political competition, but not its effectiveness or its excesses.[10] Many younger ministers share the PAP old guards' contempt for the opposition. As recently as November 1992, a publication of the party's official newsletter, *Petir*, carried a piece by the Acting-Minister for National Development, Lim Hng Kiang, entitled 'No need for Opposition Checks and Balances'.[11] This point was echoed by another young minister, Admiral (N. S.) Teo Chee Hean, a month later, with his remark that 'a two-party system would put us on the dangerous road to contention, when we should play as one team'.[12]

Such an uncompromising, innate mindset has its roots in the turbulent experiences which Lee and other early PAP founder-leaders went through, particularly in the 1950s and the early 1960s. These include the anti-colonial struggle for independence; the protracted battles with the communists, and later, the Barisan Sosialis-led Opposition Front; the communal antipathies which pitted the Malays and Chinese; and the bitter and acrimonious relationship with Malaysia's federal leaders during Singapore's short-lived merger with the federation from 1963 to 1965. Cumulatively, those early experiences and struggles produced the breed of PAP elitists who have little faith in the opposition. Thus the PAP believes that a growth-oriented, one-party dominance is indispensable to progress and stability in Singapore. This ideology accounts for the regime's authoritarianism, paternalism, and depoliticization of the populace.

Besides regulating para-political institutions such as the community centres (CCs) and residents committees (RCs), the print and broadcast mass media have been subjected to strict censorship laws. The imposition of the Undesirable Publications Act of 1967 and the Newspaper and Printing Act of 1974, have transformed the media's mission such that it now exists primarily to 'promulgate and explain government policies'.[13] The wide powers accorded to the moguls of the media, under the 1974 Act, led to 'management' (as opposed to 'ordinary') shareholders of newspapers, having about 200 times more voting power over ordinary shareholders. Since 1971 almost all local newspapers are grouped under the umbrella of the Singapore Press Holdings, under the supervision of its executive chairman, Lim Kim San, a former senior member of the Cabinet and a confidante of Lee. The regulated media, and centralized control of the state apparatus, the system of plurality voting (the first-past-the-post system) and the unitary political framework, all pose several disadvantages to people and groups outside the regime, especially the opposition.[14]

As a result, during the most part of Lee Kuan Yew's premiership, conformity was the order of the day, and this was manifested by repeated calls for orderliness, predictability and discipline. In Lee's own words, 'Singapore's economy prospered...(because) private enterprises work within a stable and congenial framework of orderly and predictable government'.[15] This rule by 'orderly and predictable government' has led to a highly stable and prosperous society which has become the envy of many Third World countries.

The party's concern is not so much with the present, since Lee and the current generation of leaders consider themselves honest and capable gentlemen whose values and commitment to Singapore are beyond reproach. The concern is for the future, especially after Lee noted the electoral trends of the younger and more educated populace, and what a future non-PAP government may do to win votes. To deal with these issues, the PAP has often emphasized its refusal to 'play to the gallery' or go for popular, soft options. It insists that its values and ideology should continue to reign large in Singapore's political landscape, especially since it regards the opposition's alternatives as untenable and short-sighted. There is thus a constant need to regularly introduce new ideas and measures to ensure that Singapore not only survives but maintains its competitive edge. A reflection of the many initiatives launched within the last decade will lead any keen observer to the conclusion that once a certain idea is publicly floated, it is almost inevitable that the idea will be implemented.

There are, of course, occasions when major ideas are refined or temporarily put in cold storage only to re-emerge when the time is ripe. The regime seems prepared to tolerate some minor changes to the implementation of their ideas, but not in its overall direction or goal. A number of unpopular ideas which were zealously pursued till realization are: 'Asian Values' (first introduced in 1978), 'Graduate Mothers' Scheme' (1984), the preferential treatment for public housing upgrading to PAP-held constituencies (1985), and the more recent policies in 1993 relating to the introduction of the Goods and Services Tax (GST) and the hefty salary increase of about 35 per cent for Cabinet Ministers.[16]

THE IDEA OF THE EP: RATIONALE AND CONSEQUENCES

The goal of protecting and preserving the values of the PAP elite and the concomitant determination to implement them expresses itself in the issue of the EP. This thesis is borne out by a closer examination of the many facets of the issue: the rationale and motivations precipitating its launching in the early 1980s; the addition of new and enhanced powers for the EP; the many and stringent rules governing the nomination of presidential candidates, and the consequences of the whole EP exercise to the body politic, and politics in Singapore in general.

Many reasons have been offered to rationalize the introduction of the EP. I shall briefly mention only three. First, the government is concerned about the protection of Singapore's long-term economic prosperity and political stability without which, it is argued, everything else will crumble. This requires safeguards over Singapore's financial reserves and its civil service. The second reason is a corollary of the first in that the government was concerned about the overwhelming power of the executive branch, and third, it may be argued that the scheme was designed to preserve the PAP's dominance.

Viewed from a *political* perspective, the first argument – concern for the long-term survivability and stability of Singapore – warrants the greatest consideration. Of course, such a stability is wholly defined from the PAP perspective, a perspective which may actually mean the further sustenance of PAP rule in this country to the detriment of the opposition cause. Indeed, since the PAP's loss of the Anson constituency by-election in 1981, Lee has been most concerned about the changing aspirations and attitudes of the electorate. It was clear that the electorate was clamouring for more opposition in Parliament, and the PAP decided that it was necessary for a series of measures to manage this change according to its mould.

I will now consider the different stages in the development of the EP scheme, especially in the periods between *elections* since 1981. This examination will demonstrate the party's concern for regime dominance in order to perpetuate its vision of good government.

The EP and the 1981 Anson constituency by-election

Since 1959, the PAP has been Singapore's sole governing party. During this period, the party secured an average 70 per cent of the total popular vote in the elections, including an all-time high of 84.4 per cent in 1968.[17] Although the PAP was initially checked by the opposition Barisan Sosialis – which won 13 of the 51 seats in the 1963 general election – it was only a temporary check. It subsequently won a monopoly of seats in 1968 when the Barisan Sosialis boycotted the polls. It is against this background that the loss of the Anson by-election must be viewed. When the Anson seat became vacant, because veteran politician and trade unionist Devan Nair was appointed Singapore's third president, a by-election was held. Lawyer, veteran politician and Secretary-General of the Worker's Party, Joshua Benjamin Jeyaretnam defeated the PAP's novice candidate. The loss of a single parliamentary seat means very little elsewhere if the ruling party or coalition's parliamentary majority is not threatened, but viewed against the backdrop of the PAP's hitherto monopoly of seats, it was shattering.

The EP and the 1984 general election

On 15 April 1984, then Prime Minister Lee Kuan Yew first publicly broached the idea of a new kind of president; one who would help safeguard the financial reserves.[18] The idea may have been tabled in the Cabinet shortly after the Anson electoral upset[19] but it was only at Lee's National Day Rally Speech in August 1984 that it was vigorously championed. The results of the December 1984 general election, particularly the shock 12.6 per cent swing against the PAP and the loss of two seats, could have further spurred Lee to speed up the implementation of the EP idea. The 1984 election brought home the point that voter preference for a more consultative style of government and their rejection of some key government policies if not addressed[20] could actually produce the 'freak' result of toppling the PAP government.

This scenario bothered Lee even before the 1984 election. In his National Day Rally Speech four months earlier, Lee had actually conjured up such an image:

> If there is a freak election result and a coalition forms the government, all the reserves are available, the larder is wide open, you can raid it. Twenty-five years of work, savings, you can go on a spending spree for five years and then we are another broken-back country.[21]

Lee said that he was seriously thinking about amending the Constitution to introduce a 'blocking mechanism' so that the government cannot squander the national reserves; it could only be spent with the assent of the president and a Special Committee.[22] Then Deputy Prime Minister Goh Chok Tong echoed Lee's sentiments when he commented on the 'structural weaknesses of parliamentary democracy' which made it vulnerable to populist pressures and overly frequent changes of government.[23] It was also around this time that Lee despaired at the one-man one-vote and first-past-the-post electoral system, hinting that it might have to be changed if a 'freak' election result was to be avoided.[24]

Lee's concern for the state's coffers is the more understandable because he was, at that time, the chairman of the Government

Investment Corporation (GIC) which regulated the state's investment ventures overseas. Significantly too, Lee mentioned that he would like to see a former PAP Cabinet Minister elected as president.[25] The nomination and subsequent election of former Deputy Prime Minister Ong Teng Cheong in the first presidential election must be viewed against Lee's personal views on the matter, as well as his imprint on the EP issue and its final outcome.

In fact, shortly before Ong's nomination as a presidential candidate, he accompanied Lee on an official visit to China. It was also Lee, who, after Ong won 58 per cent of the vote (a lower-than-expected figure), stated that Ong had received a strong mandate, and that comments to the contrary were 'utter rubbish'. Significantly too, the man chosen to replace Ong in the event of his incapacity is Lim Kim San, who is not only Chairman of the five-member Council of Presidential Advisors, but also a former Cabinet minister and a close confidante of Lee.

The EP scheme must be seen as the PAP government's response to the demands of the changing electorate. It is part of an overall quest to manage new political realities. In June 1984, despite strong criticisms from many quarters, Lee introduced the Non-Constituency MP (NCMP) scheme which aimed at enabling three defeated opposition members with the highest votes to enter parliament. The opposition vehemently opposed the scheme and charged that the PAP was trying to stage-manage its members in Parliament. Lee, however, went ahead to present two bills in Parliament, rationalizing that the initiative was to sharpen the debating skills of PAP MPs, educate Singaporeans on the role of the opposition and dispel any cover-ups by the PAP.[26] The euphoria in the opposition camp after stunning the PAP in the 1984 election led them to reject offers of NCMP seats.

Other initiatives to manage change: 1985-7

The PAP's desire to manage political change and to prevent a further slide of its electoral support became even more pronounced after the 1984 shocker. Between 1985 and 1987, a series of legal and political moves were made to recapture the lost ground as quickly as possible. These included the rejuvenation of Resident Committees and the establishment of the Feedback Unit (both in 1985), the launching of Town Councils (1986),[27] the deliberations of the National Economic Committee (1985-6),[28] the formulation of the 'National Agenda' (1987), and the introduction of Government Parliamentary Committees. The political significance of these initiatives was obvious. They were meant to foster greater bonding between the PAP government and the electorate, and even reduce and undercut the electorate's demand for a greater parliamentary presence for the opposition.[29]

The EP and the 1988 general election

By the beginning of 1988, as news spread about an impending general election, the ruling party decided to revive the issue of the EP. On 27 July 1988, then Deputy Prime Minister Goh Chok Tong tabled the first White Paper on the EP in Parliament. Later published under the title *Constitutional Amendments to Safeguard Financial Assets and the Integrity of the Public Service*, the traditional roles and powers of the president were radically expanded.[30] MPs engaged in an unusually lively debate in Parliament over the White Paper on 11 and 12 August 1988. Significantly, several PAP backbenchers were quite critical about the powers of an elected president. Dr Toh Chin Chye, former deputy prime minister and party chairman, rejected the idea thus: 'It seems too expedient to change the Constitution just to look after the reserves.... Is this going to improve the government?...[A]ny change would affect future generations.' [31]

The opposition political parties viewed the ruling party's initiative as an attempt to subvert the supremacy of Parliament, and charged that the EP's powers may even be extended in future,[32] thereby limiting the powers of Parliament and checking the rise of the opposition. As discussion mounted, there were calls for the whole issue to be put to a national referendum for the people to decide. Faced with this unexpected critical attack, the PAP, in an unprecedented move in late August, agreed to debate the issue 'live' over television with the Workers' Party and the Singapore Democratic Party.

Despite strong objections from many quarters including from within the ruling party and a widespread frustration that the issue was not put to a national referendum, the PAP proceeded relentlessly with its game-plan. This is not surprising, since the PAP's *modus operandi* dictated that once values and policies have been established, they would be zealously pursued. In fact, Lee actually regretted not pushing through the EP idea much earlier.[33]

In the 1988 general election, despite initiating many policies meant to stem the slide in its electoral support, the PAP lost another percentage point. Compared with the 1984 figure, the party's percentage of the popular votes dropped from 62.9 per cent to 61.8 per cent. The PAP even came very close to losing another four seats in the Eunos GRC to the Workers' Party, when it scraped through with a bare majority of only 1,279 votes out of the 72,000 cast.

More measures to manage change: 1988–90

Disappointed with the further drop in electoral support, the PAP redoubled its measures to accommodate the new demands of the electorate, and to recapture lost ground.[34] These initiatives and reforms can be interpreted as further measures to enhance certain core values and principles considered necessary by the government for the future stability and progress of the Republic. These political initiatives also provide means to manage political change and transition or even alternative ways to provide more 'mechanisms for political expression outside the party system' even if they were never intended to allow the opposition a level playing field *vis-à-vis* the PAP.[35] For example, Brigadier General Lee conceded that the much-criticized Nominated MP scheme could help stem the growing support for the Opposition in parliament, especially if the NMPs did well.[36]

Second White Paper on EP (1990) and Amendment No. 3 (1991)

By March 1990, the government declared that it would go ahead with legislation on the expanded powers of the EP. Senior Minister Lee alluded to the need to resolve the issue and get it passed in Parliament before his planned handing over of the premiership to Goh, which was scheduled for November 1990. On 27 August 1990, the second White Paper on the EP was released.[37] Significantly, this second paper enlarged the powers of the EP. In November, the Select Committee made public its recommendations. In the first parliamentary sitting for 1991, on 3 January, the Constitution of Singapore Amendment Bill No. 3 was passed, and with it, the consolidation of all the new enhanced powers of the EP.[38]

The EP and the 1991 general election and 1992 by-election

In August 1991, a surprise general election was called. Only three years had elapsed since the last elections in 1988 (instead of the usual four) and Goh had barely been in office as prime minister for nine months.[39] Despite reports which told Goh that the 'ground was sweet' for the PAP and notwithstanding the buoyant economic growth of more than 8 per cent, the result came as quite a shock. The PAP's total vote dipped by one point to 61 per cent from the previous election, and even more disturbing was the fact that the party lost four seats to the opposition, its biggest number since 1963.[40]

By the standard of most mature democracies, the loss of four seats has little significance, in so far as a parliamentary majority is maintained. However in the context of a PAP-dominant system, perception in the party's top leadership was different. In the words of PAP founder-member and long-time Cabinet minister, S. Rajaratnam, 'anything less than 100 per cent victory was considered a setback'.[41] Despite the setback, Goh reiterated that the 'Government will not change rational policies to win votes'.[42] To reinforce this point, Goh further added that the promised refurbishment of public housing would first be carried out in PAP-held constituencies and that he would be deaf to the calls for upgrading services in opposition-held wards.

On 19 December 1992, Goh called a by-election to honour his 1991 election promise. It was held in his electoral constituency of Marine Parade GRC, and Goh and his three team mates were expected to win handsomely. The entire PAP machinery was mobilized to secure a respectable margin and Goh and his team won a resounding victory, securing 72.9 per cent of the valid votes. The big margin did not, however, dispel the regime's concern over the gradual erosion of its electoral support.[43] Against this backdrop, the announcement was made that Singapore's first-ever presidential elections would be held on 28 August 1993.

THE FIRST PRESIDENTIAL ELECTION

So far, our chronological survey has shown that throughout the decade-long gestation and evolution of the EP scheme, its rationale and motivations can be understood against the broader political dynamic which has characterized Singapore politics over the last 30 years, and in the light of increasing electoral pressure for political change in more recent times. The key to understanding the PAP's actions is its perennial goal of dominating the entire socio-political spheres of Singaporean society, and the unwavering belief that its ideas and values must be entrenched in the nation's political culture and consciousness, however unpopular they might be.

Cast against this background, the EP initiative may be seen as the PAP's way of protecting the nest-egg it had painstakingly built up and nurtured over the years.[44] At the same time, the scheme may be designed to prevent the changing political citizenry from discarding the values and policies mapped out by the first generation PAP leaders. These twin objectives are further borne out by our following discussion. In particular, I will comment specifically on the first presidential election, the rules and other criteria imposed upon prospective candidates, the enhanced powers of the EP, the nature of the contest, and the political implications of Ong's victory.

The rules and other criteria governing prospective candidates

The rules and other criteria imposed upon potential candidates were stringent.[45] Properly operated, these rules attract only pro-establishment personalities. In this first-ever contest for the post, even pro-government figures hesitated in coming forward after they knew that they had to challenge another PAP-sponsored heavyweight in the person of Ong. An Opposition NMCP member, Dr. Lee Siew Choh, in fact accused the government of practising a 'closed-doorism which violated the basic tenets of democracy...a criterion [which was a] blatant discrimination practised in favour of a handful of the elite against the vast majority of the people in Singapore'.[46]

Although the ruling party claimed that there were around 400 qualified persons for the EP, initially not one was willing to be nominated. Finally, the one who did only surfaced after much coaxing by PAP stalwarts former Deputy Prime Minister Dr Goh Keng Swee and current Finance Minister Dr Richard Hu. Still, no sooner had he agreed, than Chua Kim Yeow, a bureaucrat-turned banker, found both ministers adopting a conspicuously 'hands-off' position. Other than his family members and his small staff at his company, Stamford Tyres, Chua was a loner in the non-campaign. Not even his six assenters, who included former Attorney General Tan Boon Teik, did anything other than act as his character referees.

In total, the PEC received four nominations. Besides Ong and Chua, the other two were from the Workers' Party: J. B. Jeyaretnam, its Secretary-General and former MP, and Tan Soo Phuan.[47] Since the law stated that only those with financial experience and who were of good character and reputation, could be considered,[48] the PEC decided to issue the Certificate of Eligibility to only two, Ong and Chua; it was not satisfied that Jeyaretnam and Tan had the prerequisite qualities and character to qualify.[49] Jeyaretnam lambasted the PEC for what he saw as a biased decision, claiming that he qualified for nomination but that the strict criterion was 'tailored' in such a way that 'nobody outside the PAP's "charmed circle" could stand for the election'.[50] Legally, there was nothing he could do against the decision, because the PEC's decision is final and not subject to judicial review.

Another criticism of the EP scheme, and one which has never been much articulated, is the extent to which it limits opportunities for minority candidates, in particular Malays, from being elected to the post in the future. Since independence, the government has pursued a tacit policy that Singapore's top post should be rotated on the basis of the candidate's ethnicity. This policy manifested itself in the choice of all the first four presidents. The stringent meritocratic and financial criteria now imposed upon presidential hopefuls might mean that such a multi-racial rotational representation of the highest office will be beyond the reach of Malays since very few of them have held high political and corporate posts. This effect may have the unintended consequence of practically undercutting one of the cornerstones of Singaporean politics and public life: multi-racialism.

The EP's enhanced powers and authority

We can argue that the more important motivation for the introduction of the EP was *political*, rather than economic. It was enacted to ensure the continuation of the PAP elite's (especially Lee's) model of governance. In this way, Lee's vision of 'good government' – such as meritocracy, integrity of leadership, abhorrence for populist policies and state welfarism – stood a better chance of survival even after his departure from the political scene, especially if the opposition could be curtailed. An analysis of the EP's impact validates this point.

If finance is the overriding factor, there are many different ways in which the government can raise funds without having to resort to the national reserves, such as selling assets of institutions (like the profitable Singapore Airlines) and state land, or privatizing the many successful state-owned corporations, or by printing more money.[51] Second, even if an opposition coalition were to succeed in forming the government, it could be prevented from raiding the coffers because the Constitution prevents it from spending what it did not itself accumulate. Third, a PAP-sanctioned president can exercise considerable leverage over an opposition-led government, given his wide discretionary powers under the amended Constitution.

The political implications of such a powerful president must suggest that the ruling party which endorses the candidate for the post, either directly or via proxy, can ensure the continued dominance of its political rule as well as its values, ideas and policies. Even in the unlikely event that the PAP is overthrown, the PAP-endorsed president, with his overarching powers, will continue to be a repository of PAP power. In short, the PAP cannot be totally annihilated from the political scene.

The contest for the EP's post

The outcome of the EP contest was highly predictable. Everyone expected Ong to win. The 'contest' was in reality a no-contest. While Ong clearly wanted the job and was prepared for it, Chua was not. He even praised Ong as being far superior to himself.[52] To compound matters, Chua had a seemingly insurmountable task given Ong's record of political achievements. As Deputy Prime Minister, Chairman of the PAP and Secretary-General of the National Trade Union Congress (NTUC), Ong was a well-known public figure. Chua, on the other hand, was only known by the financial community, having been the former Accountant-General, and later Executive Chairman of the government-owned Post Office Savings Bank. Most significantly, Chua never wanted to contest in the first place. His reluctance and lackadaisical attitude during the run-up to the election gave the public an early signal that the whole contest was a staged-managed, one-sided affair. Despite being given nine days to campaign with 12 stadiums designated as rally sites, Chua shunned them all and decided to address the people via the two 10-minute televized broadcasts offered by the state-owned television and radio stations. By contrast, Ong's posters were up at every strategic corner throughout Singapore. He was ably assisted by the NTUC which not only promised to mobilize its 230,000 members to assist him, but called upon the members each to secure five to six votes for their former union boss.[53] The Prime Minister, in his National Day Rally speech in early August, made his preference known to all: Ong was the ruling party's choice.

On polling day, 28 August 1993, some 1.7 million voters cast their votes. However when the results were announced, the seemingly reluctant and furtive Chua secured much higher than expected: 41.3 per cent as against Ong's 58.7 per cent: 670,358 voters gave their votes to Chua as opposed to 952,512 for Ong.[54] The NTUC leaders must have been somewhat disappointed since they were expecting between 60 to 70 per cent for Ong.[55] If we view this contest as between a PAP-partisan candidate and a relatively 'independent' one, particularly after Chua's *volte face* with his poignant poser to the people: 'Do you want the PAP to dominate the presidency as well?',[56] and the call by the opposition not to vote for Ong, Ong's performance was even lower than the 61 per cent received by the PAP during the 1991 general election. The official support for Ong, the mobilization of the NTUC's machinery, the open endorsement by a select cross-section of all the ethnic groups, and the conspicuous but perhaps legally questionable position adopted by the media (in all the four languages) when it 'campaigned' for Ong on polling day with two strongly argued pieces,[57] all demonstrate how clear the regime's objective was. A solid victory for Ong would also mean a victory for the PAP and the continuation of its values and manner of governance.

Although the results do not conclusively support the view that a large segment of the public has repudiated the PAP, I think it represents another signal from at least 40 per cent of the electorate seeking a new management style. It is quite obvious that more and more people are demanding greater checks and balances.[58] Equally obvious was the fact that the electoral ghosts of the 1991 general election have not been fully exorcized.[59]

The implications of Ong Teng Cheong's victory

We can interpret the election results in several ways. For a start, given Chua's sizeable voter support, it would be less difficult to persuade a credible non-partisan candidate to stand against a government-endorsed candidate in future presidential contests. Second, the two candidates set a precedent for future presidential contests which is likely to be conducted in a dignified or sedate manner without the usual personal attacks and mudslinging that one finds in Singapore's elections. Ong's victory must also imply that Singaporean politics in the next six years would be 'more of the same', with little deviation from the now-familiar PAP government's method of governance. Ong is on record as having stated, soon after fulfilling the requirement to sever his party links, that:

> I am no longer partisan and I will no longer come under the control of the party whip. So I am an independent person and my main duty, if elected as president, is to look after the interests of the nation and the people as a whole – not any sectoral interests.[60]

Given President Ong's long and close links with the regime, it is hard to envisage him embarking on the adventurous course of having to veto something which he was once bound to uphold in line with the principle of collective Cabinet responsibility. Being party to all earlier decisions of the Cabinet in matters such as utilizing financial resources, and the criteria by which top leaders were appointed, Ong cannot now be expected to change the principles and ways in which he had earlier been socialized. Indeed, it would be very difficult for him to suddenly cut off his links with the party and all it stands for. During the Select Committee hearings on the subject, Goh and Lee even remarked that it would make no difference whether a candidate remained a party member or not upon his election, because his resignation from the party would not necessarily make him less sympathetic to his party's policies.[61] Ong himself wanted Singaporeans to know that he was not planning anything new and unexpected with his first official words about how he saw his role would be. Responding to Prime Minister Goh's statement during the investiture of the EP, that 'I do not intend to bring about a situation which will give you cause to exercise your veto powers', President Ong replied:

> I look forward to developing a sound working relationship with the PM and his Government. The purpose of the elected president is to institute judicious checks and balances in our political system, not to create unworkable conflict and gridlock.[62]

Ong himself admitted that as a Cabinet minister, he had participated in the deliberations that resulted in the government's decision to have the elected presidency, and as such, it made him 'acutely conscious' of the responsibilities expected of the EP.[63] In fact, President Ong cannot do anything to prevent the present regime under Goh from spending the financial reserves amassed by Goh and his team since 1990 because the EP's veto can only be applied to reserves not accumulated by the government of the day. In the hypothetical case of irresponsible spending by the government, such as buying Rolls-Royces for ministers, the EP cannot veto it.[64] Given all these impediments and institutional constraints, Ong, will, in all probability, assume a 'more of the same' ceremonial role which his predecessors performed, notwithstanding his latent powers.

CONCLUSION

Now that Ong has the presidency, it remains to be seen whether his office will reinforce the regime's agendas, vision and future concerns. I think it will, especially as Ong has been so clearly entrenched in the PAP mould and ethos. The long-term implications of the EP are less clear. There could be greater independence of action *vis-à-vis* the Prime Minister and the Cabinet, especially if Senior Minister Lee were to succeed Ong either after six years or sooner if Ong's cancer recurs. After all, Lee's personality and past contributions to Singapore are widely known, and he himself had remarked that 'the job of the EP is not to be popular, but to be strong' and that 'he would have to take a stand against the government which may be very unpopular with many of the government supporters, and he must be prepared to do that'.[65] Reflecting on the PAP's track record, political finesse and pragmatism, we can expect the party to introduce further measures aimed at strengthening its deeply-held values that are deemed to underpin Singapore's viability. I doubt if the regime will stop at the EP in its attempt to safeguard its vision of good state and society.

NOTES

1 *Straits Times*, 4 August 1993.
2 See Leslie Fong, 'Domestic Politics: Was 1990 a Watershed?', in *Singapore in 1990: The Year in Review*, Institute of Policy Studies, Singapore, 1991: 4.
3 *Straits Times*, 21 August 1993.
4 *BBC Newshour*, London, 29 August 1993.
5 See for example, Bilveer Singh, *Whither PAP's Dominance?: An Analysis of Singapore's 1991 General Elections*, Pelanduk Publications, Petaling Jaya, Malaysia, 1992: 113.
6 Raj Vasil, *Governing Singapore: Interview with New Leaders*, Octopus Publishing Corporation, Singapore, 1992: 285.
7 R. S. Milne and D. K. Mauzy, *Singapore: The Legacy of Lee Kuan Yew*, Westview Press, Boulder, COL.: 1990: 177.
8 *Straits Times*, 10 May 1991.
9 *Straits Times*, 30 November 1993.
10 Chan Heng Chee, *The Dynamics of One-Party Dominance: The PAP at the Grassroots*, Singapore University Press, Singapore, 1978: 8.
11 *Petir*, November/December 1992:75.
12 *Straits Times*, 12 December 1992.
13 Alex Josey, *Singapore: Its Past, Present and Future*, Eastern Universities Press, Singapore, 1979: 103–4.
14 Chan Heng Chee, *The Dynamics of One-Party Dominance*: 188.
15 Lee Kuan Yew's piece in *People's Action Party 1954–1979: 25th Anniversary Issue*, CEC, PAP, Singapore, 1979: 39.
16 See Hussin Mutalib, 'Ministers' Pay: How much is Enough?', in *Singapore* (Singapore International Foundation, Singapore), January–February 1995: 23.
17 See Table on the Electoral Performance of PAP and Opposition, 1959–91, in Hussin Mutalib, 'Singapore's 1991 General Election', *Southeast Asian Affairs 1992*, Institute of Southeast Asian Studies, Singapore: 299–309.
18 *Straits Times*, 2 September 1993. See also Linda Low and Toh Mun Heng, *The Elected Presidency as a Safeguard for Official Reserves: What is at Stake?*, Times Academic Press for the Institute for Policy Studies, Singapore, 1989: 5 and 29.
19 Some parliamentarians intimated this information to the author. See also Milne and Mauzy, *Singapore*: 71.
20 Jon S. T. Quah, 'The 1980s: A Review of Significant Political Developments', in Ernest Chew and Edwin Lee (eds) *A History of Singapore*, Singapore, Oxford University Press, 1991: 385–400.
21 *Far Eastern Economic Review*, 6 September 1984, and *Foreign Broadcast Monitor*, BBC London, Newsdesk, 30 August 1993: 2.

22 Jon S. T. Quah, 'Singapore in 1990: The Politics of Transition', in Azizah Kassim and Lau Teik Soon (eds) *Malaysia and Singapore: Problems and Prospects*, Singapore Institute of International Affairs, Singapore, 1992.

23 K. S. Sandhu and Paul Wheatley (eds) *Management of Success: The Moulding of Modern Singapore*, Institute of Southeast Asian Studies, Singapore, 1989: 1087.

24 *The Economist*, 22 November 1986: 15.

25 *Straits Times*, 20 August 1984.

26 The two bills were: the Republic of Singapore (Amendment) Bill, No. 8/84 and the Parliamentary Elections (Amendment) Bill, No. 9/84. For details of the scheme, see Lee Boon Hiok, 'The Singapore Non-Constituency Opposition Member of Parliament', in *The Parliamentarian*, July 1985.

27 Aimed at allowing more citizen participation in the management of their constituencies, three town councils were launched in nine constituencies starting with those in the Ang Mo Kio area.

28 Formed to put the recessionary economy back on course, the committee was headed by Lee Hsien Loong, then a Minister of State (Trade and Industry). See *The Singapore Economy: New Directions*, Ministry of Trade and Industry, Singapore, February 1986: 231–2.

29 See for example, the article by Chan Heng Chee in Sandhu and Wheatley, *The Management of Success*: 70–89.

30 See Kevin Tan Yew Lee, Yeo Tiong Min and Yeo Ting Min, *Constitutional Law in Malaysia and Singapore*, Singapore: *Malayan Law Journal*, Singapore 1991.

31 *Far Eastern Economic Review*, 6 September 1993.

32 *Straits Times*, 13 August 1988. See also Milne and Mauzy, *Singapore*: 73.

33 During his televised National Day Rally Speech, Lee said: '[I]f I had taken this through in 1984 when I first raised it, there would not have been all this fuss'. Milne and Mauzy, *Singapore*: 73.

34 A few months after the election, it launched the widely publicized public discourses about a 'National Ideology' (later renamed 'Shared Values'). It then established the Institute of Policy Studies to secure feedback on current policy issues. Next came the formation of many advisory committees to help the regime formulate better policies on matters such as health, family and the aged.

35 Garry Rodan, 'Preserving the one-party state in contemporary Singapore', in Kevin Hewison *et al.* (eds) *Southeast Asia in the 1990s: authoritarianism, democracy and capitalism*, Allen & Unwin, Sydney, 1993: 86.

36 Garry Rodan, 'Singapore's leadership transition: erosion or refinement of authoritarian rule?', in *Bulletin of Concerned Asian Scholars*, Vol. 24, No. 1 (January–March 1992).

37 *Elected President: Safeguard Financial Assets and the Integrity of the Public Service.*

38 Since the party whip was not lifted, all PAP MPs voted in favour of the bill. SDP's Chiam See Tong voted against it. NCMP member, Dr Lee Siew Choh also voted against the bill but his vote did not count since he was constitutionally prohibited from voting on a bill to amend the Constitution.

39 For an analysis of the election, see Hussin Mutalib, 'Singapore's 1991 General Election', in *Southeast Asian Affairs 1992*: 299–309, and Bilveer

Singh, *Wither PAP's Dominance?: An Analysis of Singapore's 1991 General Election*, Pelanduk Publications, P. J. Malaysia, 1992.

40 In the 1963 general election, the PAP lost 14 seats while the opposition Barisan Socialists won 13 seats and another was lost to an Independent candidate.

41 *Sunday Times*, 29 September 1991.

42 *Straits Times*, 28 October 1991.

43 For an analysis of the by-election, see Hussin Mutalib, 'Singapore's December 1992 By-Election: Interpreting the Results and the Signals', in *Round Table*, Vol. 326, 1993: 159–68.

44 See for example, *Straits Times*, 25 August 1993.

45 For a detailed explanation of the rules, see Kevin Tan, 'Constitutional Changes' in this volume.

46 *Straits Times*, 4 January 1991.

47 Nominated MP, Chia Shi Teck, after first proposing himself as a candidate since he 'only wanted to contest because nobody else threw his hat into the ring', later withdrew when Chua agreed to contest against Ong. *Straits Times*, 17 August 1993.

48 *Straits Times*, 3 August 1993.

49 *Straits Times*, 17 August 1993. (J. B. Jeyaretnam was earlier fined in the courts and had his MP's seat denied, while Tan had repeatedly refused to pay parking fines.)

50 *Foreign Broadcast Monitor*, BBC London, Newshour, 28 August 1993: 12. He also spoke to other foreign media, including Australian Broadcasting Corporation (Radio National), which also carried other views by scholars and observers, including by this present writer.

51 This point was argued by Dr Ngiam Kee Jin of the Economics and Statistics Department, National University of Singapore, in a Forum on the Elected Presidency organized by the university's Law Faculty on 30 August 1993, two days after the presidential elections.

52 *Straits Times*, 4 September and 7 September 1993.

53 See for instance the report in *Straits Times*, 19 August 1993.

54 *Sunday Times*, 29 August 1993.

55 *Ibid.*

56 *Straits Times*, 27 August 1993, which contains the full text of Chua's second TV broadcast the day before.

57 It is doubtful that Singapore's electoral laws allow newspapers to write such one-sided pieces in support of a particular candidate on polling day since the law prohibits 'campaigning' on that day. Refer to the editorial and another piece by Han Fook Kwang in *Straits Times*, 28 August 1993.

58 *Straits Times*, 4 September 1993.

59 *Straits Times*, 4 September 1993.

60 *Straits Times*, 16 August 1993.

61 See the Report of the Parliamentary Select Committee as presented to Parliament on 18 December 1990, in particular the exchange between P. M. Goh and Brigadier General Lee with representor Walter Woon, the Vice Dean of the Law Faculty of the National University of Singapore.

62 See *Straits Times*, 2 September 1993, for the full speech and other reports of the investiture ceremony at the Istana.
63 *Straits Times*, 2 September 1993.
64 *Straits Times*, 7 September 1988.
65 *Straits Times*, 2 September 1993.

8 Notes from the margin

Reflections on the first presidential election, by a former Nominated Member of Parliament

Chia Shi Teck

INTRODUCTION

The result of the first presidential elections was finally announced at 3.30 a.m. on 29 August 1993, seven and a half hours after the casting of votes ended. A total of 369 counting stations were set up to speed up the counting process. The official indication was that the results should be in between midnight and 01.00. As the minutes ticked past 01.00, 02.00 and finally 03.00, the sense of uneasiness at the counting stations intensified.

As this election was a watershed event, and as I had also agreed to give my immediate comments on the results to the media, I stayed up for the results. A few journalists called me after 02.00 to give me updates and a feel of the air of excitement at the counting stations. There was some speculation that recounting was taking place in many counting stations, thus causing the delay. There was also a serious joke being circulated: the reluctant candidate, having won, wanted a recount to lose! Like most people in Singapore, I did not doubt that Mr Ong Teng Cheong would win the election. Notwithstanding the lack of interest of Mr Ong's contender, I did not expect Mr Ong to win more than 65 per cent of the vote. I based this feeling on the fact that the anti-government vote of 25 per cent to 40 per cent would go against Mr Ong since he was seen as a PAP man. Mr Ong's campaign did not succeed in erasing this fact. The suggestion that his years in government would be an asset in this new role did not help here.

The delay in announcing the final results was of enough concern for it to be raised in Parliament during the 12 October 1993 sitting. Prime Minister Goh Chok Tong explained that there were 1.6 million voters and the overly cautious and cumbersome procedure of reporting the results, coupled with the insufficient number of fax machines, caused the delay. The prime minister went on to confirm that there was no recount in any of the counting stations. He would not give the breakdown of votes by counting stations, saying that it was the total votes scored that mattered.

THE GOVERNMENT, THE CANDIDATES AND THE ELECTIONS

Mr Ong Teng Cheong, now President Ong, was clearly the candidate put up by the ruling party and the government. Of course, since the Constitution requires the candidate to be non-partisan, it would be unwise for either the government or the ruling People's Action Party (PAP) to openly nominate him as their candidate. As required by the Constitution, Mr Ong divested himself of all political affiliations. He resigned his membership in the PAP and that automatically meant giving up his parliamentary seat, his chairmanship of the party and his deputy prime ministership.

His nomination for the candidacy would come from another quarter – the National Trade Union Congress (NTUC) of which he was Secretary-General. Over the years, the NTUC has had a symbiotic relationship with the PAP government. So important is this relationship that a minister or person of ministerial calibre is often appointed as the Secretary-General of the Congress. One quickly thinks of men like C. V. Devan Nair, Lim Chee Onn, Ong Teng Cheong, and now Lim Boon Heng. All except Devan Nair held the post of Secretary-General and were serving cabinet ministers as well. As the top man in the NTUC, Ong naturally had the strong backing and official support of union members. There are over 200,000 union members and each was asked to get their candidate five votes a piece. If this strategy succeeded, it would immediately assure Mr Ong over 1 million votes. To run for the presidency, he would have to step down from the NTUC as well, and just a few days before his resignation from the union, he made what was probably the first election campaign speech. In his last public address as NTUC Secretary-General, Mr Ong urged the government to give workers a pay hike. Rightly or wrongly, this was perceived as probably the first salvo in the election campaign.

While the government and the PAP resisted the temptation to nominate Mr Ong themselves, they were very open about their support for his candidacy. Prime Minister Goh Chok Tong went public to ask Singaporeans to vote for Mr Ong during his 1993 National Day Rally Speech. Senior Minister Lee Kuan Yew also publicly endorsed Mr Ong. Even Finance Minister Richard Hu, who had been one of the two people instrumental in persuading Mr Chua Kim Yeow to run against Mr Ong, openly announced that his vote would go to Ong. One by one, community and ethnic leaders and groups expressed their open support for him, and quietly but surely, the entire machinery of the NTUC and the PAP worked in unison to ensure a resounding victory.

WHAT CHOICE? THE RELUCTANT CANDIDATE OR NO ELECTIONS?

The government had put in a lot of effort and spent almost 10 years paving the way for the elected presidency, equipped with very important executive powers to control the legislature. For the first time, Singapore would have a president with a direct mandate from the people. The election procedure had been ironed out, but would there really be an election? The Presidential Elections Act specifically says that if there is only one qualified candidate, he is deemed to be elected as president. In other words, you can actually have an elected president without an election. This provision could be criticized as defeating the whole idea of giving the president the people's direct mandate. I think this is the case.

Now that we had created such an institution, I felt it necessary at the time that a contest must be held to raise the people's awareness, to inform them about the importance of this new political office with important executive powers, holding the proverbial second key. The sentiment of the people was, I gather, that there would be no contest and the whole 'election' would simply fly past as a non-event. I was alarmed and sounded out several possible candidates inside and outside government to test their reactions. None of them 'dared' to go against the establishment. If everyone thought like this, there would surely be no election. I knew that I was not automatically qualified to run for the presidency, but nevertheless decided to go public with my offer to stand as candidate if no one else put his name up as a candidate.

Being then a Nominated Member of Parliament, I had the advantage and privilege of discussing the subject with many journalists. As the deadline for the government's announcement of the election date drew nearer, I invited two senior journalists, one from the *Straits Times* and the other from the Chinese *Lianhe Zhaobao* for a drink. I told them that I might consider contesting should there be no other candidate. Their initial reaction was one of shock, but after overcoming their surprise, they assured me full coverage and support. As a result, when the election finally materialized, many reporters called me for my comments. I thus had the opportunity to express my views fully. I made it clear that there should be a contest and that I was prepared to stand just to ensure that there would be a proper election. I felt that I was much too young for the job and did not automatically qualify for the pre-qualification certificate. In any case, I had neither the interest nor the temperament for the job. My offer resulted purely from my desire to attract a contest. I was confident that I would not be ridiculed for my conviction. I meant well.

Many days passed before Mr Chua Kim Yeow's candidacy was finally announced. When I heard that Mr Chua was stepping forward, I wrote in to the Presidential Election Committee to withdraw my application for the pre-qualification certificate. From the outset, that had been my plan although some people were not quite so sure and kept asking me if I was still going to stand, now that Mr Chua's candidacy had been announced. Indeed, I received a rather anxious call asking me what my stand was. I said that I would withdraw. I wanted to honour what I said when I offered myself as a candidate: that I would not contest if there was another candidate. It was clear in all my statements that I was not chasing the job. By withdrawing, I kept faith with the people of Singapore. I was, in a way, happy that the government succeeded in persuading someone to challenge Mr Ong. Later, when it became clear that the 'challenger' was unwilling to do battle, I was sadly disappointed.

My offer was not a bluff, and because it took so long for Mr Chua to announce his candidacy, I had actually made preparations for the printing of posters, banners and press advertisements. I had also read through the many submissions to the Select Committee on the Constitution Amendment Bill. There was a general consensus among the various professional bodies and individuals that the president should be truly independent and above partisan politics. I had several brainstorming sessions with my wife and decided that I would go for a straightforward and friendly campaign. I was confident that a 'gentlemanly contest' would be acceptable to the government and should set the pace for future presidential elections. I also discovered that campaigning island-wide was a very costly affair. There was a legal cap of S$600,000 on election spending. Even with that cap, few people can afford such a campaign. And even if you had the money, you needed a whole political machine behind you to mobilize the forces, otherwise a candidate would be severely handicapped in his election campaign.

The opposition parties were unable to field any candidate who met the stringent pre-qualifications under the Constitution. Indeed, the qualifiers were all likely to be establishment figures. Getting an establishment man to be the government's candidate must have been difficult enough. I imagine that trying to get one to stand against the government's preferred choice would have been impossible. From that standpoint, Mr Chua must be saluted for being very brave. He had to think about the morning after and the loss of privacy. As a former bureaucrat, he naturally fought shy of the limelight. Of course the government would have preferred him, after agreeing to offer himself as an alternative candidate, to keep 'mum' about the reason for his candidature.

ONG VERSUS CHUA: A CONTRAST OF AMBITIONS AND STYLES

From the word go, a massive and aggressive campaign was launched to get Mr Ong into office. In contrast, Mr Chua Kim Yeow, the retired Auditor-General, wanted to lie low, preferring to get over what he perceived as his 'national service' quickly. Many people were shocked, not so much to hear of his candidacy, but the reasons he gave for being talked into accepting the contest. Mr Chua said that it was the former Finance Minister Dr Goh Keng Swee and the present Finance Minister, Dr Richard Hu who pestered him into offering himself as a candidate. He accepted it as a national duty. Both of them were his former bosses. He did not want to campaign – no posters, no banners, no interviews and no speeches except the two 'compulsory' SBC shots. He also openly rejected all offers of help from well-wishers.

The way Mr Chua announced his candidacy and the approach he took caused some embarrassment to the ruling party. Mr Chua was in a high state of nerves on Nomination Day. Many who saw him enter and leave the Nomination Centre were full of sympathy for him. He even had to make way for the younger Mr Ong to walk out of the Conference Hall exit even though he was already at the door before Mr Ong. Much criticism was thrown at Mr Chua for his reluctance. Even the local press was brave enough to publish some angry letters in the Forum Page. One exasperated Singaporean blurted out:

> If Mr Chua is not convinced that he is better than Mr Ong, then how can the electorate be convinced enough to let him be President.... My message to Mr Chua is this. If you think you are the best person for the job, sell yourself to us. If not, pull out or the election will be a fruitless exercise.
>
> *Straits Times*, 4 August 1993

Even the people from the media were very upset. They finally succeeded in getting him to agree to a last-minute interview. They actually told him that he was duty bound to talk to the people of Singapore. He was told that he was doing an 'injustice' to the people. Some even asked him whether he was serious when he said that he was 'doing national service' when he agreed to be a challenger to Mr Ong. To be fair, we must remember that Mr Chua was never a politician. He could well have still been in too much of a state of shock to seriously contemplate a proper campaign strategy. Having seen how Mr Chua 'suffered', future challengers will know what to expect in the next round in 1999.

A MATTER VOTES: WHAT ARE THE PEOPLE VOTING FOR?

Now that the wheels had been set in motion, the government was anxious that there should be a proper contest, for much could be learnt and gained from this historic election. This was the first time that the whole voting population had to vote for a single candidate. A walkover would mean another six-year wait. A contest would focus voters on this new concept of having a universal franchise to elect the head of state. Of course, the election could also be used to gauge the ruling party's popularity at that point in time and to assess the sentiments on the ground, especially since there was an approved government candidate.

Originally, many people considered the presidential elections to be a non-event, a waste of time. Everyone expected a big victory for Mr Ong as he is well known and was a very popular PAP minister. It would therefore be logical to consider the votes cast in favour of his opponent as being anti-government votes. In fact, many observers believed that, had Mr Ong not been the candidate, the number of anti-government votes might have been more numerous. In other words, had the government's candidate been, say, a lesser-known or perhaps less affable minister, the results might have been totally different.

Before proceeding further, let us consider whether the results would have been different had there been a three-cornered fight? Would Mr Ong Teng Cheong still have retained the majority, leaving the other two candidates to share the remainder of the anti-government votes? There would also be a big possibility that Mr Ong might win the election without a clear cut majority (i.e. obtaining the highest absolute number of votes amongst the three candidates, but collecting under 50 per cent of the votes cast). Would such a win be good enough as a mandate? Would we accept a candidate who had only 30 per cent of the vote, as had President Roh Tae Woo in South Korea some years ago? One must not rule out the possibility that a more willing and truly independent candidate might actually end up winning the race. I think that that might well have happened.

Looking at the odds, a truly interested and qualified independent candidate would have a better chance of winning in a one-to-one fight. A three-cornered fight would have split the anti-government votes. What is perhaps more important is that a more enthusiastic and sincere campaign would have swung more votes to the independent candidate, thereby increasing his chances of pipping Mr Ong at the finish line. My own feeling is that had there been a three-cornered fight, Mr Ong would still have won, but with an even smaller majority than the one he obtained. Voters who were disappointed with Mr Chua's reluctance would have cast their votes for the third candidate. The sophistication of the voters can be discerned from the small number of spoilt votes – only slightly over 2 per cent – which is comparable to the figure chalked up in normal general elections.

The popular votes for the PAP in the last few general elections were:

Year   *PAP*
1980 – 75.5 per cent
1984 – 62.9 per cent
1988 – 61.8 per cent
1991 – 61.0 per cent

The government's popular vote has been dropping. If we take this presidential election as a barometer of the government's popularity, we can see a further drop of 2 per cent over the 1991 general election figure. This might have taken the government by surprise especially since the prime minister himself had just led his Marine Parade GRC to a resounding 75 per cent by-election victory in 1992.

The ruling party is privy to the votes cast by each electoral division and thus can gauge its own popularity. With such a close result, it is conceivable that there must have been many close shaves and even losses for the government-backed candidate in some polling stations. The ruling party may already be nursing the lost ground. The pattern of votes in the four opposition wards may also be indicative of what to expect in the next polls.

If one takes the actual votes cast in the 1991 general election and juxtaposes the results of the presidential elections, a 2 per cent downward swing for the PAP in all the single member constituencies and GRCs would have won the opposition several more seats in Parliament. The point is that for the national average to drop 2 per cent, the drop in many constituencies would have been much larger because the PAP strongholds would still carry and maintain their own percentages.

One other interesting point to consider is that, over the last two general elections, the 'better educated and more credible' opposition candidates have been gaining more votes than the national opposition average of about 40 per cent. This trend, coupled with the results of this presidential election, may encourage people of even better calibre to become opposition candidates. Another possible repercussion is that the outcome of the presidential elections may actually encourage good, well-intentioned individuals to stand as independents in the parliamentary elections. Mr Chua's proposition that he is independent of the PAP and good enough for the job can well be the argument for future independent candidates to campaign on. Many people may well vote for a good independent candidate during a general election, just to keep the PAP in check. Indeed, independents seem to have the upper hand here since they need not oppose for the sake of opposing, and therefore need not adopt a confrontational posture and are still able to play a constructive role. Independents may not be viewed as threats to the PAP government. Some may even see elected independents in a better position to play the non-partisan role of Nominated MPs. Elected independents would have the direct mandate of the voters.

THE ELECTED PRESIDENT AND THE BIGGER PICTURE

However we look at the outcome of the presidential election, we should remember that it is just another step in refining the constitution by Senior Minister Lee Kuan Yew. Having devoted a lifetime to building up Singapore, he is anxious to put in place the necessary 'instruments' to sustain Singapore's success.

To the senior minister, sensible voting must mean voting for the PAP, the good people who deliver the goods, the good people who keep their promises. When he first spoke about the weakness of the one-man-one-vote system in the aftermath of the December 1984 general election, he was visibly upset with the plunge in the PAP's popularity. It went down 13 per cent to 62.9 per cent. He indicated that he might need to alter the one-man-one-vote system because he did not want to see a freak election where irresponsible opposition candidates are elected to form the government. That would spell disaster for Singapore. During the 1984 elections, PAP ministers and MPs reasoned with voters, asking them not to act irrationally or impulsively by wasting their votes just because they were unhappy with some trivial petty local issues. They were asked to look at the big picture and swallow whatever bitter pills the ruling party might have to force down their throats for their own good. As it turned out, many voters thought otherwise. That, in Mr Lee's view, was a very dangerous trend for Singapore. If left unchecked, Singapore would soon be doomed. It was therefore necessary to fine-tune Singapore's political and constitutional system.

Many changes have been made since December 1984. Whatever reasons may be given for each change, one cannot help but sympathize with the opposition. The various changes made have served two important and conflicting functions. The first is to satisfy the growing desire of voters to have more opposition candidates; the second is to ensure that PAP rule is perpetuated. The first change to be introduced was the Non-Constituency Member of Parliament (NCMP) scheme. The Constitution was amended to allow for as many as six NCMPs who would be the best 'losers' in any general election. The message to the electorate was clear: vote for all PAP MPs and the PAP will in turn give the opposition some seats. Only Dr Lee Siew Choh of the Workers' Party agreed to take up the government's offer of an NCMP seat in the 1984–8 Parliament.

The Group Representation Constituencies (GRCs) were introduced in the 1988 general election. This scheme was meant to ensure that the minority races are assured of representation in Parliament. All constituencies are dominated by ethnic Chinese, and the PAP was concerned that if people voted along racial lines, none of the minority races would be elected into Parliament. This would be dangerous. The argument is a good one, but like most institutions, there is always room for abuse. The opposition parties considered it yet another ploy to make it even more difficult for them to enter Parliament since they had greater problems trying to recruit credible ethnic minority members.

The Nominated Member of Parliament (NMP) scheme was introduced in 1990. The Constitution allows for up to six NMPs who should be non-partisan people who can contribute to the well-being of Singapore through the parliamentary process. Again, the opposition saw this as a ploy to frustrate their chances. They perceived the NMPs' presence as adding pressure on their performance. If the NMPs performed well and overshadowed the opposition MPs, the scheme would satisfy the portion of the electorate who craved alternative viewpoints, and the opposition would lose more votes.

So far, the schemes have not always worked to the advantage of the ruling party. A loss in one GRC (now with four members) will mean a loss of four parliamentary seats. In the 1988 and 1991 general elections, the PAP almost lost Eunos GRC. Several other GRCs were also closely contested. NCMPs and NMPs under pressure to perform may indeed outdo even the PAP backbenchers and that may prove detrimental to their own credibility and that of the party.

CONCLUSION

Now that the elected president concept has been set in place, are we next to expect a change in the hallowed one-man-one-vote system? Since President Ong Teng Cheong's inauguration, Senior Minister Lee has, within a period of six months, spoken twice about the wisdom – his wisdom – of giving two votes to electors aged 35 to 60 years and who have families. He reasoned that younger voters are not mature enough and have less to lose in wasting their votes. The 35 to 60 age group have more to lose and have the future of their families to worry about, and thus act more rationally. On the other hand, those above 60 years of age might fall into the hands of politicians promising free handouts.

The slim overall margin and possible losses in more than four wards might trigger Senior Minister Lee into pushing for bigger changes more quickly. Already, several ministers, including Brigadier General George Yeo, have taken up the cudgels and spoken publicly about the perceived flaws of the present voting system, using negative examples in the West to support their arguments. The breakdown of voting patterns might suggest that the ruling party may not enjoy its two-thirds majority in Parliament for too long.

The government may continue to adopt ingenious ways to retain power, always working through the legislative process, and by constantly tinkering and amending the Constitution, making changes it considers will benefit Singapore. It may also continue to step up its efforts at 'wealth sharing schemes'. The government argues that their schemes to increase the wealth of the less fortunate are not subsidies. Subsidies suggest wasteful consumption. Any form of subsidy, once introduced into the welfare system, cannot easily be taken away without political costs being incurred. While the government may argue that all its 'give-aways' go towards increasing the wealth of the people, and that they are free to give more in good years and less or nothing in bad years, the practicalities are quite different. The government's assertion may ring true in the beginning, but like all incentive schemes, the motivational value drops after a while. More and bigger incentives are needed to satisfy the people. It is also difficult for the government to ensure that whatever 'wealth' has been given out stays with the people and is not squandered.

The poorer classes may need, for example, to sell off their Telecoms shares or their upgraded flats[1] to realize cash for consumption. The hard-headed government is in fact indirectly 'returning' some wealth to the people to meet the increased expectations. Take the upgrading programme for public housing, for example. The government had committed to spend over S$1 billion (US$715 million) each year for the next 10–15 years to upgrade the older public housing estates through retro-fitting and amenity enhancement. Apartments in upgraded estates fetch higher prices on the housing resale market. What is noteworthy is the way in which upgrading is carried out. While certain criteria have been established for selecting precincts for upgrading, Prime Minister Goh Chok Tong has said that all things being equal, it is the PAP wards which will be given priority for upgrading. His rationale was that if voters in a constituency voted for the ruling party, they had signalled that they endorsed the government's upgrading programme. By parity of reasoning, a failure to return the ruling party to that constituency can be read as the constituents' lack of enthusiasm about the government's programmes. Naturally, the opposition parties cried foul.

During a talk given by Senior Minister Lee Kuan Yew on 14 March 1996 to an audience of over 2,000 Singaporean undergraduates, a student asked if linking the public housing programme to votes was not 'money politics'. Lee's reply was:

If you can point to any single cent that a minister has gained by it, then I will say, yes, it is money politics in the sense the term is used in the popular press; in other words, you get a personal advantage out of it. But using public revenue for policies which bring you votes: that is the whole essence of politics.

Not wanting to be left out, residents in the private estates, especially the older ones, were also pressuring the government to include their estates in the upgrading programme. Some of them even bluntly reminded the government that they, too, were tax payers and that they also carried votes. The government is said to be giving serious thought to their demands. Pressures such as these are likely to arise from other sectors of the populace.

The president's role must be to ensure that none of these 'give-aways' eat into the government's reserve and that future governments are not committed to heavy financial burdens and debts. A credible opposition may also ride on the same horse and make wonderful promises to get itself voted in. If we consider the trend of decline in the government's popularity over the last few elections, it is possible that a credible opposition may wrestle power from the PAP ten years down the road. By then, all the founding members of the PAP would have left the political arena and will thus no longer be able to direct and hold the party together. The political scene will be totally different. I think that when this happens, there will be more willing challengers for the post of elected president, especially when the president's role becomes clearer and more meaningful.

NOTE

1 Singapore Telecoms was the first government department to be privatized. Shares of the newly listed public company were offered to Singapore citizens at a special discount. The Government declared that this was a means for the people to have a share in the nation's wealth, especially when the prices of these shares soar over the long term. Another major 'wealth-sharing' exercise has been the upgrading of older Housing and Development Board estates. The extent of the upgrades varies from renovations of lift-lobbies and reception areas to the construction of an additional utility room. Naturally, the upgraded flats are valued far higher than conventional flats.

9 The elected presidency

Towards the twenty-first century

Lam Peng Er

In the late 1980s, few political scientists correctly predicted the sudden collapse of the East European Marxist regimes, the demise of the Soviet Union and the Cold War structure; nor indeed did anyone anticipate the end of the one-party dominant systems of Italy and Japan.[1] Within the domestic political scene of Singapore, no one anticipated the illness of Brigadier General Lee Hsien Loong, heir apparent to Premier Goh Chok Tong, which resulted in greater uncertainties in Singapore's political succession. Such a sudden turn of events poignantly highlights the limitations or even the futility of anticipation. Paul Kennedy cautions:

> [W]ritings upon how the present may evolve into the future, even if they discuss trends that are already underway, can lay no claims to being historical truth. Not only do the raw materials change, from archivally based monographs to economic *forecasts* and political *projections*, but the validity of what is being written about can no longer be assumed. . . . Unforeseen happenings, sheer accidents, the halting of a trend, can ruin the most plausible of forecasts; if they do not, then the forecaster is merely lucky.[2]

Alvin Toffler, who made his reputation anticipating the future, writes: 'The sole certainty is that tomorrow will surprise us all'.[3] However Toffler points out:

> It seems hardly necessary to add that the future is not 'knowledge-able' in the sense of exact prediction. Life is filled with surrealistic surprises. . . . Nevertheless, as we advance into the terra incognita of tomorrow, it is better to have a general and incomplete map, subject to revision and correction, than to have no map at all.[4]

This chapter does not *forecast* the impact of the elected presidency (EP) on Singapore politics towards the twenty-first century. Rather it examines a number of hypothetical scenarios which focus on the EP interacting with other political actors in Singapore's political system. It is impossible to anticipate the personalities and the behaviour of future key political office bearers, the introduction of new political rules and institutions or the modification of existing ones, the sizzling issues of the day, the health of the global and domestic economy, and the strategic balance in the region. The unpredictable nexus of these internal and external factors may compel or deter a future president from casting a veto to prevent the government of the day from dipping into the national reserves to pay for its programmes.

This chapter makes the following propositions. First, the PAP was not oblivious to other scenarios that differed from their official rationale for the EP proposal: a 'responsible' EP checking an 'irresponsible' government. The PAP publicly canvassed other permutations concerning the power relationship between the EP and the government. Apparently, the ruling party went ahead because its anxiety in checking a roguish government via the EP outweighed the dangers of an incompetent president[5] who might paralyse the government through his wide-ranging blocking powers over the budget, appointments and detentions. Second, even in the 'best scenario' where both president and PM are 'responsible' office bearers, there is still room for conflict and a possibility of a gridlock. If conflict arises even in the most unlikely case, it may be due to fundamental differences in political judgment and philosophy rather than the key actors' lack of virtue and sincerity. Third, if the EP's ultimate powers are activated at all, it is likely to occur only in the post-Lee Kuan Yew era.

POWER MATRIX: PRESIDENT AND CABINET

Four plausible, alternative scenarios (Figure 9.1) may arise when the president interacts with the prime minister (PM) and his cabinet. Some of these scenarios and their variations were canvassed by the ruling party, the opposition parties, the press and informed public opinion.[6] They are:

1 *PAP's Scenario*: A 'responsible' president checking an 'irresponsible' government by safeguarding the national reserves, maintaining the integrity of key civil and military appointments, and preventing arbitrary arrests of citizens on the pretext of curbing ethnic and religious chauvinism.

	Good Cabinet	Bad Cabinet
Bad President	Opposition scenario	Worst scenario
Good President	Best scenario	PAP scenario

Figure 9.1 Typology of power relations between the EP and the PM

2 *Opposition Parties' Scenario*: An opportunistic and vindictive pro-PAP president bent on sabotaging a new government formed by non-PAP party or parties.[7] The discrediting of the new government will then result in the PAP regaining power in the next election.

3 *Best Scenario*: A felicitous state of affairs where Singapore is doubly blessed by the presence of a 'good' president and a 'good' PM. Since the president has no need to intervene and exercise his veto against a good and responsible government, the president will keep a low profile politically and essentially perform a ceremonial role. The EP will continue to act as a sentinel but his presidential veto will not be activated. According to one account, the 'best case scenario (is) that of a competent, dedicated government and a strong benign president who would not check the government as there was no need to'.[8] However such an interpretation simplistically assumes that there is no room for serious conflict between the two offices in the 'best scenario'.

4 *Worst Scenario*: A double jeopardy when a 'bad' president and a 'bad' PM collide or collude, thereby spelling disaster for the country. Three possible sub-plots emerge:

i   The belligerent office bearers from rival parties are unable to transcend their partisan and parochial interests, and forge a bipartisan compromise to resolve their differences. An imperfect example was the Mitterrand presidency, which was supported by the French Socialist Party, and 'cohabitating' with a government led by right-wing parties. Even if both camps were to tacitly observe a political armistice, major policy initiatives may flounder due to a lack of political consensus.

ii Both contentious office bearers come from warring factions of the same party.[9] The executives represent competing factions that may be divided by policies, personalities, power and patronage. In the case of Japan, the intense rivalry between factions of the ruling Liberal Democratic Party (LDP)[10] was often fiercer than the competition between the LDP and the opposition parties. Important party and cabinet posts were parcelled out between the factions. In 1993, the Ozawa-Hata group from the Takeshita faction within the LDP bolted and formed the Japan Renewal Party (*Shinseito*). The JRP then forged a coalition with other opposition parties and toppled the LDP from power.

Similarly in Singapore, one faction from the ruling party may bolt and become a challenger with a new party label. The ertswhile allies may separately capture the government and the presidency resulting in a political stalemate. There is a precedent in Singapore when the PAP suffered a schism. In 1961 the left-wing faction of the PAP defected and formed the Barisan Sosialis Party. The breakaway party posed a formidable challenge to the PAP until the renegades erroneously boycotted the 1968 general election and eventually faded from the political scene. Even if factions within a ruling party do not break away and mount an open electoral challenge under a different party label, the capturing of the presidency and other political posts by rival factions may lead to political instability.

iii Both venal office bearers come from the same political party, and are in cohoots with each other to loot the national reserves.[11] If the EP and the PM came from the same party, the checks and balances may not work, especially when the EP does not cut his emotional, ideological and financial ties to his former party. One requisite for holding the office of the EP is to surrender any prior party affiliation to avoid political partisanship but this requirement does not prevent the EP from retaining informal ties with his old party. While the constitution provides for a collision between the the EP and the cabinet, there are no provisions to deal with a collusion between a venal EP and a corrupt cabinet commanding a parliamentary majority.

The PAP also examined the 'good president, bad government' scenario with a twist. Premier Goh cautioned citizens not to recklessly vote 'irresponsible' parties into power simply because the country is assured of an institutional safeguard, the EP, to check a 'bad' goverment. He argued:

> Singaporeans should not now assume they can be freer with their votes and just return any government because there is a 'goalkeeper' in the system. The EP can only prevent the reserve from being drawn down and from appointing the wrong people to key jobs, but there are many ways to bankrupt a country, and the EP must not be seen as a safety net.[12]

Indeed, if such an event took place, the EP scheme would have backfired. In a somewhat bizarre manner, the EP would then have led to the very scenario the framers of the scheme strove so hard to avoid in the first place. In the very attempt to contain a 'bad government', it would instead have facilitated it. This would be a tragic self-fulfilling prophesy.

Goh also pondered over other potential outcomes:

> When you have a good government and a good president, then there is a safeguard for the system. . . . But if you have a bad government, a good president, that is only half a safeguard. If you have a bad government and a bad president, I think everything is gone for the country. So my advice is: settle for the best, both in government, as well as in the presidency.[13]

Apparently, the scenario of a 'bad president and a good government' was absent from Goh's public statements. Certainly, it would have been a poor public relations exercise to sell the new institution to Singaporeans by presenting such a scenario. By examining alternative outcomes, the ruling party is clearly aware that institutionalizing the EP may possibly open a Pandora's box. That the party insists on implementing the EP despite potential political pitfalls suggests that its leadership is convinced that the dangers of an incompetent and dishonest government is more real than the intellectual constructs of other theoretical outcomes.

THE LEE ERA AND THE EP

None of the four hypothetical cases above are likely to take place in the short term. First, presidential powers will probably remain dormant because the opposition parties, being chronically devoid of resources, organization, manpower, attractive leadership, mobilizing ideas and party unity, are not in a position to capture power. The Singapore Democratic Party (SDP) is in the midst of a fratricide, with the warring factions concentrating their energy on discrediting each other rather than forming a united front against the PAP government.[14] The profound weaknesses of the opposition parties make it virtually impossible for them to replace the PAP.

To reap the maximum number of protest votes, the opposition parties may opt for an electoral strategy of treating general elections as 'by-elections'. With this approach, the opposition parties concede half of the electoral seats to the PAP by not contesting these electoral districts. Therefore, the PAP is certain of forming a majority government and remaining in power even before polling day. First adopted in the 1991 general elections, the opposition parties shrewdly offered voters the 'best of both worlds' – the guarantee of a PAP government with a proven track record, and an opposition party or parties that will check the ruling party.[15] Assured that a 'freak' election (with the PAP ousted from power) will not occur, voters are more willing to vote for the opposition. By conceding a general election to the PAP right at the outset, the opposition removed the hypothetical possibility of a 'freak' election, the very rationale the ruling party used to justify the introduction of the EP. If the opposition parties continue to adhere to this 'by-election' approach leading to the concomittant absence of a 'freak' election, the EP's full extent of powers are unlikely to be activated.

Second, Senior Minister Lee continues to retain substantial influence in Singapore's political system. Although not directly involved in the day-to-day running of the government, Lee sits in cabinet meetings, dispenses advice to his protégés, receives prominent coverage in the local mass media, and even proposes further constitutional changes to Singapore's 'one-man-one-vote' system.[16] Goh gave a 'rare glimpse' into the relationship between Lee and the cabinet after Lee stepped down from the premiership. Goh said:

> Senior Minister Lee Kuan Yew still wields 'tremendous influence' over the government, but this does not mean that he tries to impose his views on the younger leaders. He has tremendous influence... on my thinking and my policies. I have worked with him for many years and I am not ashamed to say that I am a great admirer of him.[17]

Goh also made a tongue-in-cheek comment in the same session: 'He could probably outrun all of us in the Cabinet, perhaps with the exception of his son (Brigadier General Lee)'.[18]

On another occasion, Prime Minister Goh was asked if he was bothered by the perception that Lee was 'still running the show' as long as he remained in the Cabinet. Goh replied:

It doesn't bother me. He has a great deal of influence on me and on the other Cabinet ministers. . . . I have said openly that I would be very stupid not to use the man's wise counsel and ability to help me govern.[19]

When asked whether he envisaged having Lee in the Cabinet for some time, Goh replied: 'Yes, for quite some time'.[20] Lee has also defined his present role:

I am kind of a 12th man in an 11-man team. I don't do the job of administering the government. The Prime Minister gets me to do long-range thinking on future problems.[21]

The government's White Paper on the EP gave the analogy of a two-key safeguard mechanism: the PM would hold one key while the EP held the other.[22] In reality, Lee was the locksmith while President Ong and Premier Goh remain his political apprentices holding the keys. Since the present elected president and prime minister were 'socialized' by Lee and they share common experiences and values, they are highly unlikely to have serious disagreements, at least not serious enough to trigger the presidential veto. Given the continued presence of Senior Minister Lee, hypothetical PAP factional disputes, with one group occupying the premiership while another captures the EP, are improbable.

Political entrepreneurs aspiring to join political parties or form new ones will probably lie low until Lee departs from the political arena. The formidable presence of Singapore's Founding Father, and the high cost of joining opposition politics act as a deterrent to potential politicians outside the PAP fold from participating in politics. In the short term, the EP's ultimate powers will not be tested since it is almost impossible for the government to be captured by non-PAP elements.

Third, the international environment seems benign in the short term. The US continues to underpin East Asia's strategic balance by maintaining its military presence in South Korea and Japan; larger regional powers, especially China, India, Japan and Vietnam, are engaged in economic pursuits rather than military adventures and the international trading system remains relatively open. ASEAN (Association of South East Asian Nations), which includes Singapore, has thus far credibly and successfully harmonized the interests of member states despite lingering territorial disputes and differing national interests. The institutionalizing of the ASEAN Regional Forum and other confidence-building measures in the post-Cold War era encourage countries in the Asia-Pacific region to develop a habit of constructive multilateral consultation and diplomacy rather than to resort to arms to settle international disputes. Other multilateral economic organizations, especially APEC (Asia-Pacific Economic Cooperation), enhance free trade and regional growth. These are conditions that favour Singapore as a small trading state. Thus there is presently little economic and geo-political pressure on Singapore to adopt Keynesian pump-priming measures and heavy armaments programmes measures that will draw upon its national reserves, and arouse the scrutiny of the EP.

Taking advantage of a favourable trading and strategically stable environment, Singapore is poised to be a developed economy by the end of this century. In 1988, the then Minister of Trade and Industry Brigadier General Lee Hsien Loong made a bold long-term forecast:

> What will the economy be like in 1999? We have forecast growth of 4 to 6 per cent growth per year. Suppose we make the middle estimate 5 per cent, then our GDP will be 70 per cent higher than today. We will be a developed economy.... [The government] has been extremely prudent – some would say even parsimonous – in spending public money, so that each year there has been a budget surplus, and because of rapid growth, tax revenues have increased.[23]

Thus far Lee's rosy prognosis appears to be on course. Other analysts are also bullish about Singapore's potential for sustained economic growth.[24] The Economist Intelligence Unit projected that Singapore will enjoy a 7.9 per cent GDP growth over the previous year by 1998 (see Table 9.1). According to the Monetary Authority of Singapore, the country's de facto central bank, Singapore's potential output is expected to grow at 6–7 per cent per annum for the 1994–8 period.[25] If these short-term forecasts hit the mark, and with no visible economic or strategic threats on the horizon, the government will be assured of increasing tax revenues and need not dip into the reserves accumulated by the previous government. In these circumstances, the president will not be required to exercise his veto power.

THE POST-LEE ERA

If Lee remains intellectually sharp and in robust health for the next 10 to 15 years, he is likely to remain politically influential even if he were to surrender the last political posts he still retains.[26] Despite persistent speculation that he may seek the office of the EP sometime in the future,[27] Lee has publicly declared that he does not need to become the president to maintain his political viability. Being the charismatic

Table 9.1 Projected GDP growth, 1993–8

	Year					
	1993	1994	1995	1996	1997	1998
GDP growth (per cent)	9.8	7.3	7.3	7.5	7.7	7.9

Source: Economist Intelligence Unit, *Country Forecast: Singapore, First Quarter 1994*, pp. 3, 6–7

Founding Father with a domineering personality, he will make his presence felt, with or without formal political office, including that of the EP. It is uncharacteristic of him to stay as a bystander if his handicraft, a carefully calibrated, meritocratic socio-political system based on rewards and punishments, starts to unravel.

Lee, in his 1988 National Day Rally address, candidly expressed his resolve not to retire from politics even after stepping down from the premiership. Morever he remarked that he need not become president to remain influential. The following quote from the *Straits Times* coverage of his oration is as instructive as it is macabre:

> Mr Lee said that as a member of 'that exclusive club of founding members of new countries, first Prime Ministers or Presidents', he could not disengage himself from Singapore. 'Even from my sick bed, even if you are going to lower me into the grave and I feel that something is going wrong, I will get up. Those who believe that when I have gone into permanent retirement, really should have their heads examined', he said to loud applause from the audience. . . . Mr Lee made these remarks when he spoke of the proposal to have an elected president who would safeguard the nation's reserves and the integrity of the public service. Referring to talk that he intended becoming president, Mr Lee said to some laughter from his audience: 'I don't have to be president and I am not looking for a job. Please believe me.'[28]

While the veto powers of the EP will probably not be activated in the short run, certain convergence of domestic and international developments may trigger the blocking mechanisms in the post-Lee era.[29] The post-Lee period is not a complete enigma. By definition, Lee would have made his exit from the political stage ushering in a new epoch in Singapore politics. His political apprentices would be truly on their own for the first time. They may be challenged by counter-elites emboldened by Lee's departure; they have to strike a consensus as to whether or not greater political liberalization (a 'kinder and gentler' form of PAP government and greater space and autonomy to civil society) can be permitted without leading to political instability.

Table 9.2 Affluence and creature comforts of Singaporeans, 1973–92

Items per household	1973	1978	1983	1988	1992
Fridge	47.3	87.6	96.1	98.3	97.8
Washing machine	1.8	15.0	46.8	73.5	80.5
Air-conditioner	2.7	7.8	11.2	19.4	35.3
Television	49.0	86.9	95.2	97.9	97.5
Video cassette recorder	n.a.	n.a.	27.7	71.0	75.1
Piano, Organ	n.a.	n.a.	9.8	11.4	11.8
Personal computer	n.a.	n.a.	n.a.	11.2	20.2
Car	17.0	23.8	25.5	29.8	31.1

Source: Department of Statistics, *Singapore 1992: Statistics Highlights*, March 1993, p. 33

If present trends continue to hold, Singapore will become a very affluent society (see Table 9.2); the bulk of its population will enjoy high levels of education (Table 9.3)[30] and income. According to the 1995 World Bank Atlas, Singapore was the 18th richest country in the world in 1994 in terms of per capita GNP. By purchasing power, Singapore was ranked ninth in the same survey. Thus Singapore has moved ahead of her former colonial master, Britain, in these measurements of economic wealth (Tables 9.4 and 9.5). Increasing numbers of the electorate will probably be more demanding: voters will desire greater consultation by the government and will have more diverse and higher expectations to be met. Once the basic problems of food, shelter and employment are solved, there is the tendency especially for those with the resources of income, education and leisure to aspire for non-materialistic issues like self-actualization, concern for the ecology, a greater appreciation for aesthetics, and political participation.[31] These voters will have a greater sense of political efficacy. Some of these tendencies are already visible in the present electorate and will be even more pronounced in the next quarter of a century.

Political scientist Chan Heng Chee anticipates the following trend in Singapore:

A new and younger generation of voters is less inclined to accept the political leadership at face value. The strategic strata of the middle bureaucrats, students, and academics... are definitely expanding, and are searching for a more open, and democratic political system.[32]

Goh, in his long-term projections of various social and political trends in Singapore, noted that:

Singaporeans were becoming better educated, with 20 per cent of each cohort making it to the university and 40 per cent to the polytechnic. As a result, their needs and expectations would change. They would be more questioning, and would want to participate more in discussion and be reasoned with.[33]

Table 9.3 Education of subsequent age cohort in Singapore

	Entry ratio	
	Polytechnic	University
Year	Per cent of Primary One cohort	
1982	11	7
1983	14	8
1984	14	8
1985	15	9
1986	15	10
1987	17	12
1988	16	14
1989	18	15
1990	20	15
1991	24	14
1992	29	16

Source: Department of Statistics, *Singapore 1992, Statistics Highlights*, March 1993, p. 35. Table 4: Affluent Countries and GNP Per Capita

Dr Tony Tan, the chairman of the PAP, also noted these sociological changes in Singapore society, and warned the party to adapt and 'be alert to dangers of political sclerosis'.[34] Below is the *Straits Times* coverage of his speech to party members:

The People's Action Party must reflect the mood of the times or risk developing 'political sclerosis' and being left behind by a younger electorate... He noted that any political party which had been in power for a long time faced the danger of complacency.

The party's thinking, its policies and responses become fossilized and do not change to reflect the mood of the times.

'If we are not alert to this danger, we will wake up one day to find that we have been left behind by a younger electorate whose aspirations and aims are different from those of the party', he said.

In the post-Lee era, the question remains whether the PAP will remain

Table 9.4 Affluent countries and GNP per capita

Country	GNP per capita (US$)
1. Switzerland	36,410
2. Luxembourg	35,850
3. Japan	31,450
4. Denmark	26,510
5. Norway	26,340
6. Sweden	24,830
7. United States	24,750
8. Iceland	23,620
9. Germany	23,560
10. Kuwait	23,350
11. Austria	23,120
12. United Arab Emirates	22,470
13. France	22,360
14. Belgium	21,210
15. Netherlands	20,710
16. Canada	20,670
17. Italy	19,620
18. **Singapore**	**19,310**
19. Finland	18,970
20. Britain	17,970

Source: *World Bank Atlas* in *Straits Times*, 14 January 1995

cohesive, avoiding polarization, and with personalities engaging in power struggle. This competition for power may be intertwined with ideological disputes over continued authoritarianism or greater political liberalization. Also uncertain will be the international environment in the long run. Will there be a relatively open global trading regime and regional strategic stability? An unfortunate convergence of unfavourable domestic and international trends may force a future government to dip into the reserves, thereby activating the EP's checking mechanism.

Despite various imponderables, some analysts are optimistic about Singapore's long-term future. Paul Kennedy writes: 'Barring a war in East Asia or a massive global slump, the signs are that the four 'tigers' (Singapore, Hong Kong, South Korea and Taiwan) are better structured than most to grow in wealth and health'.[35] It is conceivable that the first quarter of the next century will be the dawn of the 'Pacific Century'.

According to this sanguine outlook, Marxist and Socialist regimes like China, Vietnam and Myanmar will be peacefully integrated into the regional political and economic framework leading to a virtuous

Table 9.5 Affluent countries by purchasing power

Country	Purchasing power per person (US$)
1. Luxembourg	29,510
2. United States	24,750
3. Switzerland	23,620
4. United Arab Emirates	23,390
5. Qatar	22,910
6. Hong Kong	21,670
7. Japan	21,090
8. Germany	20,980
9. **Singapore**	**20,470**
10. Canada	20,410
11. France	19,440
12. Norway	19,130
13. Denmark	18,940
14. Austria	18,800
15. Australia	18,490
15. Belgium	18,490
17. Italy	18,070
18. Netherlands	18,050
19. Britain	17,750
20. Sweden	17,560

Source: World Bank Atlas in *Straits Times,* 14 January 1995

circle of growth, mutual confidence building measures and peace; the freezing of regional hotspots such as disputed sovereignty over the Spratly Islands in the South China Sea[36] by claimant states; non-violent unification of the Koreas, and Japan remaining as a merchant rather than a *samurai* state.[37]

In the pessimistic scenario,[38] the region will be less than 'pacific' in the next century. The US–Japan Security Alliance unravels, undermined by persistent trade conflict, and lack of a common enemy for the erstwhile partners after the demise of the USSR. The US retreats to neo-isolationism, Japan and Korea adopt nuclear weapons, China and India acquire blue water naval fleets to project their power in the region. ASEAN is enfeebled by bickering member states that are unable and unwilling to reconcile their differences. This chain of events sparks off a vicious circle of a regional arms race. Strategic insecurity and uncertainty coinciding with the strengthening of regional trading blocs leading to heightened protectionism, trade wars and a global depression.

Acutely sensitive to Singapore's vulnerability to shifts in the international and regional environment, PAP leaders anticipate problems long before they appear on the horizon. Moreover, Singapore's one party dominant system has permitted the ruling party not to be overly distracted by the weak opposition. Thus the ruling party has the luxury to engage in long-term projections rather than constricted by election cycles of four to five years. Goh in his analysis of the future, speculatively considered the scenario that 'regional instability threatens to undermine Singapore's internal ethnic balance, particularly between the Malays and the Chinese'.[39] Lee in his last National Day Rally speech in 1990 as the PM warned:

> As I went through these 25th Anniversary celebrations, I had a sense of the unreal. You know, we are generating so much euphoria, optimism. Is it justified? Yes, we have done well, 25 years. Next 25 years can be a very different and a very unpleasant world.... Without security, without an international order, which means somebody maintaining the peace, the world cannot progress. It may be towards the next century, some limited form of international government, limited international policing is necessary, and I hope it comes about, through the UN and the Security Council. But for the time being...the United States has to take the role....Pax Britannica lasted over 120 years....After that the Americans took over. So the Americans have done it for 45 years. Can they do it for another 45? I have my reservations. Not that they lack the will. Their resources? Can they do it for another 20 years? I asked some American leaders, including the top military men, they said: 'Well, possible'. Ten years, they are confident...but 20 years, next generation of weapons – that's big expenditure. In other words, the future is going to be a very problematic one without some Pax UN or Pax America amended, hyphen Japan, hyphen EC, hyphen Soviet Union maybe, or the Russian Republic. Some such Pax must be established or you will have international lawlessness. As the Chinese saying goes, '*Dayu chi xiaoyu, xiaoyu chi xiami*' – big fish eat small fish, small fish eat shrimps. So we say, well, we become tadpoles. That is really the crux of life for Singapore.

If this bleak and threatening scenario were to emerge, the Singapore government would have to decide on the level of spending to boost military defence to maintain a credible deterrent, and to avoid massive domestic unemployment and social dislocation.[40] The government must contend with a more pluralistic and demanding electorate. Under such tremendous pressure, the government will be forced to use the national reserves. However, the president may exercise his veto because, in his political judgment, more money for armaments may result in greater insecurity if it precipitates a further regional arms race; more resources for temporary jobs creation are wasteful bcause the fundamental factors of Singapore's economic recession are not resolved.

Under the new 1994 constitutional amendments of the presidency, the EP no longer has the power to veto defence spending on specific items. However, the EP can indirectly influence the level of defence spendings because he can still veto the annual budget. Defence spending constitutes a substantial portion of the yearly budget allocation. Lee gave the following explanation:

> [A]lthough the president would not veto individual defence and security transactions, he retained the right to veto the Defence Ministry's annual budget.
>
> So the president could not stop the government from buying, say, 20 aeroplanes if it wanted to. But this was not the only door which had to be unlocked to spend the money.
>
> At the end of the year, when you budget to pay for the aeroplanes, he can say, your budget doesn't pass, make sure you cut some other item of expenditure in order that you have a balanced budget, and then I will approve it. So there still remains a check.[41]

It is possible even for a 'responsible' government and 'responsible' EP to head towards a constitutional and political showdown, not because either party is corrupt, but each side has a different conception of the national interest. Thus the crisis is precipitated by a clash of judgments rather than a lack of sincerity on the part of the EP and PM. The *Straits Times* reported:

> A difference of judgment between the elected president and the Cabinet in times of crisis could prove the undoing of Singapore, warned Dr Ong Chit Chung (PAP MP, Bukit Batok). 'I am a bit uneasy about the elected president's power to go against the advice of the Cabinet and withhold consent for the declaration of a state of emergency', he said. It would not merely be a matter of a constitutional showdown, but could be a matter of life and death for Singapore and its people.[42]

However, another view naively believes that differences over political judgment are not intractable so long as the EP is sincere.

> We do agree that different individuals will come up with different judgments. But assuming that the elected president has the country's

interests at heart...then the second judgment should be based on the merits and demerits of the programme and not whether it had been suggested by another party.[43]

The potential problem is not necessarily a question of the EP's sincerity but the issue of political judgment. Different leaders may hold different conceptions of what constitutes the national interest.

EPILOGUE

Therefore, even in the 'best' scenario, there is still room for conflict. The clash between a 'good' EP and a 'good' government may result from different judgments, political and economic philosophies, and temperament rather than a malevolent desire for political vendetta or greed. Such a scenario is but one out of many possibilities (some are benign, others are not) which may not even be presently imaginable. Will a Ross Perot-like demagogue, with all the pre-qualifications of a businessman heading a $100-million corporation arise as a presidential challenger in Singapore? Will a PAP government unexpectedly find itself 'cohabiting' with a non-PAP president when voters want to retain a good PAP government but subject it to checks from a credible candidate with no prior PAP affiliations? Will the EP and PM be mobilizing public opinion or even mass demonstrations, seeking allies in the civil service and the military, manipulating the mass media to break a political impasse rather than engaging in quiet negotiation and compromise? Will there be further constitutional improvization to the office of the EP when unexpected problems crop up? Will the cabinet try to circumvent the EP's veto by selling state assets like land, and the privatization of public utilities and other government-linked enterprises to raise funds to pay for its programmes? Will there be a situation where three or more qualified candidates split the votes in a hotly contested presidential election? If the winner were to gain victory with less than half of the popular votes, will the EP have the moral mandate to stand up to a ruling party with a strong majority in parliament? These are questions which can be answered only by the passage of time.

If the EP mechanism were to work smoothly in the future, it would affirm Lee's prescient ability and sagacity to envision problems long before they arise. The EP would then be his institutional legacy of promoting honesty in government by subjecting it to checks from a pre-qualified EP armed with a national mandate. Yet the anxiety remains that a paralyzing institution might have been unwittingly created. In the midst of a national or regional crisis, the political system may come under severe stress due to the strife between the elected president and the prime minister, who have differing conceptions of what constitutes the national interest. The fate of Singapore will then hang in the balance.

NOTES

1 Although the one party dominant systems of Italy and Japan seemed set to rule for 'half an eternity', the 'unthinkable' happened. Interestingly, Singapore also has a one party dominant system: the PAP as a perennial ruling party and permanent opposition parties that compete in periodic elections. For various examples of a one party dominant system as a type of democracy, see T. J. Pempel, *Uncommon Democracies: the One-Party Dominant Regimes* (Ithaca, NY and London: Cornell University Press, 1990).

2 Paul Kennedy, *The Rise and Fall of the Great Powers: Economic Change and Military Conflict from 1500 to 2000* (New York: Random House, 1987): 438.

3 Alvin Toffler, *Power Shift: Knowlege, Wealth, and Violence at the Edge of the 21st Century* (New York: Bantam Books, 1990): 466.

4 *Ibid.*: preface xx.

5 By imposing extremely stringent conditions which a presidential candidate must meet before he is eligible to run for elections, the ruling party tries to 'pre-qualify' and weed out 'incompetent' candidates. This is perhaps a reason why the PAP is not too perturbed by the theoretical possibility of an incompetent president emerging. However, technical and financial competence which a candidate needs to act as a sentinel over the national reserves is not identical to political competence. The latter requires political leadership, skill and judgment, attributes which cannot be guaranteed by the pre-selection of candidates.

6 Variations of these four scenarios were posited in the press. See *Straits Times*, 13 August 1988.

7 Such a perception is not limited to the opposition parties but is also subscribed by some academics. See for example, James Cotton, 'Political Innovation on Singapore: the Presidency, the Leadership and the Party', in Garry Rodan (ed.) *Singapore Changes Guard: Social, Political And Economic Directions in the 1990s* (New York: St. Martin's Press, 1993), Garry Rodan, 'Preserving the One-Party State in Contemporary Singapore', in Kevin Hewison, Richard Robinson and Garry Rodan (eds) *Southeast Asia In the 1990s* (St Leonards, NSW: Allen & Unwin, 1993) and Lily Rahim, 'Singapore: Consent, Coercion and Constitutional Engineering', *Current Affairs Bulletin*, Vol. 70, No. 7, December 1993/ January 1994.

A characteristic statement from the opposition parties was made by Non-Elected MP Lee Siew Choh who argued that: 'the Elected Presidency was really the PAP's way of preparing itself against a freak election result which might lead to it being voted out of the government. The PAP... was fearful of losing its majority in Parliament or of having an opposition-controlled Parliament'. See *Straits Times*, 4 January 1991. The opposition's suspicions were not allayed by earlier statements by the then Senior Minister (Prime Minister's Office) S. Rajaratnam who said: 'The new President would have the right to veto legislation to safeguard the country's vast financial reserves, including domestic savings and pension funds, in the event that the present PAP govenment was overthrown or become decadent'. See *Straits Times*, 23 July 1988.

8 *Straits Times*, 13 August 1988.

9 Prime Minister Goh, in an attempt to forecast the future, painted the possibility, albeit theoretical, that the ruling party breaks up into factions. See *Straits Times*, 30 November 1991.

10 Except for a haitus between August 1993 and June 1994 the LDP has been the ruling party of Japan since 1955.

11 For Scenario 4c, see *Straits Times*, 9 August 1988.

12 *Business Times*, 4 January 1991.

13 *Straits Times*, 4 January 1991.

14 On the SDP's self-destruction, see Hussin Mutalib, 'Singapore in 1993: Unresolved Agendas in an Eventful Year', *Asian Survey*, Vol. XXXIV, No. 2, February 1994: 129. The battle lines are drawn between Chiam See Tong, the founder of the SDP, and most of his erstswhile comrades in the party's Central Executive Committee.

15 Chiam See Tong said: 'With the PAP secure in power, voters will feel at ease to show more support for an opposition to check the ruling party in parliament'. See *Business Times*, 17–18 August 1991. See also *Straits Times*, 22 August 1991, which reported:

Nominations for the August 31 general elections closed yesterday. [The PAP] was declared winner in 41 of the 81 seats to be contested, the minimum number of walkovers it needed to form the next government. This is the first time since 1968 that Singaporeans know for sure that the PAP will form the government even before they cast their votes.

16 S. M. Lee proposed that those between ages 35 and 60 who are married with children be given an additional vote because they are more 'responsible' with a greater stake in the system. See *Straits Times*, May 1994. See also Lee's comments on the 'some men, two votes' system in Fareed Zakaria, 'Culture is Destiny: a Conversation with Lee Kuan Yew', *Foreign Affairs*, Vol. 72, No. 2, 1994.

17 *Straits Times*, 5 August 1991.

18 *Ibid.*

19 *Straits Times*, 5 December 1992.

20 *Ibid.*

21 *Straits Times*, 17 September 1994.

22 See for example *Straits Times*, 30 December 1991.

23 Lee Hsien Loong, 'The Singapore Economy Into the 1990s', Speech delivered at the Master of Business Administration Club, NUS, 12 February 1988.

24 See for example, Helen Hughes, 'Growth of Singapore: an External View', Working Paper No. 91/13, 1991, National Centre for Development Studies, Research School of Pacific Studies, the Australian National University.

25 *Straits Times*, 4 July 1994.

26 Lee's role is to be 'busy looking after the "long-term" challenges facing Singapore'. Lee said: 'I could run a multinational or go back to law, but I really think I can make a better contribution in government, planning for the long-term'. *Straits Times*, 12 October 1992.

27 The media reported: 'Names that have cropped up as likely presidential candidates include Senior Minister Lee Kwan Yew, Finance Minister Richard Hu and Chief Justice Yong Pung How. But Mr Lee has repeatedly said that he will not be the first elected president'. *Business Times*, 1 June 1993.

28 *Straits Times*, 15 August 1988.

29 It is obvious no one can accurately predict when the post-Lee era will begin. In this essay, the time frame of the post-Lee era is limited to the first quarter of the twenty-first century. Recent future-orientated books by Paul Kennedy and Alvin Toffler have limited their analyses to the next quarter of a century because speculation beyond that time frame is likely to become highly fantastical. Nevertheless, we ought to be reminded that one year and even one day can sometimes be a long time in politics. See Kennedy, *Preparing for the Twenty-First Century*: 19 and Toffler, *Power Shift*, Preface: xix.

30 Moreover, overseas universities, especially from the West, provide the training of a third of the Singaporeans pursuing university education. Some of them return home imbued with more 'liberal' political ideas. For these statistics, see Department of Statistics, Census of Population Office, *Singapore Census of Population 1990: Literacy, Languages Spoken and Education*: 10.

31 This argument can be traced to Maslow's Hierarchy of Needs or even the Biblical saying 'Man does not live by bread alone'. See Abraham Maslow, *Motivation and Personality*, 2nd edn (New York: Harper and Row, 1970). For writings on the propensity of citizens to take a more direct form of political participation in affluent societies, see for example, Ronald Inglehart, *The Silent Revolution* (Princeton, NJ: Princeton University Press, 1977) and *Culture Shift in Advanced Industrial Society* (Princeton, NJ: Princeton University Press, 1990).

32 Chan Heng Chee, 'Singapore: Coping with Vulnerability', in James W. Morley (ed.) *Driven By Growth: Political Change In The Asia-Pacific Region* (Armonk, NY: M. E. Sharpe, 1993): 241.

33 *Straits Times*, 30 November 1991.

34 *Sunday Times*, 15 January 1995.

35 Kennedy, *Preparing For The Twenty-First Century*: 202.

36 Segal considers the dispute over the Spratleys as a potential hotspot in the region. He writes:

> All the islands in the group are tiny... but they command the sea passage from Japan to Singapore... Chinese pursuit of territorial claims in the South China Sea might lead to a Sino–Japanese arms race and ASEAN anxiety. War may become a less useful instrument of policy in the Pacific, but peace will not be complete.
>
> (Gerald Segal, *Rethinking The Pacific* (Oxford: Clarendon Press, 1990): 233, 388.

For a more detailed discussion of the Spratleys as a bone of contention between claimant states, see Lee Lai To, 'ASEAN-PRC Political and Security Cooperation: Problems, Proposals, and Prospects', *Asian Survey*, Vol. XXXIII, No. 11, November 1993.

37 Lee commented: 'We'd all be happier, including the present generation of Japanese, if the American security alliance remains, leaving Japan to concentrate on high-definition television'. *Straits Times*, 17 December 1991.

38 A variation of such a scenario is found in Kennedy, *Preparing For the Twenty-First Century*: 151.

39 *Straits Times*, 30 November 1991.

40 The White Paper for the EP noted: '[T]he reserves, were the only assets available for coping with unforeseen crises, such as a prolonged global recession or an international financial crash'. See *Straits Times*, 30 July 1988.

41 *Straits Times*, 26 August 1994.

42 *Straits Times*, 5 October 1990.

43 *Straits Times*, 16 November 1990.

Postscript

As this collection of essays goes to press, amendments relating to the powers of the elected president are pending before Parliament.[1] In addition to substantial amendments to the powers of the elected president, this omnibus amendment bill makes changes to a number of other key important provisions in the Constitution such as the amendment provision under Article 5, as well as to the Group Representation Constituency scheme. Of germane interest are the amendments to the amendment procedure under the Constitution and the modified powers of the elected president. The Bill is only in its infant stages and no date has been set for the Second Reading and debate. As such, the Prime Minister (who tabled the Bill) has not yet articulated the reasons behind these changes. In this short *Postscript*, I will only briefly explain the relevent proposed changes in comparison with the older provisions. A more detailed analysis must be left to another time and forum.

AMENDMENTS TO AMENDMENT PROCEDURE

- The old Article 5(2A), which has been the source of confusion and the first-ever *Constitutional Reference No 1*[2] has been re-organized to take into account changes necessary upon the inclusion of a new Article 5A.
- A new Article 5A is proposed. It provides that the President 'may, acting in his discretion, in writing withhold his assent to any Bill seeking to amend [the] Constitution (other than a Bill referred to in Article 5(2A)), if the Bill ... provides directly or indirectly of the discretionary powers conferred upon the President by [the] Constitution.'[3] The practical effect of the inclusion of the new Article 5A read with Article 5(2A) is:
  Any amendment to Article 5(2A); Article 5; Part IV (fundamental

liberties); Chapter 1 of Part V (office of the Elected President); Article 93A (judicial review of presidential elections); Article 65 (prorogation and dissolution of Parliament); or Article 66 (general elections); or any other provision in the Constitution 'which authorizes the President to act in his discretion' must obtain approval of the President, acting in his discretion. If he approves, a Parliamentary two-thirds majority will suffice to effect the amendment. If the President vetoes the Bill, it will go to a national referendum and will only be passed when carried with a two-thirds majority.

In all other matters affecting the President's powers, the President has three options: He may do nothing, assent to the Bill, or veto the Bill. If he does nothing, the new Article 5A(6) provides that he will be deemed to have assented to the Bill upon 'the expiration of 30 days after [the] Bill has been presented' to him for his assent. If the President vetoes the Bill, the Cabinet can advise the President to refer the Bill to a constitutional tribunal established under Article 100 to determine if the Bill provides 'directly or indirectly for the circumvention or curtailment of [his] discretionary powers. If the tribunal is of the opinion that it does, 'the Prime Minister may at any time direct that the Bill be submitted to the electors for a national referendum.'[4] This change necessitates an amendment to Article 22H which deals with the President's veto powers in respect of amendments to his own discretionary powers.

APPOINTMENT & POWERS OF THE COUNCIL OF PRESIDENTIAL ADVISERS

- Article 37B of the Constitution has been amended to provide that instead of having one member of the Council of Presidential Advisers appointed by the President 'on the advice of the Chairman of the Public Service Commission', the President will now make the appointment on the advice of the Chief Justice.[5]
- Article 37J is amended by the insertion of a new clause 2A which provides that in 'advising or making any recommendation to the President in relation to the appointment and revocation of appointment of any person to any office referred to in Article 22, 22A and 22C (public officers, members of statutory boards and directors of government companies), 'the Council shall state whether its advice or recommendation is unanimous or the number of votes for and against it.' Further, a new Article 37J(2B) is added to provide for the

counting of votes at the meetings of the Council of Presidential Advisers which shall be by simple majority, with the Chairman having a casting vote. This amendment is in consonant with the final amendment on the President's power under Article 22A.

AMENDMENT TO PRESIDENT'S POWER TO ACT

New articles are added to Article 22, 22A and 22C (President's power to veto appointment of public officers, members of statutory boards and directors of government companies) to provide that where the 'President, contrary to the recommendation of the Council of Presidential Advisers, refuses to make an appointment or refuses to revoke and appointment ... Parliament may, by resolution passed by not less than two-thirds' majority overrule the decision of the President.'[6]

KEVIN TAN

1   See Constitution of the Republic of Singapore (Amendment) Bill, Bill No 30/96 dated 1 Oct 96 [hereinafter *Constitutional Amendment 1996*]which was tabled by Prime Minister Goh Chok Tong in his own name.
2   See [1995] 2 *Singapore Law Reports* 201.
3   See section 3 *Constitutional Amendment 1996*.
4   See new clause 5A(4).
5   See new clause 37B(1)(c)
6   See new clauses 22(2), 22(3), 22A(1A), 22A(1B), 22C(1A), and 22C(1B).

Index

Anson constituency by-election (1981) 19, 173–4
Anti-British League 17
Association of South East Asian Nations (ASEAN) 206–7, 212
Attorney General v. Wain 126

Bagehot, Walter 105
Barisan Sosialis 2, 102, 168, 171, 173, 203
Bartley, Robert 161
Becker, Gary 153, 154
British Constitution 105
British governors 9, 53
Buchanan, James 6, 146, 154, 155, 161, 162
by-elections: (1992) 177–8; Anson constituency (1981) 19, 173–4

candidates: censorship 171; competence 70–2; ethnicity 13–16, 180; first presidential election 189–90; partisanship 68, 72, 94–5, 97–8; political affinity 57–8, 62; pre-selection criteria 110–12, 179–80; qualifications 56–7, 63, 70–2, 94–8, 110; reluctant 190–92
Central Provident Fund 147, 149–50, 159
Chan Heng Chee 209
Chen, John 62
Chia Shi Teck 6–7, 78; on first presidential election 188–99; relationship with Wee Kim Wee

20–1; on Wee Kim Wee's retirement 30, 36
Chiam See Tong 31, 32, 62
Chua Kim Yeow 7, 42, 78, 179; election campaign 167, 181, 192–3; political independence 132; qualification for office 97; reluctance 190–2
civil liberties 115, 125–32; civil society 4
Commonwealth countries 103
Community Centres 171
Confucianism 104, 105
Constitutional Amendments to Safeguard Financial Assets and the Integrity of the Public Service (White Paper, 1988) 145, 176
constitutions: British 105; cultural context 104; as curb on Parliament 103; nature of 108–9; of Singapore *see* Singapore Constitution; written 116–17
Coomaraswamy, Punch 11
Corrupt Practices Investigation Bureau 56, 59, 64, 109, 114
Council of Presidential Advisors (CPA): composition 56, 59; and presidential power of veto 119, 124; remuneration 66; role 59, 122–3
Currency Board 151

defence spending 214
Derbyshire City Council v. Times Newspapers Ltd 126, 131

Diplock, Lord 108–9
Doshi, Tilak 6
Dzafir, Ridzwan 13–14

economy 145–6; future prospects 207,
209–15; growth and role of public
savings 146–51; public choice
model 152–6; public savings
management 156–60
Elected Presidency Bill 21
elected presidency scheme 53–80;
acting president 59; and 1988
general election 176–7; candidates
see candidates; consequences
173–8; and constitution *see*
Singapore constitution; final
scheme (1991) 63–5; financial
provisions 60–1, 151–6; first White
Paper 53–5; introduction of 102;
and legal control of government
100–35; Oath of Office 57–8, 62;
personnel boards 66; political
context 168–72; political
motivations 167–84; Presidential
Elections Committee (PEC) 58,
71–2, 95–6, 111, 191; presidential
powers *see* presidential powers;
problems 70–6; public reaction
167; rationale 54–5, 91–2, 109,
151–6, 172–3; second White Paper
(1990) 54, 55–6, 177; Select
Committee's Report *see* Select
Committee's Report; Supreme
Court Special Tribunal 66, 74–5;
see also presidency; presidents
elections, presidential 63–4;
competitiveness 68–9; deposits 77;
election expenses 98; first 178–83,
188–99; Presidential Elections
Committee (PEC) 58, 71–2, 95–6,
111, 191; single candidate 77–8
ethnicity: Group Representative
Constituencies 91, 102, 107–8,
196–7; institutionalization 13; as
presidential selection criterion
13–16, 180; presidents 13–16, 37,
68; wives of presidents 16, 37

Fay, Michael Peter 113
Feedback Unit 175

foreign reserves 159
freedom of speech 126–7, 131

general elections: (1984) 174–5;
(1988) 176–7; (1991) 177–8;
opposition votes gained 195; PAP
percentage votes 194
Goh Chok Tong 144; advice to voters
203–4; 1992 by-election 177–8; on
candidates' qualifications 71; on
democracy 170, 174; endorsement
of Ong 189; on future of Singapore
209; housing policy 198;
relationship with Lee government
205–6; relationship with Wee Kim
Wee 20, 21; response to Select
Committee Report 61–2; on Wee's
selection 30–1
Goh Choon Keng 62
Goh Keng Swee 179, 192
Goode, Sir William 9, 53
government: by cabinet 105; fusion of
powers 105; legal control of
100–35; opposition *see* opposition,
parliamentary; parliamentary
systems *see* parliamentary systems;
presidential system 108; separation
of powers 116–18, 123–32
Government Investment Corporation
151, 175
Group Representative Constituencies
(GRCs) 91, 102, 107–8, 196–7

Hamilton, Alexander 103
Hayek, F.A. 6, 155
housing policy 198
Hu, Richard 159, 179; support for
Chua 192; support for Ong 189–90
Huang Jianli 4–5
human rights 115, 125–32
Hume, David 162
Huntington, S. 3, 154

ill-health 10, 21–3
Internal Security Act 55, 59, 102, 109,
115, 127–8
Ismail, Samad 17
Ismail Bin Abdul Aziz 11
Istana 23–4, 29

Japan 203
Japanese Occupation 17
Jennings, Ivor 105
Jeyaretnam, J.B. 111, 173–4, 179
Jeyaretnam, Joshua Benjamin v. Lee Kuan Yew 126
judiciary 127–30

Kennedy, Paul 200, 211
Keynes, J.M. 153
Koh Lam Son 62
Kranji National Cemetery 27, 28
Krueger, Anne 153
Krugman, Paul 149

Lam Peng Er 7
Lee Hsien Loong: Constitutional Amendment (No 2) Act 65, 73–4; economic forecast 207; illness 40, 200
Lee Kuan Yew: alleviates Yusof's loneliness 24; constitutional safeguards 144–5; on democracy 161, 170; on economy 172; endorsement of Ong 189; as Founding Father 2–4; future prospects 207–8; on future of Singapore 213; housing policy 198; influence on presidency 204–7; on man's frailty 109; on Nair's alcoholism 25; on national reserves 174–5; on Ong as People's President 42–3; promotion of elected presidency scheme 174; relationship with Nair 12; relationship with Sheares 11; relationship with Wee 13; role in presidential appointments 11–13, 53; support for Nair 18–19; support for Sheares 20; support for Yusof 20; on voting system 195–6, 197; on Wee Kim Wee 15–16, 17, 35; on Yusuf's health 22; on Yusof's Malay background 14–15; on Yusof's wife 16
Lee Siew Choh 62–3, 179, 196
Legislature 89–90
liberties, fundamental 115, 125–32
Lim Boon Heng 62, 189
Lim Chee Onn 189

Lim Hng Kiang 171
Lim Kim San 12, 171, 175
Lincoln, Abraham 116
Ling How Doong 31, 36
Lingens v. Austria 126
Low Thia Kiang 67

Machiavelli, Niccolò 1
Madison, James 100
Maintenance of Religious Harmony Act 56, 59, 64, 109, 115, 127, 129–30
Malayan Communist Party 17
Malayan People's Anti-Japanese Army 17
Malaysia: expulsion from 10; merger with 9–10, 171
Marbury v. Madison 116, 121
Marshall, David 17
Marshall, John 116–17, 121
Mauzy, D.K. 170
Mill, John Stuart 162
Milne, R.S. 170
MND Holdings 151
Modigliani, Franco 157
Monetary Authority of Singapore 151
Mutalib, Hussin 7

Nair, C.V. Devan 2, 189; adjustment to presidency 24–5; alcoholism 25–6; detention by British 17, 18; ethnicity 13, 68; Internal Security Department investigation 19; Japanese Occupation 17; and PAP 17–18; pension 25–6; as People's President 32, 33–5, 38–9; political engagement 16, 17–20, 41; presidential selection 10, 12, 38, 53, 173; resignation 10, 15, 24–6; trade union activities 17–18; visit to Sarawak 26
Nair, Mrs 16
National Agenda 175
National Cemetery 27, 28
National Economic Committee 175
national security 128–9
National Trade Union Congress 39–42, 102, 189–90
New York Times v. Sullivan 126

Newspaper and Printing Act (1974) 171

Nominated Members of Parliament (NMPs) 90, 102, 106–7, 177, 196–7

Non-Constituency Members of Parliament (NCMPs) 90, 102, 106–7, 175, 196

Nwabueze, Ben O. 125

Oath of Office 57–8, 62

Oliverio, Oscar 39, 40, 42

Olson, M. 154

Ong Ah Chuan v. Public Prosecutor 125

Ong Chit Chung 214

Ong Teng Cheong: candidature for elected presidency 10, 12, 13, 39, 189–90; election campaign 181–2, 192–3; election to presidency 37, 39–43, 78, 175; ethnicity 39–40; ill-health 40–41; implications of victory 182–3; on nature of presidency 124, 125; as People's President 42; political background 16, 41–2; political independence 182; qualification for office 97; refers to Special Tribunal 75; on role of presidency 183

opposition, parliamentary: creating 105–8; GRC scheme 91, 102, 107–8, 196–7; lack of 4; Nominated Members of Parliament (NMPs) 90, 102, 106–7, 177, 196–7; Non-Constituency Members of Parliament 90, 102, 106–7, 175, 196; offers to voters 205; PAP backbenchers as 106; PAP intolerance of 170–1; response to elected presidency scheme 169; votes gained in general elections 195

Othman bin Wok: friendship with Yusof 24; presidential candidacy 11, 15

parliamentary systems 52, 55, 88–9; in Singapore 89–91; Westminster 52, 102–4, 104–8; *see also* government

People's Action Party (PAP) 2–4; antipathy to opposition 168, 170–1; backbenchers as 'opposition' 106; constitutional reforms 101; defeat in Anson constituency 19, 173–4; future prospects 210; 1988 general election 176–7; 1991 general election 177–8; general election votes 194; inhibition of opposition 102; Nair's involvement 17–18; and Ong's nomination 41–2; opposition to referendum 118; political domination 79–80, 106, 168–72; and presidential selections 19, 39

People's President: concept 10, 31–7; Wee Kim Wee 31–2, 35–7, 42–3

Phey Yew Kok 25

presidency: candidates *see* candidates; constitutional development 52–80; constitutional safeguards 144–6; elected presidency scheme *see* elected presidency scheme; evolution 9–10; financial provisions 72; as human rights watchdog 115, 125–32; influence of Lee Kuan Yew 204–7; and legal control of government 100–35; modifications of office 38–43; nature of institution 124–5; post-Lee 207–15; as safeguard against corruption 114–15; selection process 11–13; *see also* presidents

presidents: accountability 110; attendance at functions 113; as check on government 118–32; conflict with Government 72–5, 119–22; ethnicity 13–16, 37, 68; health problems 21–3; immunity from suits 60, 64; independence 132–3; interaction with cabinet 201–4; misconduct/misbehaviour 122; partisanship 133; People's President concept 10, 31–7; peoples' right to elect 92–4; political engagement 16–21; powers *see* presidential powers; problems in office 23–31; removal from office 60, 64–5, 75–6, 110;

temporary 121; term of office 61, 64, 110; as watchdog 114–18, 125–32; *see also* presidency
Presidential Council for Minority Rights 102, 130
Presidential Council for Religious Harmony 58, 115, 129
presidential elections *see* elections, presidential
Presidential Elections Act (1991) 63, 77–8, 92–3, 95–6, 190
Presidential Elections Committee (PEC) 58, 71–2, 95–6, 111, 191
presidential powers 58–9, 64; enlargement 112–14; financial veto 114; limited 67–8, 72–4; patronage 113; removal of 120–2; spending of reserves 65, 91–2; transfer of surpluses 66; veto 67, 92, 109, 113, 118–19, 124
Proclamation of Emergency provisions 58
Puan Noor Aishah (Yusof's wife) 16, 27
public housing 198
public savings: and economic growth 146–51; management 156–60
Pye, Lucian 105

Rajah, A.P. 11
Rajaratnam, S. 12, 178; Nair's resignation 26; proposal of Wee Kim Wee 15; on Wee's unsuitability 31
referendums: on constitutional reform 120; on creation of constitution 117–18
Rendel Constitutional Commission (1954) 88, 107
Residents Committees 171, 175
Roh Tae Woo 194
Rousseau, Jean-Jacques 1

savings and investment *see* public savings
Select Committee's Report 56–61, 177; Parliament's response 61–3
Sheares, Benjamin Henry: death 22, 28; ethnicity 13, 68; funeral 28–9, 37; ill-health 22; political

engagement 16–17, 19; presidential appointment 10, 11; ties with the people 32–3
Sheares, Dr Joseph 33
Sheares, Mrs 16
Sheng-Li Holdings 151
Sidek bin Saniff 35–6
Singapore Constitution; Amendment Bill (1990) 54; Amendment No 2 Act (1994) 65–7, 74; Amendment No 3 Act (1991) 76, 91, 109–10, 115–16, 145–6, 177; amendments (1965–79) 102; Bill of Rights 125; Constitutional Commission (1966) 93; constitutional provisions 69–70; judicial review 103, 116–17; legitimacy 116–18; provision for parliamentary gap 104–8; Rendel Constitutional Commission (1954) 88, 107; safeguards 144–6; United Kingdom imposed (1958) 88–9; Wee Chong Jin Constitutional Commission (1966) 107
Singapore Democratic Party 176, 204–5
Singapore Malay Union (Kesatuan Melayu Singapura) 17
Singapore Press Holdings 171
Smith, Adam 147, 153
Soin, Kanwaljit 67
Stigler, George 153
Story, Justice Joseph 144
Supply Bills 61, 72, 119, 124
Supreme Court: advisory capacity 66; removal of president 75–6; Special Tribunal 66, 74–5

Tan, Kevin 5
Tan, Tony 209
Tan Boon Teik 179
Tan Cheng Bock 36, 67; relationship with Wee Kim Wee 20–21
Tan Soo Khoon 56
Tan Soon Phuan 111, 179
Tang Guan Seng 36
Temasek Holdings 151
Teo Chee Hean, Admiral N.S. 171
Thio Li-ann 5–6
Toffler, Alvin 200
Toh Chin Chye 176

Town Councils 175
Tun Salleh Abas 76, 122

Undesirable Publications Act (1967)
171
Utusan Melayu 17

Vasoo, S. 62

wealth sharing schemes 197–8
Wee Cho Yaw 32
Wee Chong Jin 11; Constitutional
Commission (1966) 107
Wee Kim Wee: adjustment to
presidency 24; ethnicity 13, 15–16,
37, 68; ill-health 22; office under
elected presidency scheme 76–7; as
People's President 31–2, 35–7,
42–3; political engagement 16, 17,
20–1; presidential selection 10,
12–13, 21, 53; presidential style 21;
retirement 29–31; as unelected
elected president 38
Wee Kim Wee, Mrs 16
Westminster parliamentary system
52, 102–4, 104–8

Winslow, V.S. 6, 71–2
wives of presidents 16, 37
Wong, Aline 36
Wong Lin Ken 29
Woon, Walter 31, 67
Workers' Party 111, 173, 176–7, 179,
196

Yang di-Pertuan Agong 10
Yang di-Pertuan Negara (Head of
State of Singapore) 9–10, 17, 21,
53, 89
Yeo, Brigadier General George 197
Yeoh Ghim Seng 11
Yusof bin Ishak, Encik: death 27–8;
friendship with Othman Wok 24;
funeral 27–8, 37; ill-health 21–2;
loneliness in office 23–4; Malay
background 13–15, 37, 68, 89;
political engagement 16, 17, 19;
presidential selection 9–10, 11;
prolonging of presidency 23; ties
with the people 32; as Yang di-
Pertuan Negara 9–10, 17, 21, 53,
89